THE PHILOSOPHY OF ALAIN LOCKE
Harlem Renaissance and Beyond

THE
PHILOSOPHY OF
ALAIN LOCKE

Harlem Renaissance and Beyond

Edited by
LEONARD HARRIS

Generously Donated to
The Frederick Douglass Institute
By Professor Jesse Moore
Fall 2000

TEMPLE UNIVERSITY PRESS
Philadelphia

TEMPLE UNIVERSITY PRESS, Philadelphia 19122
Copyright © 1989 by Temple University. All rights reserved
Published 1989
Printed in the United States of America

The paper used in this publication meets the minimum
requirements of American National Standard for Information
Sciences—Permanence of Paper for Printed Library Materials,
ANSI Z39.48-1984

Library of Congress Cataloging-in-Publication Data
The Philosophy of Alain Locke : Harlem renaissance and beyond / edited
by Leonard Harris.
    p. cm.
  Bibliography: p.
  Includes index.
  ISBN 0-87722-584-2 (alk. paper)
   1. Locke, Alain LeRoy, 1886–1954—Philosophy.   I. Harris,
Leonard, 1948–
E185.97.L79P48 1989
191—dc 19   88-12235
                                                                CIP

Frontispiece pastel portrait
by Winold Reiss, c. 1925.
Courtesy of The National Portrait Gallery,
Smithsonian Institution. Gift of
Lawrence A. Fleischman and Howard
Garfinkle with a matching grant from
the NEA.

Preface

I was born in Cleveland, Ohio, April 12, 1948, the second son of a milkman, Eugene Harris Sr., and the last of five children borne and raised by Agnes Chapel Harris. My mother hailed from a family of eleven; my father was an only son, orphaned at birth by his mother's death, reared by his grandfather Big Bill Harris of Tuskegee, Alabama, also an only son and black as the African soil.

At eighteen, the age by which Harrises leave home willingly or not, I barely graduated from Glenville High School, barely survived the gang wars we Del Amours were forever in, and escaped with my mother's passion for education to Central State University, Wilberforce, Ohio. In 1966 at least half of my fights, brick throwings, and hurled curse words had been aimed at whites in frustration during the civil rights movement in Cleveland. At Central, at least half were aimed at blacks during my days as a hippie/black militant.

But philosophy bequeathed me a place for my mind to be, a place that seemed not to notice, a place to be invisible except as I was one with ideas.

In September, 1969, at Miami University in Oxford, Ohio, I began graduate studies in philosophy. Miami made me a believer—all white, deadly white, even the fraternity house behind my apartment building had as its logo a white master lording over a slave. I saw a white rat on campus and knew that I had reached hell.

The philosophy department held open its arms: Bubbling Bob Harris, Rick Momeyer, Martin Benjamin, and Carl Hedman acted like humans and were as honestly perplexed about their worlds as I. And a strong black woman, Marian Musgrave of the Department of English, who joined Miami's faculty from Central in September, 1969, had given me ultra-blues in English at Central and was now at Miami. Occasionally I rode to her hometown, Cleveland, with her and listened as she sang songs in German. Her existence was enough to make me buy another dictionary just in case of God knows what.

At Cornell University in September, 1970, Allan Wood, David Lyons, Norman Kretzman, Nicholas Sturgeon, and James Turner gave me the blues, deservedly, but all of the white graduate students in philosophy had the peculiar eye disease of not seeing any person of color. Three years of utter loneliness followed, but for the Africana Studies Center and the Caribbean Student Association. I lived with the peculiar bedfellows called analytic and social philosophy until they became visible; I then came to perceive that what previously appeared as ideas in abstract were actually abstract ideas in a social context, an understanding that enlivened my task of discovering and revealing the historical being of African people who were one with this peculiar form of visibility.

I am indebted to the Morgan State University Press and Research Committee, particularly Dr. Ruthe Sheffey, for material support while preparing this anthology; to Lucius Outlaw, Clifford DuRand, Otto Begus, Marcia Rittenhouse, and Robert Birt for their steadfast willingness to read and critique my writing; to Johnny Washington for his work *Alain Locke, Philosopher* (Westport, Conn.: Greenwood Press, 1986) and his years of steadfast interest in Locke scholarship; to Jeffrey Stewart for his suggestion that Alfred M. Dunham, brother of Katherine Dunham, possibly had something to do with Locke's revived interest in philosophy after it lay dormant for seventeen years; to Esme E. Bhan of the Moorland-Spingarn Research Center, Howard University, for her guidance through the Locke material and her patience; to Robert Williams for his presentation at the December, 1985, American Philosophical Association meeting in which he linked the works of George Santayana and Locke; to George R. Garrison for his efforts to open the pages of *Teaching Philosophy* to articles on Locke, and to Peter Hare for his receptiveness not only to Locke material but to the panorama of Afro-American philosophic endeavors; to Albert Mosley for his always insightful comments and brotherhood in struggle; to John McDermott for making the Society for the Advancement of American Philosophy open to discourse about American philosophers of whatever race or culture and forging humanism in the numerous corridors he travels; to Robert Ginsberg for making the review pages of the *Journal for Social Philosophy* a source open to developments in Afro-American philosophic works; to Howard McGary and the Committee on Blacks in Philosophy of the American Philosophical Association for assuring an open forum for edifying and critical dialogue; to Thomas Harper for supporting my efforts to edify the youth; and to Sherron Jones-Harris, James Williams, Barbara Monroe, Margarette Tarrence, Donna Martin, Diane Gibson, and Allan Williams for the love they have shared.

For Leonard Nawatu Harris, Jarrard Lemir Harris, Jamila Rehema Harris, Leonard Robinson, M'wey Robinson, Daniel Harris, Michael Foster, Tony Foster, Kevin Harris, Candice Harris—the ascending generation.

Contents

IV. IDENTITY AND EDUCATION

AN INTERPRETATION

Introduction

Rendering the Text

LEONARD HARRIS

If, as Alain Locke believed, all philosophies are "in ultimate derivation philosophies of life," and not embodiments of objective reality, then we can fruitfully enter his philosophy by entering his life.

Locke's was a life full of enigmas. He was born in Philadelphia, Pennsylvania, on September 13, 1885, the only son of Pliny Ishmael Locke and Mary Hawkins Locke. However, he used September 13, 1886, as his birth date throughout his career. He was named Arthur Locke by Pliny and Mary, but at his death in Washington, D.C., on June 9, 1954, he was known by the name he had taken: Alain LeRoy Locke.[1]

Locke studied to become a professional philosopher but became renowned for his ideas on race, for his role as an aesthete of the Harlem Renaissance, and as progenitor of the view that black literature, drama, art, and music are the conveyers of what is uniquely and genuinely African American. As an undergraduate student at Harvard between 1904 and 1907, he attended courses taught by Josiah Royce, George Herbert Palmer, Ralph Barton Perry, and Hugo Munsterberg. He graduated *magna cum laude* in philosophy in March, 1907. Two months later it was announced that Locke received a Rhodes Scholarship. Remarkably, Gustaf Westfeldt wrote to the British Embassy in Washington, D.C., requesting that the granting of Rhodes Scholarships to Negroes be discontinued because such awards would make the scholarships unpopular in the South. Although Rhodes Scholarships retained the right of admission, five Oxford colleges refused to admit Locke. He eventually attended one of the youngest and poorest colleges, Hertford College, from 1907 to 1910. When a Thanksgiving dinner for Rhodes Scholars held at the American Club excluded Locke because of his race, Horace Kallen was one of the few Americans who refused to attend the dinner in protest. In "Oxford Contrasts," Locke critiqued Oxford University's stringent class distinctions and rejection of learning techniques incompatible with its institutionalized education system.[2] He also contrasted America's explicit racial prejudice to Oxford's indifference, making non-whites invisible.

After studying Greek, philosophy, and *Literae Humaniores* in England, and after studying at the University of Berlin in 1910 and 1911, taking particular interest in the works of Christian Freiherr von Ehrenfels and Alexius Meinong, Locke returned to America with no possibility of finding university employment except at traditionally black colleges. He joined the faculty of Howard University in 1912 as an Assistant Professor of the Teaching of English and Instructor in Philosophy and Education under Lewis B. Moore, Professor of Philosophy and Education and Dean of the Teachers College.

Locke received an Austin Fellowship to attend Harvard in 1916 and 1917 to complete work for his doctorate in philosophy. He wanted to study under Josiah Royce, but Royce died before he returned to Harvard. Instead of Royce, Locke studied under and submitted his doctoral dissertation to Ralph Barton Perry on September 17, 1917, and was awarded his doctoral degree in the spring of 1918. His dissertation was entitled "Problems of Classification in Theory of Value" and was an extension of an article prepared while at Hertford. Locke maintained a high regard for Royce's uniqueness, as a Californian who was out of place among the Bostonians and other New Englanders at Harvard and as the only major American philosopher during the early 1900s to publish a book condemning racism.[3] He developed a passion, like Perry, for the works of William James. But unlike Perry, Locke sought to understand the way conceptions of experience might account for the role of racial identity in human affairs. And unlike Perry, Locke focused on metanormative rather than normative value theory; seeking the unifying elements of phenomena at the meta-level was characteristic of Locke's entré into experience.

Mary Hawkins Locke died in the home of her only child on April 23, 1922. A follower of Felix Adler and a teacher in Camden and Camden County, New Jersey, she had directed Locke's early education. From a family of free blacks, missionaries to Africa with the Society of Friends, and soldiers who fought against the South in the

American Civil War, Mary Hawkins Locke had succeeded in shaping her ascending generation. Her wake, held in Locke's Washington, D.C., home shortly after her death, was notable for the presence of her inanimate body, which rested on a chaise lounge and was addressed by Locke in the present tense. A possible explanation for such peculiar behavior is that Locke was disaffected from the tenets of his family's Episcopalian background and was seeking a spiritual home; one he seems to have eventually found, at least during the 1920s and 1930s, in the Bahá'í faith. On May 19th and 21st, 1921, for example, Locke participated in an Inter-Racial Amity conference, convened at the suggestion of 'Abdu'l-Bahá to Mrs. Agnes S. Parsons in 1920 when she was on pilgrimage in Haifa. The Bahá'í belief in the unity of humanity was expressed in practical terms by inter-racial meetings (then a fairly unusual situation in Christian America). The Bahá'í belief in the ultimate spiritual unity among the plurality of religious faiths and the treatment of death as a passing into another present, instead of the traumatic ending of a condemned born sinner hoping for an uncertain redemption, were appealing to Locke. As Locke had published his impressions of England in "Oxford Contrasts" (1909) and his African experiences in "Impressions of Luxor" (1924), he later published his impressions from a 1930 visit to Haifa, a spiritual center of the Bahá'í faith, in "Impressions of Haifa."[4] Locke maintained a deep appreciation for the Bahá'í perception of human and spiritual unity.

Although enamored at a young age by the lifestyle of classical Greek culture, educated at institutions offering little positive incentive to study African culture or race relations, and attracted also to the spirituality of the Bahá'í, Locke felt that the promotion and study of African culture and race relations were integral to his being. In 1915 and 1916 he fought to offer a course on race relations against the wishes of the Howard University administration. The administration denied him the opportunity to offer the course in its curriculum, but he eventually taught the course to a study group under the aegis of the National Association for the Advancement of Colored People (NAACP). In addition, Locke went on an extensive tour of Egypt and Sudan in 1924, reporting his visit to Tutankhamen's tomb and other experiences in "Impressions of Luxor."[5] He consistently promoted African art exhibits, developed a major collection of African art, and encouraged recognition of the cultural commonalities of all African people. He did so while chairing the Department of Philosophy at Howard University from 1917 to 1925 and again from 1928 to 1954.

To reduce the power of forces pursuing equitable pay between blacks and whites, the Howard University administration fired Locke in June of 1925, along with several other black faculty members. No longer employed at Howard, Locke's intellectual productivity became prolific and his relationships with numerous artists and philanthropists flourished. Using a collection of articles prepared for the *Survey Graphic* in March, 1925, as his base, Locke anthologized a collection of articles, poetry, spiritual songs, and pictures of artwork that became the standard-bearer for the Harlem Renaissance—*The New Negro*.

The New Negro was part of a movement already in motion— E. Franklin Frazier, Booker T. Washington, and others had written or published articles and books proclaiming the existence of a "New Negro." Locke's version of the New Negro, contrary to Washington's, emphasized Afro-American cultural continuities with Africa, that is, affirming positively what was valued as inferior by white culture; affirming positively an African identity even though Americanized in many ways; and applauding the folkways, rhythms, symbols, and rituals of black life. In addition, Locke applauded the inevitable urbanization of blacks while other philosophers romanticized small-town and rural living. Locke's associations with W. E. B. Du Bois, Langston Hughes, and Claude McKay developed through the 1920s and 1930s. Du Bois's notion of the Talented Tenth, for example, was supported by Locke. As Du Bois became progressively radical and eventually rejected the idea of an educated elite leading blacks and functioning as a role model, so too did Locke. Langston Hughes was Locke's ideal author: urbane, steeped in the traditions of black folk literature, and portraying its contours with a sense of their universal value. But McKay was critical of Locke's efforts to involve Hughes in the literature of advocacy, that is, the literature of blacks that self-consciously portrayed the struggles of blacks against racism, the universal human pathos of oppression, and the cares of an African people transplanted to America. Locke perceived the artist as a community representative. This view stood at odds with McKay's conception of the artist as an individual expressing an utterly unique vision. In promoting African art and the Africanity of the African diaspora in the Americas, Locke exaggerated the spiritual and virtuous character of African culture. His exaggerations were at times used as a pedagogical method to alter unfavorable attitudes about black culture. As I argue elsewhere, however, Locke's philosophic conceptions were not supportive of a nativistic or atavistic conception of cultural virtues.[6] Rather, his notion of the New Negro was constituted to alter the nature of public discourse about African people and to re-envision African self-concepts across various social strata.

The conception of black culture as Rousseauean primitive and virtuous during the Harlem Renaissance was encouraged by romantic white eccentrics. Locke was never dependent for money, status, or access to publishers on romantic white eccentrics such as Mrs. Rufus Osgood Mason, née Charlotte Louise van der Veer Quick, a white "godmother" who was a patron at times for Harlem Renaissance figures such as Zora Neale Hurston, Langston Hughes, Louise Thompson, Aaron Douglas, and Richmond Barthé. Hurston, for example, received maintenance money, subventions for her books, and advice, if not orders, from Mrs. Mason on what to write and how to edit black folklore.[7] Locke, like Mrs. Mason was himself a patron but one given less to controlling others than to the shaping of ideas.

Between 1935 and 1939 the Harlem Renaissance died. Many of the jazz, blues, and literary geniuses of the era were either dead or living in self-imposed exile in France. Marcus Garvey had been deported, Booker T. Washington's accommodationist educational policies were largely confined to the South, and Du Bois was increasingly radical and under government surveillance. The National Negro Congress, an organization that applied pluralist principles by sponsoring conferences for competing black civic and political groups, was increasingly dysfunctional. With the beginnings of the depression in 1929 and the advent of World War II in 1938, publishers and philanthropists supportive of black literature greatly declined. As early as 1931, but certainly by 1937, Locke was supportive of the new thrust of "proletarian" literature such as Richard Wright's *Native Son*. New social realities, forms of domination, distortions, and misconceptions required revising the focus of emancipatory articulations. Proletarian art and literature as tools for liberation, particularly liberation from cultural and racial oppressions, was considered the next phase after the outdated focus on the exotic that accompanied the New Negro movement. Locke thus distanced himself from many of his former associates and his own popular identity.

Although the productive activity of many of Locke's friends either significantly declined or ended, Locke's activism increased in philosophy and the field of adult education, a field he first became involved in as a delegate to a Carnegie Corporation–sponsored Adult Education Conference in 1924. By 1936 Locke helped form the Associates in Negro Folk Education (ANFE), which published the Bronze Booklets, an adult education project. The ANFE labored under the twin constraints of limited funds from the Carnegie Corporation and a conservative board.[8] By 1945, Locke was elected president of the American Association for Adult Education (AAAE), a primarily white group. Within its corridors, Locke continued to promote the importance of cultural studies as a central feature for adult education. Locke not only left a series of books on black music and art as education tools prior to his administrative role but he published frequently while president of the AAAE. His seminal work during that time is "The Need for a New Organon in Education," a critique of the fetishization of the inferential rules of logic, the valorization of science, and a defense of the importance of our affective domains as integral to critical reasoning. Locke's editorship with Bernard Stern of *When Peoples Meet: A Study of Race and Culture Contact* resulted from presentations at the American Council on Education Conference, Chicago, 1941. He offers "critical relativism" as a preferable reasoning modality.

Locke did not publish an article in philosophy until 1935, at the age of fifty, seventeen years after receiving his doctoral degree and ten years after the publication of *The New Negro*. The most he did directly in the field of professional philosophy from 1918 to 1935 was a presentation entitled "Cultural Relativism" on February 7, 1930, before the Harvard Philosophy Club.

It is speculated that Alfred Dunham, brother of Katherine Dunham and a prize student of Alfred North Whitehead at Harvard, rekindled Locke's interest in publishing philosophical articles. Dunham wrote Locke at least from February 28, 1928, keeping Locke informed of his activities in Chicago and, later, his encounters with philosophers at Harvard. For example, in a letter written from the Hotel Grand, Chicago, and dated Saturday, M. (no year), Dunham described a feature of Du Bois's relation to philosophy. During a conversation with Du Bois, Du Bois informed Dunham that he had been advised by William James against pursuing a career in philosophy when he was a student at Harvard. James did so, according to Du Bois's autobiographies, because James did not believe Du Bois could secure employment as a philosopher. In a letter dated December 19 (no year), Dunham conveyed Ralph B. Perry's awareness of Locke's work and noted Perry's regret that his and Locke's travel plans prevented them from meeting again. By 1933, Dunham discussed in letters to Locke the latter's plans for Dunham's eventual role at the helm of Howard's Department of Philosophy. But again, as with Royce's death, Locke's plans for a relationship centered around philosophical discourse was marred. Dunham was plagued with mental illness shortly after joining the faculty of Howard University. He did not complete his doctoral degree, was frequently hospitalized throughout his remaining life, and died in 1951, leaving Locke the sole Harvard-educated black philosopher.

Whether or not Dunham played as significant a role as the above suggests in rekindling Locke's interest in philosophy, 1935 marked Locke's reentry into the doing of philosophy directly rather than through the mediation of other literary genres. Locke did not again publish nor write an article in philosophy as detailed as his 1935 "Values and Imperatives," a revised version of his doctoral dissertation and bearing features of his 1930 presentation on cultural relativism before the Harvard Philosophy Club. However, he continued to develop arguments only implied in "Values and Imperatives" in several unpublished and published articles until his death. "Value," for example, an unpublished review of the history of value theories written after "Values and Imperatives," was also his most direct statement on the nature of value. The most important scholars who invited or made available opportunities for Locke to publish philosophical writings after 1935 were R. M. MacIver, Lyman Bryson, Horace Kallen, Max Otto, Sidney Hook, and Bernard Stern, all actors in the cultural pluralist movement.

The following may not all be unexplainable, but taken together, they are enigmatic. Locke studied the pragmatists of America and value theorists of Europe but was not conceptually confined to their worlds of philosophic debate; rather, he referenced their philosophies as a conduit for the expression of his own views. He considered African art as the art of grand civilizations at a time when most black and white university-educated scholars believed that African works were either not art or at best the product of primitives unworthy of applause. At a time when the denegration of black folkways was a national pastime, he considered the folkways of African people as the source of classical artistic texts. He was forceably removed from university teaching but nonetheless created provocative intellectual works while shepherding a host of young literary radicals. He remained an important literary critic after the movement of New Negro literature he helped spawn was dead. He avoided the patriotic romanticism of American democracy, rural communalism, and the noncontextual pretenses of cultural pluralists when they dominated public and philosophic discourse. He provided leadership in adult education by promoting cultural education and rejecting the festishization of standard logic; and he began the formal doing of philosophy when he was fifty years old. These are but a few of the enigmas in the life of one of the most intellectually versatile persons in black intellectual history and American philosophy.

Creative moments are often enigmatic. Unlike the enigmatic character of his life, Locke's intellectual sojourn as a philosopher is in less need of explanation than appreciation. Locke contextualized his own philosophy and in doing so provided further reason to believe his views on value relativism and cultural pluralism.

THE SOJOURN THROUGH PHILOSOPHY

Locke sojourned through philosophy, rather than live entrapped and imprisoned in American pragmatism and European value theory traditions of rhetoric. It was as if he traveled, consuming the finest in a genteel fashion, observing like an anthropologist the norms and habits of self-possessed provincials portending cosmopolitanism, all in preparation to return home from the caverns and hinterlands of a T. S. Eliot wasteland. Unlike Royce, for example, who traveled from California to the urbane East, consumed by a desire to clarify and defend believed atextual abstractions, Locke contextualized philosophical metaphors and their excrescences. In his published philosophy articles Locke emphasized the importance of human loyalties in shaping belief systems, a central notion in Royce's philosophy and argument in *Race Questions, Provincialism, and Other American Problems*(1908). But unlike Royce, Locke did not make a fetish of loyalty nor predicated being of it or ideas as such. Locke rejected Royce's metaphysics but found ideas within Royce's conceptual arena that helped account for the realities shaping Locke's world.

It was theoretical space the traveler took home: insisting that a functional constraint of value relativism was our universally shared feature of humanity while simultaneously affirming the truth of the relativity of value judgments. He warranted the heuristics of collective identity by culture in conjunction with recognizing the forever-moving process of individual transvaluations and the transpositions of value categories such as truth, beauty, and virtue; rejected reifications of ethnic identities but simultaneously saw self-respect and dignity as being mediated through collective identities. He rejected experimental science as a privileged model of reasoning and all forms of scientism but promoted objectivity (aprivileged) in social science. He applauded pragmatism's success at negating Cartesian dualism and dethroning metaphysical absolutism with value relativism and metaphysical pluralism, but insisted on imperatives of tolerance, reciprocity, and parity as conditions for the possibility of the peaceful coexistence of cultures.

The preoccupations of James, Dewey, Perry, Royce, and Santayana were the metaphysics and epistemologies of Hume, Hobbes, John Locke, Kant, Hegel, Marx, Darwin, and Spencer. Alain Locke shared their preoccupations but with important differences. The Negro, for Locke, was not a problem but a nation in formation; philosophy was not the search for truth unencumbered by provincialism but a search that bore a provincialism reified and masquerading, including pragmatism. As Houston Baker Jr.'s depiction of Locke's *The New Negro* affirms: "In an American era populated by Tom Buchanans in the upper echelon, Theodore Bilbo and Woodrow Wilson in local and national politics, Lothrop Stoddard and William Graham Sumner in scholarship, Octavus Roy Cohen in popular media, and Snopeses everywhere, Locke's discursive act was veritably one of *extreme deformation* [de-forming a master code of symbols to fit a re-formed agenda]—of what I want to call here . . . *radical marronage*" (a banding together, communal project, an independence).[9] The master symbolic codes and rhetorical forms of the world of philosophy he entered were re-formed and encoded with messages that were arguably warranted and allowed space for African people.

Locke's philosophical thought synthesized elements from William James's metaphysical and experiential pluralism, Christian Freiherr von Ehrenfels' Gestalt conception of value as an intrinsic feature of cognition not derivative of other cognitive features, Alexius Meinong's emphasis on value as essentially a feeling (*Wertgefühle*) and not a Kantian judgment of preference, desire, interest, or utility, and Wilbur Urban's categorization of values and their forms and qualities. Locke's attachment to the ideas of Ehrenfels and Meinong stemmed from his research at Hertford and Berlin. He drew on their works and the works of Urban to discuss the categorization of value and the location of value in the panorama of human consciousness, two issues of increasingly less importance to him in his later works. Arguing for the central role of valuing in shaping human experience, however, remained an integral part of his work. Also central was his effort to unmask a paradox definitive of human life—that is, that values are necessarily relative modes of feeling, but the possibility of social life without some values functioning as social imperatives is unlikely. For example, individual authoritative imperatives are characteristically transilient and become projected as the sort society at large should follow. Consequently, social imperatives seem required to ameliorate conflicts that arise over conflicting transilient imperatives. Locke's version of cultural pluralism rejected an image of a romanticized future world without social norms regulating cultural life.

Reading Locke's articles in philosophy as a body of texts establishes the importance of William James's view of human experience as a theoretical starting point. Locke did not engage in a systematic critique of James's writings. Rather, his strategy was to reference James' arguments as sufficient warrant for rejecting absolutism, dogmatism, and universalism. Locke characteristically then proceeded to develop his own version of experience. He applauded James's conception of experience as the continual interaction of cognitive and pragmatic factors; James's rejection of the copy (or correspondence) theory of truth that held that true propositions parallel objective reality; James's arguments for a coherence theory of truth that emphasized the revisability of warranted propositions; and James's epistemic relativism, his notion that descriptions of psychological or objective states of affairs are not value free and that ideas are not isolated moments of cognition but features of a continual flow of interacting factors. In addition, Locke favored James's rejection of Cartesian dualism, for example, rejecting the view that ideas were fixed entities or stayed cognitive activity. Rather, ideas were understandable relations, and thoughts were always a stream or process. However, Locke believed that James's pragmatic method of decision making, as a description of how we characteristically make decisions or as a prescriptive method for so doing, was incomplete. Promoting experimental science as a universally applicable model reflected a degree of Western cultural bias and an unwarranted empiricism. James reacted against the works of John Locke, Hume, Hegel, Royce, and Bradley. Alain Locke reacted against the works of James, Dewey, Royce, Hegel, and Marx. An emphasis on the importance of collective identities and a rejection of experimental science and codified methods of decision making mark, in general, the differences in James's and Locke's theoretical foci.

Locke was disillusioned, like the poet and recluse Santayana, with the possibility of using philosophical discourse as a way of solving human social problems, but he consistently held that the clarification of concepts and symbols we use to describe ourselves is an important step toward reducing conceptual conflicts. Like Santayana, he was disillusioned with the importance American and Continental philosophers attached to empiricism. Also like Santayana, who was proud that his Spanish and Catholic heritage differentiated him from others, Locke took pride in his differences. But unlike Santayana, Locke was involved in shaping the life-world of his racial group. He was also more attracted to the Bahá'í faith than Christianity. Locke's social involvements were more like Dewey's than Santayana's because he was a philosophic gadfly making abstract ideas pertinent to practical reality. Like Kallen, Locke held cultural pluralism to be a practical model through which congenial relations between conflicting cultural groups could be achieved. But unlike Kallen and other major American philosophers, Locke took substantively into account the implications of his philosophy for an understanding of racial identity and race relations.

Between the 1920s and 1940s, Kallen, Randolph Bourne, Dewey, George Herbert Mead, William I. Thomas, Robert Park, Melville J. Herskovits, and Franz Boas significantly shaped and vitalized the cultural pluralist movement.[10] Not associated in a formal group, as individuals they each rejected the nativism of anti-immigration movements in America. They rejected the instinctivism and hereditarianism of eugenic accounts that pictured the cultures of ethnic and racial groups as biologically determined. They promoted the view that culture is, among other things, an ever-emerging phenomenon and not pre-given before socialization nor an inalterable set of habits necessarily manifest in each individual member of an ethnic group. The integrity of each culture, cultural interaction, and freely chosen forms of association were preferred over forced Americanization and forced assimilation. Moreover, pluralists were united in their efforts to show that a pluralist philosophy was incompatible with ideas justifying totalitarian political systems. Cultural pluralists held many different and often conflicting views on the value of diverse cultures and their futures, but the human potential to change and the integrity of cultures were consistent themes in their works. Locke was a fellow shaper of America's cultural pluralist panorama, but again with a difference.

In Locke's social world of interest, as distinct from the social worlds of interest among other value theorists and cultural pluralists, the personal character virtues of African people as a people, and inferentially as individuals, were stereotyped, denigrated, and considered manifestations of their inferior natures. The beliefs of African people, as expressed through their cultures, were presumed by racists to reflect an innate human nature and, by implication, race-based innately differential modes of valuing. Arguments for the belief in innately different human natures between races frequently held that such differences were endogenous to the cultural properties of races across historical reference systems. That conception of human nature was associated with an equally erroneous view, on Locke's account, of monist philosophy. Monist philosophers believe that a thing's essence is identical to its invariant properties across reference systems. Although Locke agreed with monists that the properties of a thing could be invariant across reference systems, he believed that different reference systems constituted valuation differently, giving us a variety of preferences or norms. Who and what we are is shaped by the reference systems within which our common denominators as human beings are situated. Our commonalities do not exist as isolated essences but rather in relation to the ways we manifest ourselves within social life. As Locke once wrote, "All philosophies, it seems to me, are in ultimate derivation philosophies of life and not of abstract, disembodied 'objective' reality; products of time, place and situation, and thus systems of timed history rather than timeless eternity."[11] Locke's belief in our common humanity and his simultaneous emphasis on cultural discontinuities did not reflect an inconsistency but the manifest features of his conception of identity. The process of ethnogenesis, for example, an area of study that Locke helped popularize along with Charles S. Johnson, Park, Thomas, and Kallen, was predicated on the view that ethnic/racial identities are constantly formed and re-formed. The symbolic creation and re-creation of identity is pictured and portrayed for Locke in art, literature, and drama.[12] He held that the world is subject to remain culturally diverse; that cultural plurality has social advantages that cultural uniformity lacks; that personal concepts of worth such as self-respect, self-pride, and self-esteem, in an already racially and ethnically diverse world, are tied to our valuations of group identities. Locke did not argue like Kallen or other pluralists that the world is determined to result in an end state of permanently culturally separate communities and that such an end state is morally preferable to a culturally uniform end state.[13] Nor did he argue that cultural plurality is necessary because of different historical memories or inalienable instincts.[14] His notion of the fluid character of identity, for example, having bounded characteristics yet subject to flow in a variety of ways, was grounded on his conception of valuing as a force shaping our concept of our self-worth. The commonness of nature as human does not, in a naturalistic fashion, mean we will become culturally uniform. Analogously, the existence of an androgynous world would not necessarily mean the existence of a world without sexual distinctions. That is, even if there were no gender distinctions such that biological females and males normally perceived one another as being shaped differently or attached presumptions of attitudes, feelings, or powers to what physical features were apparent, it does not follow that there would be no modes of differentiating by sexual preferences or that such preferences would not be advertised by individuals through their dress, speech, and association. Locke's focus on identity theoretically requires that we see collective identity as always in transition, historically constituted, and the mediating social phenomenon through which self-definitions are generated.

Locke's versions of cultural pluralism and value relativism were thus constituted with the peculiarities of racial identity substantively taken into account. The ethnogenesis of racial identity and the concepts of experience best suited to account for it were Locke's central concern. Locke did not confuse racial identity with ethnic identity, nor did he assume that historical analysis or conceptions of experience relevant to the persistence or legitimacy of ethnic identities were simplistically transferable to race. Locke was certainly influenced by his teachers and numerous others, but to seek the origin of his views in other than his own creativity would be a tacit denial of his independence of mind. His sense of independence, paradoxical life, and intellectual influences were best described by him in 1935 in the contextualization of his philosophy.

Philadelphia, with her birthright of provincialism flavored by urbanity and her petty bourgeois psyche with the Tory slant, at the start set the key of paradox; circumstance compounded it by decreeing me as a Negro, a dubious and doubting sort of American and by reason of the racial inheritance making me more of a pagan than a Puritan, more of a humanist than a pragmatist.

Verily paradox has followed me the rest of my days: at Harvard, clinging to the genteel tradition of Palmer, Royce and Munsterberg, yet attracted by the disillusion of Santayana and the radical protest of James; again in 1916 I returned to work under Royce but was destined to take my doctorate in Value Theory under Perry. At Oxford, the Austrian philosophy of value; socially Anglophile, but because of race loyalty, strenuously anti-imperialist; universalist in religion, internationalist and pacifist in worldview, but forced by a sense of simple justice to approve of the militant counter-nationalisms of Zionism, Young Turkey, Young Egypt, Young India, and with reservations even Garveyism and current-day "Nippon over Asia." Finally a cultural cosmopolitan, but perforce an advocate of cultural racialism as a defense counter-move for the American Negro, and accordingly more of a philosophical mid-wife to a generation of younger Negro poets, writers, artists than a professional philosopher.

Small wonder, then, with this psychography, that I project my personal history into its inevitable rationalization as cultural pluralism and value relativism, with not too orthodox reaction to the American way of life.[15]

Locke provides an example of an effective rapprochement between a life committed to studying epistemology, aesthetics, or metaphysics and the social reality of racism. He contextualized philosophy itself, including his own, and thereby avoided the Kantian, Cartesian, Hegelian, and Roycean pretensions of having reached an Archimedean point whereby cultural groundings were transcended. Locke faced his cultural groundings, engaged in their critique, and offered a way of valuing that requires us to continually engage in emancipatory revaluation and transvaluation.

THE PHILOSOPHY OF ALAIN LOCKE

Locke's philosophy can be described as radical pragmatism. It is radical in the sense that he believed pragmatism, as a philosophical movement, had become a conservative dogma by the late 1930s. In addition, for Locke, as a philosophy pragmatism failed to appreciate its own ethnocentrism because, under James, it privileged experimentalism and the scientific method. The scientific method and attitudes associated with it were for Locke but one set of methods and attitudes among many by which we can secure meaningful and useful knowledge, knowledge that is itself always subject to revision. Moreover, Locke's critique of metaphysical absolutism centers less on the idea of the given or block universe than on absolutisms' tendency to coincide with or justify prescriptions of cultural uniformity. His critique of pragmatism's approach to values, particularly Dewey's, centers on its approach to value absolutes.

Locke's philosophy can also be described as radical scientific humanism. Radical because the search for common cognates definitive of humanity were of paramount importance to him, but not because a comprehensive list of human commonalities were discoverable. Moreover, cultural diversity for Locke was inherently valuable. A multitude of ways of valuing is characteristic of our being and not a temporal phase of human history. Believing in our unified or common species being for Locke did not require prescribing cultural uniformity. Humans were not more-or-less genuinely human because they saw themselves as members of a culture guided by objectively calculated social choices. Although understanding physical nature and explaining social behavior should be subject to the cannons of the scientific method, these spheres of understanding for Locke do not exhaust our spheres of equally worthwhile interests.

Locke's philosophy can also be fruitfully described as radical value relativism. Radical, because values are not simply the foundational wellspring of our ideations for Locke, nor simply always relative to a given context. They were always in flux in a way that made categorizations of value types a heuristic exercise. In addition, norms such as reciprocity, tolerance, and parity should, for Locke, be universally institutionalized to regulate social relations. Although, like all forms of valuation, these norms are not an inherent property of human nature but possible socially constituted preferences.

Locke's philosophy is strikingly similar to modern deconstruction authors, but again, there are important differences. Locke critiqued the ways Western culture hid itself from its own theoretical limitations; one involved the inability (like any culture) to escape its own problem of enunciation. That is, the problem of trying to escape the limitations of one's own language and its cannons of rationality. The cannons of Kantian rationality, at least on the accounts of deconstructionists, for example, cannot be used to critique the cannons of Kantian rationality. Analogously for Locke, Western theoretical and value biases cannot be used to escape those biases. The technically sterile language of American professional philosophy, for example, cannot be successfully used to critique the technically sterile language of American professional philosophy; the formalism of neo-classical art and literature cannot be used to escape the formalism of neo-classical art and literature. Western culture too often hid its own biases by denying it had any. Like the American Philosophical Association, holding national conventions at hotels in southern cities that refused blacks accommodations while priding itself on its unprejudiced objectivity, Western culture hid its biases under a cloak of abstractions and jaundiced pragmatic formulas that legitimated the status quo. Once pragmatism, like the slogans popularized by the

New Negro movement, became a standard-bearer, "smugly complacent," and a code word for the professionalized status-seekers within academies of culture, it lost its subversive power. The ideas and attitudes for which they were initially arrayed to combat were no longer the forces in as great a need of critique. Whether this is true of some forms of the deconstruction movement is debatable, but at least, Locke's approach to de-forming and re-forming reality warrants consideration of the limitations of the deconstruction movement.

The worlds of African people, however, represented a counterstandpoint to Western cultural biases for Locke. That standpoint was used to both see and be seen; to critique without the presumption of having escaped the inescapable limitations of cultural context; and it was sufficiently visceral for Locke to promote continual re-relativizing and transvaluation. Locke's cultural strategy involved continual reconstitution of the nature of public dialogue by and about African people for the negation of forms of domination.

It is appropriate, I believe, to describe Locke's epistemology, metaphysics, value theory, and cultural strategy, as Lockean.

The philosophy of Alain Locke is a philosophy of critical reflection as itself the basis of rationality. It is not a system of logical rules or criteria of truth conditionals but rather, to borrow from J. Habermas, a system for communicative competency between collective agents. *Critical relativism* is the reasoning modality that conditions the possibility of communicative competency and reflections on facticity.[16] Locke's conception of social identity, as historically conditioned and a manifestation of our loyalties, helps to shape and reshape our sense of self-worth. By affirming the synergism of social identities, but rejecting the predication of being of character virtues and collective agency, we neither lose warrant for applauding our differences nor legitimate the fetishizing of their temporal existence. Locke's value pluralism gives warrant to the need for continued revaluations because values are manifestations of various feeling-form-qualities and historical conditions. Locke's metaphysical pluralism is deconstructive in character, in part, because on Locke's account axiology always entails a normative dimension and metaphysics entails prereflective hierarchies. Locke exposes the way uniformitarian universals lead to or condition pluralities.[17] Moreover, Locke requires that we continually revalue our conceptions of reality because they are always subject to our fallability. Locke's cultural pluralism, with its emphasis on the importance of tolerance, reciprocity, and parity, is the pragmatic and constructive feature of his philosophy.

The philosophy of Alain Locke rejects the conception of philosophy as itself a value-free endeavor, as an atextual sphere of intellectual dialogue over universalizable principles of rationality, knowledge, and nature or a domain of discourse that is or should be unconcerned with the human condition. Locke's critical philosophy valuates, revalues, and transvalues the symbol systems of art, drama, and literature endemic to collective agents in terms of their universal qualities manifested through folk particularities, and does so in light of both their social functions and message-conveying power.

Locke's philosophy entails a conception of social identity that is arguably the capstone of his system of thought. Locke goes beyond the subject-object, individual-collective, ideal-material dichotomies. A social identity entails for Locke the positive valuation of an interest, an affective feeling, a method of representation, and a system or process of continual transvaluation of symbols. A social identity is a form of entification; entification occurs when being is predicated of a group such that it is believed to have an existence independent of the individual (similar to Sartre's totalities). Our loyalties to social groups, for Locke, are often irrational and unpredictable, but we shape our senses of self through our loyalties to groups. The social heuristics of the group are immersed as a person's individual heuristics. Symbols and traditions, associated with the group, for example, are accorded regard, and one sees one's self as a representative sample of the group. In another vein, racial identity, when color is the demarcating factor, is itself the symbol denoting group membership. The Negro race and the Negro culture were for Locke two distinct phenomena that by dint of history were identified as synonymous. Loyalty to the uplift of the race for Locke was thus, *mutatus mutandis,* loyalty to the uplift of the culture.

Locke was not an assimilationist, separatist, instinctivist, or nativist. That group identities are without a rational basis in the sense that they parallel or reflect or manifest a hidden nature or universal essence does not warrant, for Locke, an inference that they are irrelevant or unimportant features of personhood nor that they are subject to dissipate in a foreseeable future. Locke thus eludes easy classification. However, he has been criticized as an idealist, assimilationist, and aristocratic elitist. One can find periods in Locke's long history of literary criticism and isolated statements to support attributing to him each of these orientations. However, upon examination, these orientations tell us less about the consistent threads of his philosophy than his attitude toward a given cultural issue within what he considered a temporal historical phase of cultural development.

For Locke, a social identity is conditioned by our individual valuations, but they are not subjectively molded or caused in isolation from our historicity and material condition. Analogous to James's negation of an 'idea' as a fixed entity, an instance of thought, and analogous to James's negation of the 'objective world' as a fixed entity, an isolated phenomenon to be apprehended by an all-seeing and naked eye unencumbered by interpretation, Locke negated racial, ethnic, religious, and political identities as fixed entities. He also negated identity as objectively given, anthropologically shaped by immutable biologies; he negated identities as reducible to simplistic formulas of the given. Locke's philosophy may not provide us with all the answers about the nature of values and human experience that we need, but the views he tendered provide us with substantive building blocks.

LEGACY

Heads of state such as Léopold Senghor and Kwame Nkrumah; leaders such as W. E. B. Du Bois, Marcus Garvey, George Padmore, Paul Robeson, A. Philip Randolph, and Ralph Bunche; authors such as Charles S. Johnson, E. Franklin Frazier, Carter G. Woodson, and Arthur Schomburg; artistic giants such as Richard Wright, Langston Hughes, Zora Neale Hurston, Claude McKay, Sterling Brown, Jean Toomer, Aaron Douglas, Wallace Thurman, Roland Hayes, Myron O'Higgins, Ann Perry, Lena Horne, James Baldwin, Ralph Ellison, Chester Hines, Kelly Miller, Richmond Barthé, René Maran; philosophers ranging from Otto Abel to Horace Kallen to the modern Afro-American philosophers Eugene Clay Holmes, William T. Fontaine, William Banner, Broadus Butler; and dignitaries ranging from Eleanor Roosevelt to Mary McLeod Bethune were all enriched by the frail traveling philosopher Locke.

Locke's legacy is a picture of *homo humanitas* as a unified species with diverse ways of being in the world, a diversity endemic to its nature, but a diversity that need not lead to heinous cultural conflict. Locke's legacy includes critiques of metaphysical absolutism, of epistemological foundationalism, and of romantic approaches to cultural pluralism, and denials of our cultural and racial contextuality. The foundation for peaceful living among the world's warring psychological tribes requires for Locke a way of valuing that does not negate the legitimacy of the "other's" differentiated existence but provides an authoritative way of regulating value conflicts. That way entails accepting that our values at any given time are always subject to revaluation and transvaluation. Their warrant, consequently, is always relative. As such, the egregious domination of one culture by another loses justifiability, and the recognition of our relativity may help prevent cultural conflict.

Between 1912 and 1954 the majority of Afro-American and African students of philosophy attending universities in the United States were either taught by Locke or one of the black philosophers he was instrumental in hiring at Howard University. Eugene Clay Holmes was the last Afro-American philosopher at Howard hired by Locke to continue the tradition he started. Locke's students and philosophers who have known or were taught by his intellectual heirs populate universities throughout the United States.

Locke helped build a cultural movement, the Harlem Renaissance, that was enlivened by his value theory. The adult education movement, and the central role that critical thinking skills have in educational curricula, are both indebted to Locke's stalwart efforts. The Black Aesthetic movement, African Philosophy, and debates on Black Philosophy have frequently relied on some feature of Locke's philosophy to frame their discussions.[18] His legacy as an aesthete during the Harlem Renaissance and influence on the modern Black Aesthetic movement have been well documented. Recognition of his importance as an American philosopher is steadily growing.

Russell J. Linnemann, editor of *Alain Locke: Reflections on a Modern Renaissance Man*, established that Locke participated in and helped shape the life of human letters across fields of study.[19] Locke significantly influenced the character of cultural pluralism manifest in black social thought. Johnny Washington's *Alain Locke and Philosophy: A Quest for Cultural Pluralism* interprets Locke's philosophic ideas and arguments concerning topical issues ranging from what Black Philosophy is to education, integration, and African art and culture.[20] Washington's text is the first attempt to comprehensively understand Locke's value theory and arguments on topical issues.

PURPOSES OF THE ANTHOLOGY

I have edited this anthology to provide ready access to Locke's articles in philosophy, including several previously unpublished articles, and to make possible an appreciation of his role as a modern philosopher. Instead of offering the surface structure of his principles present in topical book reviews, newspaper articles, and short essays, this anthology presents the deep structure of Locke's value theory and analyses of that theory. Locke's articles in philosophy form the deep structure of his thought and stand as evidence that he designed convincing argument methodologies in support of cultural pluralism and value relativism; that William James, Wilbur Urban, Christian Freiherr von Ehrenfels, and Alexius Meinong provided crucial conceptual building blocks for Locke's value theory; and that his value theory has warrant. Locke's articles and influence also stand as a repudiation of the belief that Afro-Americans have not had a presence in American philosophy, though American philosophy was a bastion of segregation. Moreover, it establishes that American philosophy is a patchwork quilt of ideas.

Locke's philosophy is usually culled from topical articles on art, literature, and drama, his doctoral dissertation, and his 1935 "Values and Imperatives" article. These are inadequate sources for understanding Locke's philosophy and the way it informs his views on cultural issues. The December 1, 1973, Alain L. Locke Symposium sponsored by the *Harvard Advocate*, for example, was designed to discuss Locke's cultural contributions. The conference focused on Locke's guiding ideas in order to understand why he described poetry, drama, jazz, and African artifacts the way he did. The proceedings were published in the *Advocate*.[21] The discussants included Harold Cruse, Albert Murray, Ralph Ellison, Nathan I. Huggins, and Hollie West, and the discussion focused on interpreting Locke's philosophy. Of Locke's articles in philosophy, participants referred to his dissertation and its 1935 revised form, "Values and Imperatives." The conceptual driving force of Locke's topical ideas lies in his philosophy, and its development continued beyond 1935.

There is more than one way to read a body of texts. Jeffrey Stewart's *The Critical Temper of Alain Locke*, for example, interprets Locke's concept of race by relying on Locke's criticism and appraisal of novels.[22] His anthology thus features Locke's annual reviews of black literature and relies on narratives directly addressing the concept of race. Articles and discussions in books abound on his role in the development of the Harlem Renaissance. The subtleties of his criticism of novels are common in texts on black literary criticism. Locke, as a person, has been satirized in novels and praised in journals and symposiums. However, other than "Values and Imperatives," Locke's articles of formal philosophy have not been republished. This anthology is intended to make available the original texts informing Locke's theoretical project.

STRUCTURE OF THE ANTHOLOGY

Each section of this anthology features works by Locke directly arguing for, criticizing, or expressing a fundamental notion of race, culture, civilization, identity, or value. Nearly all of the works featured here have not been republished. Three articles, "Good Reading," "A Functional View of Value Ultimates," and "Value," were not published during Locke's life. The intention is to provide a reading of Locke that moves through the philosophic strain of his intellectual productions. The works in each section are thus ordered historically. Reading Locke's works in this fashion provides a close encounter with the deep structure of his foundational concepts, not as seen through a prism of topical literary or dated political concerns but as he conveys his guiding ideas.

The first section, entitled Epistemological Foundations, features Locke's formal articles on value theory and cultural pluralism. Each article is preceded by a review of its major claims, clarification of what important terms meant during the period in which Locke was writing, and an explication of the significance of Locke's viewpoint.

The second section, Valuation: Commentaries and Reviews, offers

Locke's approach to valuation in context of Bahá'í commentaries and reviews of books by or about Otto, Santayana, and Perry. This section pictures, in succinct form, Locke's view of the way universality, cross-cultural unity, and peace can occur and be mediated by reciprocity.

The third section, Identity and Plurality, provides a selection of topical articles indicative of Locke's application of his value theory in his understanding of the relationship of culture and race. No one-to-one match exists between propositions of his theory and beliefs on the nature of race and culture, but rather a connection such that his approach to the relationship of race and culture is informed by, or is consistent with, the major thrust of his value theory. Articles for this section were selected according to whether they presented, on their own merit, an indication of Locke's beliefs in relation to his conception of race, race relations, and conflict resolution through cultural pluralism. Particular attention was paid to articles that reflected a prominent feature of his philosophy and have not been previously reprinted.

Fourth, the Identity and Education section consists of articles addressing the role of educational institutions in a racially segregated society, a pedagogical approach to racial studies in adult education that both avoids ethnocentricism but provides a sense of black self-regard, and a critique of the misguided teaching of formal logic. Articles for this section are intended to convey Locke's application of value relativism in education, his argument for the importance of cultural studies, and his suggestion that critical relativism should surplant formal logic.

The last section, An Interpretation, is the editor's rendering of the not-always-apparent implications and methodologies that Locke employs. It also takes account of the weaknesses of value theory and suggests further areas of research into Locke's philosophy.

NOTES

1. See Jeffrey C. Stewart, *The Critical Temper of Alain Locke: A Selection of His Essays on Art and Culture* (New York: Garland Publishing, 1983); and John Edgar Tidwell and John Wright, "Alain Locke: A Comprehensive Bibliography of His Published Writings," *Callaloo* 4 (February–October 1981), 175–192.

2. Alain Locke, "Oxford Contrasts," *The Independent*, July 15, 1909, pp. 139–142. Also published as "Oxford: By a Negro Student," *The Coloured American Magazine*, September 1909, pp. 185–190. See "A Rhodes Scholar Question," unpublished, 14 leaves, Alain Locke Collection, Moorland-Spingard Research Center, Howard University, Box O-R.

3. See Josiah Royce, *Race Questions, Provincialism, and Other American Problems* (New York: Macmillan, 1908); and Royce, *Philosophy of Loyalty* (New York: Hafner, 1908).

4. Alain Locke, "Impressions of Haifa," *The Bahá'í World: A Biennial International Record* 3 (1928–1930), 280, 282. For Locke's encounter with the Bahá'í faith in 1921, see Louis Gregory, "Inter-Racial Amity," *Bahá'í World* 11 (1926–1928), 281–285.

5. Alain Locke, "Impressions of Luxor," *Howard Alumnus* 11 (May 1924), 74–78.

6. Leonard Harris, "Identity: Alain Locke's Atavism," *Transactions of the Charles S. Peirce Society* 24 (Winter 1988), 65–73. See also Ernest D. Mason, "Alain Locke on Race and Race Relations," *Phylon* 40 (1979), 342–350.

7. Ardie Sue Myers, "Relations of a Godmother Patronage During the Harlem Renaissance" (M.A. thesis, George Washington University, 1981), p. 55.

8. Manning Marable, "Alain Locke, W. E. B. Du Bois, and the Crisis of Black Education During the Great Depression," in Russell J. Linnemann (ed.), *Alain Locke: Reflections on a Modern Renaissance Man* (Baton Rouge: Louisiana State University Press, 1982), pp. 63–76.

9. Houston Baker, Jr., *Modernism and the Harlem Renaissance* (Chicago: University of Chicago Press, 1987), p. 75.

10. See Fred Wacker, "The Fate of Cultural Pluralism Within American Social Thought," *Ethnic Groups* 3 (1981), 125–138.

11. Alain Locke, "Values and Imperatives," in Sidney Hook and Horace Kallen (eds.), *American Philosophy Today and Tomorrow* (New York: Lee Furman, 1935), p. 313.

12. On ethnogenesis, see L. Singer, "Ethnogenesis and Negro-Americans Today," *Social Research* 29 (1962), 419–432; J. Sarna, "From Immigrates to Ethnics: Toward a New Theory of Ethnicization," *Ethnicity* 8 (1978), 370–378; and G. Stocking Jr., *Race, Culture, and Evolution* (New York: Free Press, 1968). On the problems of immigrants, Americanization, and Chicago School sociologists and the problems of cultural pluralism, see Wacker, "The Fate of Cultural Pluralism Within American Social Thought."

13. See Horace Kallen, *Culture and Democracy in the United States: Studies in the Group Psychology of the American Peoples* (New York: Boni and Liveright, 1924).

14. See William B. Harvey, "The Philosophical Anthropology of Alain Locke," in Linnemann (ed.), *Alain Locke: Reflections on a Modern Renaissance Man*, p. 23.

15. Locke, "Values and Imperatives," in Hook and Kallen (eds.), *American Philosophy Today and Tomorrow*, p. 313.

16. See "The Need for a New Organon in Education," *Goals for American Education* (New York: Conference on Science, Philosophy and Religion, 1950), pp. 201–212.

17. See Ernest Mason, "Deconstruction in the Philosophy of Alain Locke," *Transactions of the Charles S. Peirce Society* 24 (Winter 1988), 85–106.

18. See Addison Gayle, *The Black Aesthetic* (New York: Doubleday, 1971).

19. See Linnemann (ed.), *Alain Locke: Reflections on a Modern Renaissance Man.*

20. See Johnny Washington, *Alain Locke and Philosophy: A Quest for Cultural Pluralism* (Westport, Conn.: Greenwood Press, 1986).

21. See Archie Epps, Nathan I. Huggins, Harold Cruse, Albert Murray, and Ralph Ellison, "The Alain L. Locke Symposium," *Harvard Advocate* (December 1, 1973), 9–29.

22. See Stewart, *The Critical Temper of Alain Locke.*

I. Epistemological Foundations

1. Values and Imperatives

On February 7, 1930, Locke presented "Cultural Relativism" (see Box C, Alain Locke Collection, Moorland-Spingarn Research Center) before the Harvard Philosophy Club. Features of that presentation, which focused primarily on the usefulness of value relativism, were integrated into "Values and Imperatives." In his 1917 Harvard doctoral dissertation, Locke had constructed his categorization of values. However, unlike in his dissertation, in this article Locke holds that how we categorize values is less important than understanding our transposition of values.

In this article, Locke argues for the rejection of metaphysical absolutism; for the inherent constitution of valuation as a process of transvaluation and transposition; for the need of value imperatives without appeal to absolutes; and for the pragmatic or functional use of value relativism and the proper categorization of values. Locke holds that "values are rooted in attitudes, not in reality and pertain to ourselves, not to the world." By "values" Locke generally means feelings, attitudes, beliefs, preferences, attenuations for moral principles, aesthetic objects, religious beliefs, racial and ethnic loyalties, and political persuasions. By "imperatives" he means compelling rules, guidelines, and actions. Our imperatives function as authoritative guides. Public policies, social behavior, and artistic judgments, for example, are "imperatives" if we believe in them and act with

"Values and Imperatives," *American Philosophy Today and Tomorrow*, ed. Horace M. Kallen and Sidney Hook (New York: Lee Furman, 1935), pp. 312–333.

certainty as if our policies, behaviors, and judgments are the best ones. Social life requires imperatives. Even if everyone in a given society were value relativists, the expressed or unexpressed regulating rules they followed would function as authoritative guides. By metaphysical absolutism or absolutist universals Locke means the view that there is an "essence" to the nature of things; that one method of interpreting and portraying experiences is inherently preferable to all others; or that one system of living should be universalized and legitimated. Locke's critique of metaphysical absolutism has been compared to Jacques Derrida's.[1] His view of transvaluation might also be compared to those of Wilbur Urban and Friedrich Nietzsche.

Locke situates himself as a value relativist by distinguishing his relativism from value monism, that is, the view that value has an essence of which all forms of valuing are reducible. However, he rejects value anarchism, that is, the view that facts, preferences, terms, relations are to be recognized as coequal factors shaping human experience. (He normally attributes this view to James, but here, as elsewhere, he is less concerned with James's views than with deploring the tendency to believe that value relativism warrants value anarchy.) After situating himself, he constructs a categorization of value types and preconditions for the resolution of value conflicts. His categorizations are reminiscent of Alexius Meinong's and Wilbur Urban's. Locke focuses on feelings and their forms rather than prioritizing interest (Perry) or utility (Mill) as the font of values. He aligns himself with coherence theories

1. Ernest Mason, "Deconstruction in the Philosophy of Alain Locke," *Transactions of the Charles S. Peirce Society* 24 (Winter 1988), 85–106; and Houston A. Baker, Jr., *Modernism and the Harlem Renaissance* (Chicago: The University of Chicago Press, 1987).

of truth, in contrast to correspondence theories that hold that some set of values correspond or reflect an objective truth. Consistent with his relativist position, Locke eschews the belief that a scientific reasoning methodology is the key to certain knowledge or a route to proper value conflict resolution.

Locke rejects Deweyian, Kantian, anarchist, positivist, and instrumentalist approaches to under-standing and resolving our quest for certainty. Locke implies support for a Marxian approach to ending institutionalized monopolies. However, the problem of the existence of "psychological tribes" and quests for uniformity would exist on Locke's account in a classless society. Locke provides the basic outline of his functionalist approach to value ultimates, an approach that he develops and applies in future articles.

Values and Imperatives

All philosophies, it seems to me, are in ultimate derivation philosophies of life and not of abstract, disembodied "objective" reality; products of time, place and situation, and thus systems of timed history rather than timeless eternity. They need not even be so universal as to become the epitomized *rationale* of an age, but may merely be the lineaments of a personality, its temperament and dispositional attitudes projected into their systematic rationalizations. But no conception of philosophy, however relativistic, however opposed to absolutism, can afford to ignore the question of ultimates or abandon what has been so aptly though skeptically termed "the quest for certainty." To do that is not merely to abdicate traditional metaphysics with its rationalistic justification of absolutes but also to stifle embryonic axiology with its promising analysis of norms. Several sections of American thought, however, have been so anxious to repudiate intellectualism and escape the autocracy of categoricals and universals that they have been ready to risk this. Though they have at times discussed the problems of value, they have usually avoided their normative aspects, which has led them into a bloodless behaviorism as arid as the intellectualism they have abandoned or else resulted in a completely individualistic and anarchic relativism which has rightly been characterized recently as "philosophic Nihilism." In de-throning our absolutes, we must take care not to exile our imperatives, for after all, we live by them. We must realize more fully that values create these imperatives as well as the more formally super-imposed absolutes, and that norms control our behavior as well as guide our reasoning. Further, as I shall later point out, we must realize that not in every instance is this normative control effected indirectly through judgmental or evaluational processes, but often through primary mechanisms of feeling modes and dispositional attitudes. Be that as it may, it seems that we are at last coming to the realization that without some account of normative principles, some fundamental consideration of value norms and "ultimates" (using the term in a non-committal sense), no philosophical system can hope to differentiate itself from descriptive science or present a functional, interpretive version of human experience.

Man does not, cannot, live in a valueless world. Pluralism has merely given temporary surcease from what was the central problem of monism,—the analysis and justification of these "ultimates," and pragmatism has only transposed the question from the traditional one of what ends should govern life to the more provocative one of how and why activity creates them. No philosophy, short of the sheerest nominalism or the most colorlessly objective behaviorism, is so neutral that it has not some axiological implications. Positivism least of all; for in opposing the traditional values, positivism has set up countervalues bidding us find meaning in the act rather than project meaning from the plane of reason and the subjective approach; and further, as pragmatism and instrumentalism, has set up at the center of its philosophy a doctrine of truth as itself a functional value. So, by waiving the question of the validity of value ultimates as "absolutes," we do not escape the problem of their functional categorical character as imperatives of action and as norms of preference and choice.

Though this characteristically American repudiation of "ultimates" was originally made in the name of the "philosophy of common sense," common sense and the practical life confronts us with the problem all the more forcefully by displaying a chronic and almost universal fundamentalism of values in action. Of this, we must at least take stock, even if we cannot eventually justify it or approve of it. The common man, in both his individual and group behavior, perpetuates the problem in a very practical way. He sets up personal and private and group norms as standards and principles, and rightly or wrongly hypostasizes them as universals for all conditions, all times and all men. Whether then on the plane of reason or that of action, whether "above the battle" in the conflict of "isms" and the "bloodless ballet of ideas" or in the battle of partisans with their conflicting and irreconcilable ways of life, the same essential strife goes on, and goes on in the name of eternal ends and deified ultimates. Our quest for certainty, motivated from the same urge, leads to similar dilemmas. The blind practicality of the common man and the disinterested impracticality of the philosopher yield similar results and rationalizations. Moreover, such transvaluations of value as from time to time we have, lead neither to a truce of values nor to an effective devaluation; they merely resolve one dilemma and set up another. And so, the conflict of irreconcilables goes on as the devisive and competitive forces of our practical imperatives parallel the incompatibilities of our formal absolutes.

We cannot declare for value-anarchism as a wishful way out, or find a solution in that other alternative blind alley of a mere descriptive analysis of interests. That but postpones the vital problems of ends till the logically later consideration of evaluation and post-valuational rationalizations. To my thinking, the gravest problem of contemporary philosophy is how to ground some normative principle or criterion of objective validity for values without resort to dogmatism and absolutism on the intellectual plane, and without falling into their corollaries, on[1] the plane of social behavior and action, of intolerance and mass coercion. This calls for a functional analysis of value norms and a search for normative principles in the immediate context of valuation. It raises the question whether the fundamental value modes have a way of setting up automatically or dispositionally their end-values prior to evaluative judgment. Should this be the case, there would be available a more direct approach to the problem of value ultimates, and we might discover their primary normative character to reside in their functional rôle as stereotypes of feeling-attitudes and dispositional imperatives of action-choices, with this character reenforced only secondarily by reason and judgment about them as "absolutes." We should then be nearer a practical understanding of the operative mechanisms of valuation and of the grounds for our agreements and conflicts over values.

Normally, one would expect a philosophical tradition dominated, as contemporary American thought has been, by an activist theory of knowledge, to have made a problem like this central. We might very profitably pause for a moment to take stock of the reasons why this has not been so. In the first place, in the reaction away from academic metaphysics, there has been a flight to description and analysis too analogous to science and too committed to scientific objectivism. It is impossible to reach such problems as we have before us effectively in terms of pure positivism, of the prevalent objectivism, or of the typical view that until quite recently has dominated American value theory,—the view namely that end-values exist only in so far as values are rationalized and mediated by processes of evaluation and formal value judgments. Added to this, is our characteristic preoccupation with theories of meaning limited practically to the field of truth and knowledge. Because of this logico-experimental slant, we again have made common cause with the current scientific attitude; making truth too exclusively a matter of the correct anticipation of experience, of the confirmation of fact.[2] Yet truth may also sometimes be the sustaining of an attitude, the satisfaction of a way of feeling, the corroboration of a value. To the poet, beauty is truth; to the religious devotee, God is truth; to the enthused moralist, what ought-to-be overtops factual reality. It is perhaps to be expected that the typical American philosophies should concentrate almost exclusively on thought-action as the sole criterion of experience, and should find analysis of the emotional aspects of human behavior uncongenial. This in itself, incidentally, is a confirming example of an influential value-set, amounting in this instance to a grave cultural bias. When we add to this our American tradition of individualism, reflecting itself characteristically in the value-anarchism and *laissez faire* of which we have already spoken, it is easy to explain why American thought has moved tangent to the whole central issue of the normative aspects and problems of value.

In saying this, do we say anything more than that values are important and that American philosophy should pay more attention to axiology? Most assuredly;—we are saying that but for a certain blindness, value-theory might easily have been an American forte, and may still become so if our predominantly functionalist doctrines ever shed their arbitrary objectivism and extend themselves beyond their present concentration on theories of truth and knowledge into a balanced analysis of values generally. Ironically enough, the very type of philosophy which has insisted on truth as a value has, by rigid insistence on the objective criterion and the experimental-instrumental aspects of thought, disabled itself for pursuing a similarly functional interpretation of the other value modes and their normative principles.

Human behavior, it is true, is experimental, but it is also selectively preferential, and not always in terms of outer adjustments and concrete results. Value reactions guided by emotional preferences and affinities are as potent in the determination of attitudes as pragmatic consequences are in the determination of actions. In the generic and best sense of the term 'pragmatic,' it is as important to take stock of the one as the other.

Fortunately, within the last few years a decided trend toward axiology and the neglected problems of value has developed, properly enough under the aegis of the *International Journal of Ethics*, promising to offset this present one-sidedness of American philosophical interests. Once contemporary American thought does turn systematically to the analysis of values, its empirical and functionalist approach will be considerably in its favor. Such a philosophic tradition and technique ought to come near to realizing the aim of Brentano, father of modern value-theory, to derive a functional theory of value from a descriptive and empirical psychology of valuation and to discover in value-experience itself the source of those normative and categorical elements construed for centuries so arbitrarily and so artificially in the realm of rational absolutes.

There is little or no hope that this can be obtained *via* a theory of value which bids us seek whatever objectivity and universality values may have outside the primary processes of valuation, whether in the confirmations of experience or the affirmations of evaluative judgments. For these positions lead only, as far as the direct apprehension of value goes, to Protagorean relativism,—each man the measure and each situation the gauge of value, and then an abysmal jump to the objective criterion of the truths of science, valid for all situations, all men and all times.

What seems most needed is some middle ground between these extremes of subjectivism and objectivism. The natural distinctions of values and their functional criteria surely lie somewhere in between the atomistic relativism of a pleasure-pain scale and the colorless, uniformitarian criterion of logic,—the latter more of a straightjacket for value qualities than the old intellectualist trinity of Beauty, Truth and Good. Flesh and blood values may not be as universal or objective as logical truths and schematized judgments, but they are not thereby deprived of some relative objectivity and universality of their own. The basic qualities of values should never have been sought in logical classes, for they pertain to psychological categories. They are not grounded in types of realms of value, but are rooted in modes or kinds of *valuing*.

In fact, the value-mode establishes for itself, directly through feeling, a qualitative category which, as discriminated by its appropriate feeling-quality, constitutes an emotionally mediated form of experience. If this be so, the primary judgments of value are emotional judgments—(if the inveterate Austrian term "*feeling-judgments*" is not allowable philosophical English), and the initial reference for value predication is based on a form-quality revealed in feeling and efficacious in valuation through feeling. Though finally validated in different ways and by different criteria, beauty, goodness, truth (as approval or acceptance), righteousness are known in immediate recognitions of qualitative apprehension. The generic types of value are basic and fundamental feeling-modes, each with its own characteristic form criterion in value perception. For the fundamental kinds, we can refer to inveterate common-sense, which discriminates them with approximate accuracy—the moral and ethical, the aesthetic, the logical and the religious categories with their roughly descriptive predicates. For an empirical psychology of values, however, they need to be approached directly from the side of feeling and value-attitudes, and re-discriminated not in terms of formal definition but in terms of technical description of their affective-volitional dimensions and factors.

Normally a value-mode is conveyed while the value is being apprehended. Otherwise the quality of the value would be indeterminate, and this is usually contrary to fact. Though we may still be in doubt regarding its validation, its quantity, place in the value series and other specific issues of the value situation, we are usually certain of the value-mode. This is why we should think of a value-quality primarily in terms of feeling or attitude and not of predicates of judgment; why we should speak of a value-reference rather than a value claim. And if the value type is given in the immediate apprehension of the particular value, some qualitative universal is given. It supplies the clue to the functional value norm,—being felt as good, beautiful, etc.—and we have this event in mind when we say that in the feeling-reference to some value-mode, some value ultimate becomes the birthmark of the value. If values are thus normatively stamped by form-qualities of feeling in the original value experience, then the evaluative judgment merely renders explicit what was implicit in the original value sensing, at least as far as the modal quality of the value is concerned. This could only be true on one of two assumptions, *viz.*, that some abstract feeling-character functioned dispositionally as a substitute for formal judgment, or that the feeling-attitude itself moulded the value-mode and reflected sympathetically its own pattern. If the latter be the case, a value-type or category is a feeling-mode carved out dispositionally by a fundamental attitude.

Of course, this notion of a feeling-reference or form-quality constituting the essential identity and unity of a value-mode is not easily demonstrable; it may be just a hypothetical anticipation of what an experimental analysis of valuation might later establish and prove. However, the main objection to such a conception of a value form-character has been undermined, if not overthrown, by the Gestalt psychology, which has demonstrated the factual reality of a total configuration functioning in perceptual recognition, comparison and choice. There is therefore nothing scientifically impossible or bizarre in assuming a form-quality felt along with the specific value context and constituting its modal value-quality and reference. In the absence of direct evidence of this configurational element in valuation, the most corroborative circumstantial evidence is to be found in the interchangeability or rather the convertibility of the various kinds of value. The further we investigate, the more we discover that there is no fixity of content to values, and the more we are bound, then, to infer that their identity as groups must rest on other elements. We know that a *value-genre* often evades its definition and breaks through its logical barriers to include content not usually associated with it. The awe-inspiring scene becomes "*holy*," the logical proof, "*beautiful*," creative expression, a "duty," and in every case the appropriate new predicates follow the attitude and the attitude cancels out the traditionally appropriate predicates. For every value coupled by judgmental predication, thousands are linked by identities of feeling-mode; for every value transformed by change of logical presuppositions, scores are switched by a radical transformation of the feeling-attitude. We are forced to conclude that the feeling-quality, irrespective of content, makes a value of a given kind, and that a transformation of the attitude effects a change of type in the value situation.

In this connection, a competent analyst concludes[3]: "We are compelled to recognize that in the aesthetic value situation anything animate or inanimate, natural or artificial, deed or doer, may be the object. This consideration alone makes it clear that beauty and goodness cannot always, if ever, be the same." Yet with all this qualitative distinctness, the artist may feel duty toward his calling, obligation toward his unrealized idea, because when he feels conflict and tension in that context, he occupies an entirely different attitude toward his aesthetic material. Instead of the repose or ecstasy of contemplation or the exuberant flow of creative expression, he feels the tension and pull of an unrealized situation, and feeling obligation and conflict, senses along with that a moral quality. The changed feeling-attitude creates a new value; and the type-form of the attitude brings with it its appropriate value category. These modes co-assert their own relevant norms; each sets up a categorical imperative of its own, not of the Kantian sort with rationalized universality and objectivity, but instead the psychological urgency (shall we say, necessity?) to construe the situation as of a particular qualitative form-character. It is this that we term a functional categorical factor, since it operates in and through feeling, although it is later made explicit, analyzed, and validated by evaluative processes of judgment and experiential test.

The traditional way of accounting for the various kinds of value, on the other hand, starting out as it does from the side of evaluation, leans too heavily upon logical definition. It substitutes the terminology of predicates for the real functional *differential*. A comparison, even in incomplete, suggestive outline, between a logical and a psychological classification of values will show how much more neatly a schematization of values in terms of the mechanics of value-feelings fits the facts than the rough approximations of the traditional logical classification. More than this, such a classification not only states the basis on which the primary value groups generically rest, but reveals the process out of which they genetically arise.

Taking feeling-modes as the basic factor of differentiation, the religious and ethical, moral, logical and aesthetic types of value differentiate very neatly on the basis of four fundamental feeling-modes of exaltation, tension, acceptance, and repose or equilibrium. There are sub-divisions for each value-mode determined by the usual polarity of positive and negative values, and also for each mode a less recognized but most important sub-division related to the directional drive of the value-feeling. This latter discriminates for each type of value an 'introverted' and an 'extroverted' variety of the value, according as the feeling-reference refers the value inward toward an individualized value of the self or projects it outward toward value-sharing and the socialized plane of action. We may illustrate first in terms of the moral values. Every definition of the moral or ethical situation recognizes the characteristic element of conflict between alternatives and the correlated sense of tension. The classification we are discussing would transpose a typical pragmatic definition such as "the conflict of mentally incompatible goods defines a moral situation" into a psychological category of value grounded in the form-feeling of tension, inducing the moral attitude toward the situation irrespective of content. Where the value reference is introverted or directed inwardly toward the self, this tension expresses itself as a compulsion of inner restraint or as "conscience": where an extroverted reference directs the tension toward a compulsion outward to action, the tension becomes sensed as "duty" or obligation. Or, to illustrate again, in the mode of the religious values, we have the mechanisms of introverted exaltation determining positively the ecstasy and sense of union of the religious mystic and negatively his sense of sin and separation, with the outward or extroverted form of the religious value expressing itself in the convictions of "conversion" and salvation (active union with God) and the salvationist crusade against evil (the fear and hate of Satan).

Tabular illustration follows.

This view, if correct, leads to the conclusion that there is a form-feeling or form-quality characteristic of each fundamental value-type, and that values are discriminated in terms of such feeling factors in the primary processes of valuation. The view further regards these modalities of feeling as constituting the basic kinds of value through the creation of stereotyped and dispositional attitudes which sustain them. The substantial agreement of such a table with the traditional classification of values merely indicates that the established scheme of value judgments has traced the basic value modes with fair correctness. However, there are differences more significant than the similarities. These differences not only make possible a more accurate classification of the types of value, but make evident a genetic pattern of values by which we may trace more accurately their interrelations, both of correlation and of opposition.

Over and above greater descriptive accuracy in value analysis, then, this view may be expected to vindicate itself most effectively

Modal Quality Form-Quality and Feeling-Reference	Value Type or Field	Value Predicates	Value Polarity	
			Positive	*Negative*
EXALTATION: (Awe Worship)				
a. Introverted: (Individualized): Inner Ecstasy	*Religious*	Holy—Unholy	Holiness	Sin
b. Extroverted: (Socialized): Religious Zeal		Good—Evil	Salvation	Damnation
TENSION: (Conflict-Choice)				
a. Inner Tension of "Conscience"	*Ethical*	Good—Bad	Conscience	Temptation
b. Extrovert: Outer Tension of Duty	*Moral*	Right—Wrong	Right	Crime
ACCEPTANCE or AGREEMENT: (Curiosity—Intellectual Satisfaction)				
a. Inner Agreement in Thought	*Logical Truth*	True (Correct) and Incorrect	Consistency	Contradiction
b. Outer Agreement in Experience	*Scientific Truth*	True—False	Certainty	Error
REPOSE or EQUILIBRIUM				
a. Consummation in Contemplation	*Aesthetic*	Beautiful—Ugly	Satisfaction	Disgust
b. Consummation in Creative Activity	*Artistic*	Fine—Unsatisfactory	Joy	Distress

a: Value: introverted type.
b: Value: extroverted type.

in the field of the genetics and the dynamics of values. Here it is able to account for value conversions and value opposition in terms of the same factors, and thus apply a common principle of explanation to value mergings, transfers and conflicts. It is with this range of phenomena that the logical theories of value experience their greatest difficulties. We are aware of instances, for example, where a sequence of logical reasoning will take on an aesthetic character as a "beautiful proof" or a "pretty demonstration," or where a moral quality or disposition is appraised not as "good" but as "noble," or again, where a religious ritual is a mystical "reality" to the convinced believer but is only an aesthetic, symbolic show to the non-credal spectator. The logical way of explaining such instances assumes a change of the judgmental pre-suppositions mediating the values, or in other cases, puts forward the still weaker explanation of the transfer of value predicates through metaphor and analogy. But by the theory that values are constituted by the primary modal quality of the actual feeling, one does not have to go beyond that to explain the accurate appropriateness of the unusual predicates or the actuality of the attitude in the valuation. They are in direct functional relation and agreement. As a *quod erat demonstrandum,* the proof or demonstration is an enjoyed consummation of a process, and is by that very fact aesthetic in quality. Likewise, the contemplation of an ethical deed, when the tension of the act is not shared, becomes a detached appreciation, though it needs only the sharing of the tension to revert to the moral type of valuation. In fact, moral behavior, when it becomes dispositional, with the smooth feeling-curve of habit and inner equilibrium, normally takes on a quasi-aesthetic quality, as reflected in the criterion of taste and *noblesse oblige* rather than the sterner criterion of "must" and of "duty." And of course, to the disinterested spectator, the religious ritual is just like any other work of art,—an object of reposeful, equilibrated projection. Once a different form-feeling is evoked, the situation and the value type are, *ipso facto,* changed. Change the attitude, and, irrespective of content, you change the value-type; the appropriate new predicates automatically follow.

The same principles hold, moreover, in explaining the conflicts and incompatibilities of values as value-groups. Of course, there are other types of value conflicts, means-ends and value-series problems, but what concerns us at this point are those graver antinomies of values out of which our most fundamental value problems arise. One needs only to recall the endless debate over the *summum bonum* or the perennial quarrel over the respective merits of the value Trinity. How, even after lip service to the parity of Beauty, Truth and Good, we conspire for the priority of one pet favorite, which usually reflects merely our dominant value interest and our own temperamental value bias. The growth of modern relativism has at least cooled these erstwhile burning issues and tempered the traditional debate. Indeed from our point of view, we see these grand ultimates, for all their assertion of fraternal harmony, as doomed to perpetual logical opposition because their basic value attitudes are psychologically incompatible. Repose and action, integration and conflict, acceptance and projection, as attitudes, create natural antinomies, irresolvable orders of value; and the only peace a scientific view of value can sanction between them is one based not upon priority and precedence but upon parity and reciprocity.

As we dispose of this traditional value feud, we become aware of the internal value conflicts within the several value fields, those schisms within common value loyalties which are becoming all the more serious as the traditional value quarrel subsides. There is the feud between the mystic and the reformer in religion, between the speculative logician and the inductive experimentalist in the pursuit of truth, yes,—even the one, less sharp and obvious, between the aesthete and the artist. An affective theory of valuation throws these internal dilemmas into an interesting and illuminating perspective. In each of these cases, the modal value-feeling is, of course, held in common and the same ideological loyalties shared, but these sub-groups are still divided by the basic difference in their orientation toward their common values. Here we see the functional importance of that distinction in feeling-reference or feeling-direction which so closely parallels the Jungian polarity of introversion and extroversion that these terms have been adopted to describe it. These directional drives, determined emotionally in the majority of cases, deciding whether the value is focussed inwardly or outwardly, individuated or socialized, are of the utmost practical importance. For they are the root of those civil feuds within the several value provinces between the saint and the prophet, the mystic and the reformer, the speculative theorist and the practical experimentalist in the search for truth, the aesthete and dilettante versus the creative and professional artist, and finally between the self-righteous moral zealot and the moral reformer. And as each of these attitude-sets becomes dispositional and rationalized, we have the scientific clue to that pattern of value loyalties which divides humanity into psychological sub-species, each laying down rationalizations of ways of life that, empirically traced, are merely the projections of their predominant value tendencies and attitudes.

Thus our varied absolutes are revealed as largely the rationalization of our preferred values and their imperatives. Their tap-root, it seems, stems more from the will to power than from the will to know. Little can be done, it would appear, either toward their explanation or their reconciliation on the rational plane. Perhaps this is the truth that Brentano came near laying hands on when he suggested a love-hate dimensionality as fundamental to all valuation. Certainly the fundamental opposition of value modes and the attitudes based upon them has been one of the deepest sources of human division and conflict. The role of feeling can never be understood nor controlled through minimizing it; to admit it is the beginning of practical wisdom in such matters. As Hartmann[4] has well observed,— "Every value, when once it has gained power over a person, has a tendency to set itself up as a sole tyrant of the whole human *ethos,* and indeed at the expense of other values, even of such as are not inherently opposed to it." We must acknowledge this, though not to despair over it, but by understanding how and why, to find principles of control from the mechanisms of valuation themselves. Without doubt many value attitudes as separate experiences are incompatible and antithetic, but all of us, as individuals, reconcile these incompatibilities in our own experience when we shift, for variety as often as for necessity, from one mode of value to the other. The effective antidote to value absolutism lies in a systematic and realistic demonstration that values are rooted in attitudes, not in reality, and pertain to ourselves, not to the world. Consistent value pluralism might eventually make possible a value loyalty not necessarily founded on value bigotry, and impose a truce of imperatives, not by denying the categorical factors in valuation, which, as we have seen, are functional, but by insisting upon the reciprocity of these norms. There is not necessarily irresolvable conflict between these separate value modes if, without discounting their emotional and functional incommensurability, we realize their complementary character in human experience.

At the same time that it takes sides against the old absolutism and invalidates the *summum bonum* principle; this type of value pluralism does not invite the chaos of value-anarchy or the complete *laissez faire* of extreme value individualism. It rejects equally trying to reduce value distinctions to the flat continuum of a pleasure-pain economy or to a pragmatic instrumentalism of ends-means relations. Of course, we need the colorless, common-denominator order of factual reality and objectivity (although that itself serves a primary value as a mechanism of the coordination of experience), but values simply do not reduce to it. To set values over against facts does not effectively neutralize values. Since we cannot banish our imperatives, we must find some principle of keeping them within bounds. It should be possible to maintain some norms as functional and native to the process of experience, without justifying arbitrary absolutes, and to uphold some categoricals without calling down fire from heaven. Norms of this status would be functional constants and practical sustaining imperatives of their correlated modes of experience; nothing more, but also nothing less.

Such "ends" totalize merely an aspect of human experience and stand only for a subsistent order of reality. They should not confuse themselves with that objective reality nor attempt to deny or disparage its other value aspects and the subsistent orders they reflect. This totalizing character is purely functional in valuation, and it is a mockery of fact either to raise it to the level of transcendental worship or to endow it with objective universality. This conceded, there is little sense and less need to set facts and values over against each other as antagonistic orders; rather should we think of reality as a central fact and a white light broken up by the prism of human nature into a spectrum of values. By proposing these basic value-modes as coordinate and complementary, value pluralism of this type proposes its two most important corollaries,—the principles of reciprocity and tolerance. As derivative aspects of the same basic reality, value orders cannot reasonably become competitive and rival realities. As creatures of a mode of experience, they should not construe themselves in any concrete embodiment so as to contradict or stultify the mode of which they are a particularized expression.

Should such a view become established,—and I take that to be one of the real possibilities of an empirical theory of value, we shall then have warrant for taking as the proper center of value loyalty neither the worship of definitions or formulae nor the competitive monopolizing of value claims, but the goal of maximizing the value-mode itself as an attitude and activity. The attitude will itself be construed as the value essence,—which it really is, and not as now the intellectualized *why* or the traditional and institutionalized *how* associated with the value category. In such a frame of reference, for example, romanticism and classicism could not reasonably think of themselves as monopolizing the field of art, nor Protestantism, Catholicism or even Christianity conceive themselves the only way to salvation. In such a perspective, Nordicism and other rampant racialisms might achieve historical sanity or at least prudential common-sense to halt at the natural frontiers of genuinely shared loyalties and not sow their own eventual downfall through forced loyalties and the counter-reactions which they inevitably breed. Social reciprocity for value loyalties is but a new name for the old virtue of tolerance, yet it does bring the question of tolerance down from the lofty thin air of idealism and chivalry to the plane of enlightened self-interest and the practical possibilities of effective value-sharing. As a working principle, it divorces proper value loyalty from unjustifiable value bigotry, releases a cult from blind identification with creed and dogma, and invests no value interest with monopoly or permanent priority.

However, no one can sensibly expect a sudden or complete change in our value behavior from any transformation, however radical, in our value theory. Relativism will have to slowly tame the wild force of our imperatives. There will be no sudden recanting of chronic, traditional absolutisms, no complete undermining of orthodoxies, no huge, overwhelming accessions of tolerance. But absolutism is doomed in the increasing variety of human experience. What over a century ago was only an inspired metaphorical flash in the solitary universal mind of a Goethe,—that phrase about civilization's being a fugue in which, voice by voice, the several nations and peoples took up and carried the interwoven theme, could in our day become a systematic philosophy of history like Pareto's. His historical and functional relativism of cultural values, with persistent normative constants ("residues") and variable and contingent specific embodiments ("derivatives"), is but an indication of the possibilities of relativism extended to historical and social thought. Cultural relativism, to my mind, is the culminating phase of relativistic philosophy, and it is bound to have a greater influence than any other phase of relativism upon our conception and practise of values.

Our present way of socializing values on the basis of credal agreement, dogmatic orthodoxies, and institutionally vested interests is fundamentally unsound and self-contradictory. As a practise, it restricts more than it protects the values that have called institutions into being. Organized for value-sharing and value promotion, they often contradict their own primary purposes. One way of reform undoubtedly is to combat the monopolistic tradition of most of our institutions. This sounds Marxian, and is to an extent. But the curtailing of the struggle over the means and instrumentalities of values will not eliminate our quarrels and conflicts about ends, and long after the possible elimination of the profit motive, our varied imperatives will still persist. Economic classes may be absorbed, but our psychological tribes will not thereby be dissolved. So, since there may be monopolistic attitudes and policies with respect to ends and ideals just as well as monopolies of the instrumentalities of human values—(and of this fact the ideological dogmatism of contemporary communism is itself a sad example), it may be more effective to invoke a non-Marxian principle of maximizing values.

Contrary to Marxian logic, this principle is non-uniformitarian. It is the Roycean principle of "loyalty to loyalty," which though idealistic in origin and defense, was a radical break with the tradition of absolutism. It called for a revolution in the practise of partisanship in the very interests of the values professed. In its larger outlines and implications it proclaimed a relativism of values and a principle of reciprocity. Loyalty to loyalty transposed to all the fundamental value orders would then have meant, reverence for reverence, tolerance between moral systems, reciprocity in art, and had so good a metaphysician been able to conceive it, relativism in philosophy.

But if reciprocity and tolerance on the large scale are to await the incorporation of the greater community, the day of our truce of values is far off. Before any such integrations can take place, the narrowness of our provincialisms must be broken down and our sectarian fanaticisms lose some of their force and glamor. A philosophy aiding this is an ally of the larger integration of life. Of this we may be sure, such reconstruction will never bring us to a basis of complete cultural uniformity or common-mindedness about values. Whatever integrations occur, therefore, whether of thought or social system,—and undoubtedly some will and must occur,—cultural and value pluralism of some sort will still prevail. Indeed in the atmosphere induced by relativism and tolerance, such differentiation is likely to increase rather than just continue. Only it is to be hoped that it will be less arbitrary, less provincial and less divisive.

One thing is certain,—whatever change may have occurred in our thinking on the subject, we are still monists and absolutists mainly in our practise of value, individual as well as social. But a theoretical break has come, and seems to have set in simultaneously from several quarters. Panoramically viewed, the convergence of these trends indicates a new center for the thought and insight of our present generation, and that would seem to be a philosophy and a psychology, and perhaps too, a sociology, pivoted around functionalistic relativism.

NOTES

1. Compare Professor Frank H. Knight's comment on Charner Perry's, "The Arbitrary as Basis for Rational Morality," *International Journal of Ethics* 53 (1933), 148: "In the present situation of the western mind, the crying need is to substantiate for social phenomena a middle ground between scientific objectivity and complete skepticism. On the one hand, as Scylla, is the absurdity of Behaviorism. . . . On the other side is the Charybdis of Nihilism, perhaps momentarily the nearer and more threatening of the two reefs. Of course, the two are related; nihilism is a natural correlate of 'scientificism.' . . . In any case, there is no more vital problem (pragmatically) than that of distinguishing between utterance that is true or sound and that which is effective in influencing behavior."

2. Compare Dewey, *The Quest for Certainty*, p. 21: "Are the objects of desire, effort, choice, that is to say, everything to which we attach value, real? Yes,—if they can be warranted by knowledge; if we can know objects having their value properties we are justified in thinking them real. But as objects of desire and purpose they have no sure place in Being until they are approached and validated through knowledge."

3. Herbert E. Cory, "Beauty and Goodness," *International Journal of Ethics* 36 (1926), p. 396.

4. Hartmann, N., *Ethics*, Vol. II (London, 1932), p. 423.

2. Pluralism and Intellectual Democracy

The Conference on Science, Philosophy and Religion was one of many organizational efforts by cultural pluralists between the 1920s and 1950s to discuss the similarities and differences of ethnic groups. The massive migration of peoples from Europe to the United States shortly before and after World War I, and again before and after World War II, occasioned a reassessment of the American identity, the rights of immigrants, and the value of a multicultural society. Locke participated in all of the conferences, chairing the fourth conference in the series. Lyman Bryson, Louis Finfelstein, and R. M. MacIver were the primary organizers of the series.

In this article, Locke intends to foil "tyrannies of authoritarian dogmatism and uniformitarian universality." By uniformitarian universality he means a system of beliefs purporting to convey necessarily true propositions and holding that such truths should be held by, or otherwise imposed on, all persons. The notion applies to both a philosophical position and the political reality of totalitarian states. How value relativism combats such systems frames his discussion. He employs William James's legacy by applauding James's role as a philosopher engaged in a battle against dogmatism and intellectual or metaphysical absolutism. But he rejects James's "anarchic" pluralist picture of experience.

"Pluralism and Intellectual Democracy," Conference on Science, Philosophy and Religion, Second Symposium (New York: Conference on Science, Philosophy and Religion, 1942), pp. 196–212.

Locke recommends naturalizing epistemology. By so doing, a rapprochement between empiricism and rationalism would be possible. He affirms the existence of "functional constraints"—that is, universal values characteristically exhibited by all persons. One of those constraints or constants, that all values are endogenous, can be used to help warrant democratic principles of cultural tolerance and reciprocity. Tolerance and reciprocity have at best been ideals. Recognizing that loyalty to traditions is tenacious, Locke suggests relativism as a way of recognizing that our loyalties are historically situated and not objectively given. Tolerance and reciprocity are thereby recommended as mediating imperatives. Moreover, relativism suggests that we distinguish form from symbol and the values so attached, for example, distinguishing the institution from whether there is the reality of democracy. Locke tells his readers that American institutions are not the *sine qua non* of democracy. They are the symbols that have been mistaken for the form and value or worth attached to them as if they are the only means empowered to convey the form. Locke discusses the ways that an appropriate systematic value relativism and cultural pluralism foster attitudes compatible with democracy.

Pluralism and Intellectual Democracy

When William James inaugurated his all-out campaign against intellectual absolutism, though radical empiricism and pragmatism were his shield and buckler, his trusty right-arm sword, we should remember, was pluralism. He even went so far as to hint, in a way that his generation was not prepared to understand, at a vital connection between pluralism and democracy. Today, in our present culture crisis, it is both timely to recall this, and important, for several reasons, to ponder over it.

In the first place, absolutism has come forward again in new and formidable guise, social and political forms of it, with their associated intellectual tyrannies of authoritarian dogmatism and uniformitarian universality. We are warrantably alarmed to see these vigorous, new secular absolutisms added to the older, waning metaphysical and doctrinal ones to which we had become somewhat inured and from which, through science and the scientific spirit, we acquired some degree of immunity. Though alarmed, we do not always realize the extent to which these modern Frankensteins are the spawn of the older absolutistic breeds, or the degree to which they are inherent strains, so to speak, in the germ plasm of our culture.

In the second place, in the zeal of culture defense, in the effort to bring about the rapprochement of a united front, we do not always stop to envisage the danger and inconsistency of a fresh crisis uniformitarianism of our own. There exists, fortunately, a sounder and more permanent alternative, the possibility of a type of agreement such as may stem from a pluralistic base. Agreement of this common denominator type would, accordingly, provide a flexible, more democratic nexus, a unity in diversity rather than another counter-uniformitarianism.

Third, we should realize that the cure radical empiricism proposed for intellectual absolutism was stultified when it, itself, became arbitrary and dogmatic. With its later variants—behaviorism, positivism, and what not—it fell increasingly into the hands of the empirical monists, who, in the cause of scientific objectivity, squeezed values and ideals out completely in a fanatical cult of "fact." Not all the recalcitrance, therefore, was on the side of those disciplines and doctrines, which, being concerned with the vital interests of "value" as contrasted with "fact," are after all functionally vital in our intellectual life and tradition. Today, we are more ready to recognize them and concede these value considerations a place, though not necessarily to recognize or condone them in the arbitrary and authoritarian guise they still too often assume.

In this connection, it is encouraging to see empiricism abdicating some of its former arbitrary hardness and toning down its intransigent attitudes toward the more traditional value disciplines. This is a wise and potentially profitable concession on the part of science to the elder sisters, philosophy and religion, especially if it can be made the *quid pro quo* of their renunciation, in turn, of their dogmatic absolutisms. The admirable paper of Professor Morris, prepared for this conference, does just this, I think, by redefining a more liberal and humane empiricism, which not only recognizes "values," but provides, on the basis of sound reservations as to the basic primacy of factual knowledge, for reconcilable supplementations of our knowledge of fact by value interpretations and even by value systems and creeds. This reverses the previous tactic of empiricists to deny any validity to values and so to create a hopeless divide between the sciences of fact and the value disciplines. Here again, in this more liberal empiricism, pluralism, and particularly value pluralism, has a sound and broadly acceptable basis of rapprochement to offer. Such rapprochement being one of the main objectives as well as one of the crucial problems of this conference, it is perhaps relevant to propose the consideration of pluralism as a working base and solution for this problem. This would be all the more justified if it could be shown that pluralism was a proper and congenial rationale for intellectual democracy.

James, pluralistically tempered, did not take the position, it is interesting to note, which many of his followers have taken. He did propose giving up for good and all the "game of metaphysics" and the "false" and categorical rationalizing of values, but he did not advocate sterilizing the "will to believe" or abandoning the search for pragmatic sanctions for our values. As Horace Kallen aptly states it,

James insisted that each event of experience must be acknowledged for what it appears to be, and heard for its own claims. To neither doubt nor belief, datum nor preference, term nor relation, value nor fact, did he concede superiority over the others. . . . He pointed out to the rationalist the co-ordinate presence in experience of so much more than reason; he called the monist's attention to the world's diversity; the pluralist's to its unity. He said to the materialist: You shall not shut your eyes to the immaterial; to the spiritualist: You shall take cognizance also of the nonspiritual. He was a rationalist without unreason; an empiricist without prejudice. His empiricism was radical, preferring correctness to consistency, truth to logic.[1]

I do not quote for complete agreement, because I think we have come to the point where we can and must go beyond this somewhat anarchic pluralism and relativism to a more systematic relativism. This becomes possible as we are able to discover through objective comparison of basic human values certain basic equivalences among them, which we may warrantably call "functional constants" to take scientifically the place of our outmoded categoricals and our banned arbitrary "universals." However, the present point is that James did not intend to invalidate values in his attack on absolutes and categoricals or to abolish creeds in assailing dogma. Nor was he intent on deepening the divide between science, philosophy and religion: on the contrary, he was hoping for a new rapprochement and unity among them, once philosophy and religion had renounced absolutist metaphysics and its dogmatisms.

Is such rapprochement possible? As we have already seen, only if empiricists and rationalists both make concessions. Further, these concessions must be comparable, and provide, in addition, a work-able base of contact. From either side this is difficult. And lest the concession proposed for the value disciplines seem unequal or un-duly great, let us make note of the fact that it is a very consider-able concession, from the point of view of orthodox empiricism, to concede the scientific monism of mechanism, determinism and ma-terialism. The scientific point of view, by making a place for values, makes obviously the concession of pluralism. In a complementary concession, the value disciplines, it seems to me, should make the concession of relativism. Frankly, this asks that they dethrone their absolutes, not as values or even as preferred values, but nonetheless as arbitrary universals, whether they be "sole ways of salvation," "perfect forms of the state or society," or self evident intellectual systems of interpretation. Difficult as this may be for our various traditional value systems, once they do so, they thereby not only make peace with one another, but make also an honorable peace with science. For, automatically in so doing, they cease to be rival interpretations of that objective reality which it is the function of science to analyze, measure and explain, or monopolistic versions of human nature and experience, which it is, similarly, the business of social science to record and describe.

Such value pluralism, with its corollary of relativity, admittedly entails initial losses for the traditional claims and prestige of our value systems. But it also holds out to them an effective *pax romana* of values, with greater and more permanent eventual gains. It calls, in the first place, for a resolving or at least an abatement of the chronic internecine conflict of competing absolutes, now so hopelessly snared in mutual contradictoriness. Not that there must be, in consequence of this relativistic view, an anarchy or a complete downfall of values, but rather that there should be only relative and functional rightness, with no throne or absolute sovereignty in dispute. To intelligent partisans, especially those who can come within hailing distance of Royce's principle of "loyalty to loyalty," such value reciprocity might be acceptable and welcome. As we shall see later, this principle has vital relevance to the whole question of a democracy of values, which basically entails value tolerance.

There would also be as a further possibility of such value relativism a more objective confirmation of many basic human values, and on a basis of proof approximating scientific validity. For if once this broader relativistic approach could discover beneath the expected culture differentials of time and place such functional "universals" as actually may be there, these common-denominator values would stand out as pragmatically confirmed by common human experience. Either their observable generality or their comparatively established equivalence would give them status far beyond any "universals" merely asserted by orthodox dogmatisms. And the standard of value justification would then not be so very different from the accepted scientific criterion of proof—confirmable invariability in concrete human experience. After an apparent downfall and temporary banishment, many of our most prized "universals" would reappear, clothed with a newly acquired vitality and a pragmatic validity of general concurrence. So confirmed, they would be more widely acceptable and more objectively justified than would ever be possible either by the arbitrary fiat of belief or the brittle criterion of logical consistency. Paradoxically enough, then, the pluralistic approach to values opens the way to a universality and objectivity for them quite beyond the reach of the *a priori* assertions and dogmatic demands which characterize their rational and orthodox promulgations.

More important, however, than what this view contributes toward a realistic understanding of values, are the clues it offers for a more practical and consistent way of holding and advocating them. It is here that a basic connection between pluralism and intellectual democracy becomes evident. In the pluralistic frame of reference value dogmatism is outlawed. A consistent application of this invalidation would sever the trunk nerves of bigotry or arbitrary orthodoxy all along the line, applying to religious, ideological and cultural as well as to political and social values. Value profession or adherence on that basis would need to be critical and selective and tentative (in the sense that science is tentative) and revisionist in procedure rather than dogmatic, final and *en bloc*. One can visualize the difference by saying that with any articles of faith, each article would need independent scrutiny and justification and would stand, fall or be revised, be accepted, rejected or qualified accordingly. Fundamentalism of the "all or none" or "this goes with it" varieties could neither be demanded, expected nor tolerated. Value assertion would thus be a tolerant assertion of preference, not an intolerant insistence on agreement or finality. Value disciplines would take on the tentative and revisionist procedure of natural science.

Now such a rationale is needed for the effective implementation of the practical corollaries of value pluralism—tolerance and value reciprocity, and one might add, as a sturdier intellectual base for democracy. We know, of course, that we cannot get tolerance from a fanatic or reciprocity from a fundamentalist of any stripe, religious, philosophical, cultural, political or ideological. But what is often overlooked is that we cannot, soundly and safely at least, preach liberalism and at the same time abet and condone bigotry, condemn uniformitarianism and placate orthodoxy, promote tolerance and harbor the seeds of intolerance. I suggest that our duty to democracy on the plane of ideas, especially in time of crisis, is the analysis of just this problem and some consideration of its possible solution.

In this connection it is necessary to recall an earlier statement that we are for the most part unaware of the latent absolutism at the core of many of our traditional loyalties, and of the fact that this may very well condition current concepts and sanctions of democracy. The fundamentalist lineage of "hundred per-centism," for all its ancient and sacrosanct derivation, is only too obvious. It is a heritage and carry-over from religious dogmatism and extends its blind sectarian loyalties to the secular order. So hoary and traditional is it that one marvels that it could still be a typical and acceptable norm of patriotism, political or cultural. Equally obvious is the absolutist loyalty of the secular dogma of "my country, right or wrong." Such instances confront us with the paradox of democratic loyalties absolutistically conceived, dogmatically sanctioned and undemocratically practiced. Far too much of our present democratic creed and practice is cast in the mold of such blind loyalty and *en bloc* rationalization, with too many of our citizens the best of democrats for the worst of reasons—mere conformity. Apart from the theoretical absolutistic taint, it should be disconcerting to ponder that by the same token, if transported, these citizens would be "perfect" Nazis and the best of totalitarians.

But to come to less obvious instances—our democratic tolerance —of whose uniqueness and quantity we can boast with some warrant, seems on close scrutiny qualitatively weak and unstable. It is uncritical because propagated on too emotional and too abstract a basis. Not being anchored in any definite intellectual base, it is too easily set aside in time of stress and challenge. [So it] is tolerance only in name, [or] it is simply indifference and *laissez faire* rationalized. We are all sadly acquainted with how it may blow away in time of crisis or break when challenged by self-interest, and how under stress we find ourselves, after all, unreasonably biased in favor of "our own," whether it be the mores, ideas, faiths or merely "our crowd." This is a sure sign that value bigotry is somehow still deep-rooted there. Under the surface of such frail tolerance some unreconstructed dogmatisms lie, the latent source of the emerging intolerance. This is apt to happen to any attitude lacking the stamina of deep intellectual conviction, that has been nurtured on abstract sentiment, and that has not been buttressed by an objective conception of one's own values and loyalties.

Democratic professions to the contrary, there is a reason for all this shallow tolerance, this grudging and fickle reciprocity, this blind and fanatical loyalty persisting in our social behavior. Democracy has promulgated these virtues and ideals zealously, but as attitudes and habits of thought has not implemented them successfully. First, they have been based on moral abstractions, with vague sentimental sanctions as "virtues" and "ideals," since, on the whole, idealistic liberalism and good-will humanitarianism have nursed our democratic tradition. Rarely have these attitudes been connected sensibly with self-interest or realistically bound up with a perspective turned toward one's own position and its values. Had this been the case, a sturdier tolerance and a readier reciprocity would have ensued, and with them a more enlightened type of social loyalty.

But a more enlightened loyalty involves of necessity a less bigoted national and cultural tradition. Democratic liberalism, limited both by the viewpoint of its generation and by its close affiliation with doctrinal religious and philosophical traditions, modeled its rationale of democracy too closely to authoritarian patterns, and made a creed of democratic principles. For wide acceptance or easy assent it condoned or compromised with too much dogmatism and orthodoxy. Outmoded scientifically and ideologically today, this dogmatism is the refuge of too much provincialism, intolerance and prejudice to be a healthy, expanding contemporary base for democracy. Our democratic values require an equally liberal but also a more scientific and realistic rationale today. This is why we presume to suggest pluralism as a more appropriate and effective democratic rationale.

We must live in terms of our own particular institutions and mores, assert and cherish our own specific values, and we could not, even if it were desirable, uproot our own traditions and loyalties. But that is no justification for identifying them *en bloc* with an ideal like democracy, as though they were a perfect set of architectural specifications for the concept itself. So the only way of freeing our minds from such hypostasizing, from its provincial limitations and dogmatic bias, is by way of a relativism which reveals our values in proper objective perspective with other sets of values. Through this we may arrive at some clearer recognition of the basic unity or correspondence of our values with those of other men, however dissimilar they may appear on the surface or however differently they may be systematized and sanctioned. Discriminating objective comparison of this sort, using the same yardstick, can alone give us proper social and cultural scale and perspective. Toward this end, value pluralism has a point of view able to lift us out of the egocentric and ethnocentric predicaments which are without exception involved. This should temper our loyalties with intelligence and tolerance and scotch the potential fanaticism and bigotry which otherwise lurk under blind loyalty and dogmatic faith in our values. We can then take on our particular value systems with temperate and enlightened attachment, and can be sectarian without provincialism and loyal without intolerance.

Since the relativist point of view focuses in an immediately transformed relationship and attitude toward one's own group values, it is no rare and distant principle, but has, once instated, practical progressive applicability to everyday life. It has more chances thus of becoming habitual. Most importantly perhaps, it breaks down the worship of the form—that dangerous identification of the symbol with the value, which is the prime psychological root of the fallacies and errors we have been discussing. We might pose it as the acid test for an enlightened value loyalty that it is able to distinguish between the symbol and form of its loyalty and the essence and objective of that loyalty. Such critical insight, for example, would recognize a real basic similarity or functional equivalence in other values, even when cloaked in considerable superficial difference. Nor, on the other hand, would it credit any merely superficial conformity with real loyalty. And so, the viewpoint equips us not only to tolerate difference but enables us to bridge divergence by recognizing commonality wherever present. In social practice this is no scholastic virtue; it has high practical consequences for democratic living, since it puts the premium upon equivalence not upon identity, calls for co-operation rather than for conformity and promotes reciprocity instead of factional antagonism. Authoritarianism, dogmatism and bigotry just cannot take root and grow in such intellectual soil.

Finally, we may assess the possible gains under this more pragmatic and progressive rationale for democratic thought and action briefly under two heads: what these fresh and stimulating sanctions promise internally for democracy on the national front and what they require externally on the international front in terms of what is vaguely—all too vaguely—styled world democracy.

For democracy in its internal aspects, much of pluralism's gains would consist in a more practical implementation of the traditional democratic values, but there would also be some new sanctions and emphases. So far, of course, as these things can be intellectually implemented, new support would unquestionably be given to the enlargement of the democratic life, and quite as importantly, some concern taken for the correction of its aberrations and abuses. On the corrective side, particular impetus needs to be given toward the liberalizing of democracy's tradition of tolerance, to more effective protection and integration of minority and non-conformist groups, for the protection of the majority itself against illiberalism, bigotry and cultural conceit, and toward the tempering of the quality of patriotism and sub-group loyalties. As to new sanctions, the campaign for the re-vamping of democracy has already put special emphasis on what is currently styled "cultural pluralism" as a proposed liberal rationale for our national democracy. This indeed is but a corollary of the larger relativism and pluralism under discussion. Under it, much can be done toward the more effective bridging of the divergencies of institutional life and traditions which, though sometimes conceived as peculiarly characteristic of American society, are rapidly becoming typical of all cosmopolitan modern society. These principles call for promoting respect for difference, for safeguarding respect for the individual, thus preventing the submergence of the individual in enforced conformity, and for the promotion of commonality over and above such differences. Finally, more on the intellectual side, additional motivation is generated for the reinforcement of all the traditional democratic freedoms, but most particularly for the freedom of the mind. For it is in the field of social thinking that freedom of the mind can be most practically established, and no more direct path to that exists than through the promotion of an unbiased scientific conception of the place of the national culture in the world.

For democracy in its external aspects both the situation and the prospects are less clear. However, the world crisis poses the issues clearly enough. Democracy has encountered a fighting antithesis, and has awakened from considerable lethargy and decadence to a sharpened realization of its own basic values. This should lead ultimately to a clarified view of its ultimate objectives. The crisis holds also the potential gain of more realistic understanding on the part of democracy of its own shortcomings, since if totalitarianism is its moral antithesis as well as its political enemy, it must fight internally to purge its own culture of the totalitarian qualities of dogmatism, absolutism and tyranny, latent and actual.

Yet as a nation we are vague about world democracy and none too well equipped for its prosecution. It was our intellectual unprepared-ness as a nation for thinking consistently in any such terms which stultified our initiative in the peace of 1918 and our participation in the germinal efforts of a democratic world order under the League of Nations plan, or should we say concept, since the plan minimized it so seriously? Today again, we stand aghast before a self-created dilemma of an impracticable national provinciality of isolationism and a vague idea of a world order made over presumably on an enlarged pattern of our own. There is danger, if we insist on identi-fying such a cause arbitrarily with our own institutional forms and culture values of its becoming a presumptuous, even though well-intentioned idealistic uniformitarianism. Should this be the case, then only a force crusade for democratic uniformitarianism is in prospect, for that could never come about by force of persuasion.

It is here that the defective perspective of our patriotism and our culture values reveals its seriously limiting character. This is intellec-tually the greatest single obstacle to any extension of the democratic way of life on an international scale. Surely here the need for the in-sight and practical sanity of the pluralistic viewpoint is clear. There is a reasonable chance of success to the extent we can disengage the objectives of democracy from the particular institutional forms by which we practice it, and can pierce through to common denomina-tors of equivalent objectives.

The intellectual core of the problems of the peace, should it lie in our control and leadership, will be the discovery of the neces-sary common denominators and the basic equivalences involved in a democratic world order or democracy on a world scale. I do not hazard to guess at them; but certain specifications may be stated which I believe they will have to meet, if they are to be success-ful. A reasonable democratic peace (like no other peace before it) must integrate victors and vanquished alike, and justly. With no shadow of cultural superiority, it must respectfully protect the cul-tural values and institutional forms and traditions of a vast congeries of peoples and races—European, Asiatic, African, American, Australasian. Somehow cultural pluralism may yield a touchstone for such thinking. Direct participational representation of all considerable groups must be provided for, although how imperialism is to concede this is almost beyond immediate imagining. That most absolutistic of all our secular concepts, the autonomous, sacrosanct character of national sovereignty, must surely be modified and voluntarily abridged. Daring reciprocities will have to be worked out if the basic traditional democratic freedoms are ever to be transposed to world practice, not to mention the complicated reconstruction of economic life which consistent reciprocity will demand in this field. One suspects that the practical exigencies of world reconstruction will force many of these issues to solution from the practical side, leaving us intellectuals to rationalize the changes *ex post facto*. Out of the crisis may yet come the forced extension of democratic values and mechanisms in ways that we have not had courage to think of since the days of democracy's early eighteenth century conception, when it was naively, but perhaps very correctly assumed that to have validity at all democracy must have world vogue.

What intellectuals can do for the extension of the democratic way of life is to discipline our thinking critically into some sort of realistic world-mindedness. Broadening our cultural values and tempering our orthodoxies is of infinitely more service to enlarged democracy than direct praise and advocacy of democracy itself. For until broadened by relativism and reconstructed accordingly, our current democratic traditions and practice are not ready for worldwide application. Considerable political and cultural dogmatism, in the form of culture bias, nation worship, and racism, still stands in the way and must first be invalidated and abandoned. In sum, if we refuse to orient ourselves courageously and intelligently to a universe of peoples and cultures, and continue to base our prime values on fractional segments of nation, race, sect, or particular types of institutional culture, there is indeed little or no hope for a stable world order of any kind—democratic or otherwise. Even when the segment is itself a democratic order, its expansion to world proportions will not necessarily create a world democracy. The democratic mind needs clarifying for the better guidance of the democratic will.

But fortunately, the same correctives needed for the sound maintenance of democracy are also the most promising basis for its expansion. The hostile forces both within and without are of the same type, and stem from absolutism of one sort or another. The initial suggestion of a vital connection between democracy and pluralism arose from the rather more apparent connection between absolutism and monism. But so destructive has pluralism been of the closed system thinking on which absolutist values and authoritarian dogmatisms thrive that it has proved itself no mere logical antithesis but their specific intellectual antidote. In the present crisis democracy needs the support of the most effective rationale available for the justification and defense of its characteristic values. While we should not be stampeded into pluralism merely by the present emergency, it is nonetheless our handiest intellectual weapon against the totalitarian challenge, but if, as we have seen, it can also make a constructive contribution to the internal fortification of democracy, then it is even more permanently justified and should on that score be doubly welcomed.

NOTES

1. Horace Kallen, "William James and Henri Bergson," pp. 10–11. [Complete reference unknown.—ed.]

APPENDIX

Lyman Bryson: I am heartily in accord with this paper, on all of its chief points, and I admire the conciseness and clarity with which it states so much that is *à propos* of the deliberations of this Conference. My comments are only notes added in the hope that they are what Professor Locke himself might have said in a longer discussion.

More could be made, I believe, of the dangers of the overweening desire for personal integration that fails to take into account the fact that the personality, also, is in some ways better off for the practice of a judicious pluralism. By this I mean that we have a natural tendency toward an agglutination of values. If we are loyal to one set of institutions, such as what we call "democracy," we are uncomfortable unless we assert that the other values, to which we may also be loyal, such as what we call "Christianity," are necessary to democracy. At our Conference meetings we have heard many assertions that democracy can exist only in a Christian state, in spite of history and all contemporary facts to the contrary.

We are not content to say that democracy and the Christian-Judaic tradition are highly sympathetic with each other, or useful to each other. They must be, each to the other, *sine qua non*. Professor Locke might have pointed out that within each single pattern of loyalties an organic diversity may make not for weakness but for flexibility and strength.

The author might also have pointed out, as was perhaps implied in some of the things he did have space for, that unity becomes the more desirable as the issues rise in the levels of generality. Thus, roughly, we need not agree on how freedom should be used but we would still agree that it was a value to be supremely prized. We might agree on the importance of exercising political suffrage but disagree in our use of it. And still above this, we might argue about freedom but agree that values, to be desirable, must contribute to the strength and dignity of men. The value that has been repeatedly called the chief good of democratic peoples, the supreme worth of the individual, is just such a value of the highest possible generality and we are dogmatic in our assertion of it. Diversity does not have the same utility on all levels but, one must add, an authoritarian determination of the levels on which diversity can be permitted is a very effective enslavement. I would have enjoyed a discussion of this point in the paper.

I could wish, also, that there had been more space to consider the importance of diversity, or plural systems of values, in relation to social change. It is when a culture is undergoing transformation, when diversity is most difficult to maintain, that it is of greatest importance. It is true, I think, that pluralistic groups change with less cost and more efficiency, whenever environment makes change rationally desirable, than do any other kinds of groups. This is one of the strongest arguments in favor of democratic procedures in all forms of social decision.

Erwin R. Goodenough: The Conference was originally called together to see what scientists, philosophers, and theologians could do to unite the more abstract thought and thinkers of the present in defending democracy. We were alarmed at what we had seen happen to our ideas (and our kind) in Russia, Italy and Germany, and we met to defend our way of life and thought and to strengthen the organization of society which makes such life and thought possible.

This paper is one of the few which seemed to me presented in the original spirit of our meeting. That philosophy which recognizes the conflict of various suggested ultimates and axioms and the complete inadequacy of our data to select between them (as witnessed by the inability of reasoning philosophers of different schools to convince each other by reasoning); that philosophy which tries to take the very conflict as its starting point and develop a *modus vivendi* out of it, is called pluralism. It is satisfactory to no one, or to very few, as an ultimate philosophy. Certainly Professor Locke is peering behind and beyond it as steadily, as wistfully, as any idealist. He proposes it, and I enthusiastically support it, precisely for what it is—a way of uniting for action in a world of conflict and ignorance. It is a typically American philosophy, or at least Anglo-Saxon, and it is not coincidence that it is best understood in the countries most bitterly opposed to totalitarianism. Over and again the various absolutist philosophies suggested in the Conference have shown that once in power they would be dangerously like the closed systems (at least in being closed), which we want to oppress. Here is genuinely the philosophy of democracy—not a very brilliant philosophy, as democracy itself is not a very brilliant form of organizing society, but still the philosophy which made democratic arguments, from those in the village store to those in the Senate, possible. I am sure that if we go on to discuss more practical problems at next year's meeting, our discussion will be based, tacitly if not otherwise, upon the wise principles Professor Locke has set forth. I am still more sure that if our discussion of practical problems is not thus based, it will get nowhere.

Lawrence K. Frank: In emphasizing the need for pluralistic understanding, this paper has pointed to an exceedingly important problem that will face the post–World War. If we look forward to the construction of some sort of world order in which the peoples of different cultures and religions can participate, we will need a pluralistic understanding and a broader, more sympathetic approach to many of the exigent questions of human welfare and social order; otherwise a parochial devotion to our own metaphysics and religious convictions, however precious to us, will inevitably hamper us in any attempt to achieve world order and peace in concert with peoples whose cultural traditions and beliefs are so radically different from our own.

In pleading for a relativistic approach to our own values and to those of other peoples and in calling for a recognition of equivalents in cultures rather than demanding identity, Dr. Locke has contributed something that merits the careful consideration of all those participating in this conference. Without such understanding, we are more than liable to continue the same dogmatic intolerance that has so long blighted Western European culture and blinded us to the values and virtues which other peoples, often with longer and richer historical pasts than we, cherish as their way of life.

3. Cultural Relativism and Ideological Peace

This is Locke's second published presentation for the Conference on Science, Philosophy and Religion in their Relation to the Democratic Way of Life. In it, Locke focuses on prospects for the implementation of cultural pluralism. The prospects for a peaceful culturally plural world rests on instituting three principles: cultural equivalence (warranted by the existence of cultural cognates or correlates); cultural reciprocity (negating beliefs of human superiority and inferiority because such beliefs are normally codeterminant with judgments of cultural worth); and limited cultural convertibility (accepting that there are limited degrees of commensurability and translatability of meanings and values between cultures). An enduring peace between nations requires the negation of authoritarian dogmatism and of universalism.

On Locke's account, cultural relativity negates uniformitarian dogmatism and bigotry, but given tenacious value loyalties, imperatives guided by cultural pluralism and based on the verifiable characteristics we all have in common are needed. Cultural constraints, constants, or cognates are here termed "universally human factors" (in previous articles, they were variously termed "functional contraints" or "constants").

Locke holds that metaphysical absolutism mis-

"Cultural Relativism and Ideological Peace," *Approaches to World Peace*, ed. Lyman Bryson, Louis Finfelstein, R. M. MacIver (New York: Harper & Brothers, 1944), pp. 609–618.

guidedly confuses unity and universality. The unity of peoples can exist without uniformity of cultural modalities. A naturalism that supposes the universality of human nature and entails a uniform code of conduct is thereby erroneous. To tender a decoding: The cultural distinctiveness of peoples is irrelevant to their standing as members of the human family. In addition, absolutist or fundamentalist ideas breed their opposite—sectarian disunity.

Cultural Relativism and Ideological Peace

Now that a considerable body of opinion within the Conference has crystallized around the position of value pluralism and relativism, with special emphasis this year, it seems, on the principle and concept of "cultural relativity," it seems opportune to turn from the initial task of establishing and vindicating this point of view to the next logical step—and the more practical one, of discussing its possible implementation. Already several papers[1] in this year's symposium have addressed themselves to one or more aspects of this practical side of the problem, and it is a pleasant duty to acknowledge general indebtedness to them at the outset of this further attempt to discuss some of the practical implications of the concept of cultural relativism. Three such principles of practical application seem to derive so directly and logically from the core principle in question that they may warrantably be regarded as three *basic corollaries of cultural relativity*.

In proceeding to discuss them, extended argument for the general position offered earlier by papers presented to this and previous Conferences, including one of my own written for the Second Conference,[2] may be taken to justify the assumption that there is little need or obligation to retrace in detail the argument for the main position itself. Here it should suffice to point out, for immediate perspective particularly, the practical and important relevance of cultural relativity to the main issue of this year's discussion topic—the prospects and techniques of "an enduring peace."

There seems to be, in fact, a twofold bearing of the culture-relativity principle upon our chosen Conference problem. One can readily recognize, in the first place, without needing to assume any direct logical connection between cultural relativity and pacifism or any demonstrable correlation between attitudes of tolerance and a predisposition to peace, that the relativistic philosophy nips in the psychological bud the passion for arbitrary unity and conformity. This mind-set, we know only too well and sorrowfully, constitutes the intellectual base and ideological root of all those absolutistic dogmatisms that rationalize orthodoxy. In so doing, they fortify with convictions of finality and self-righteousness the countless crusades for conformity which provide the moral and intellectual sanctions, not only for war but for most of our other irreconcilable culture conflicts. In this indirect but effective way, cultural relativism, as its influence spreads, may become an important force for ideological peace through disavowing and discouraging the chief intellectual sanctions for belligerent partisanship.

Relativism, it should be noted, contradicts value dogmatism and counteracts value bigotry without destroying the sense of active value loyalty. For scientific relativism, some interpretations notwithstanding, does not propagate indifference, scepticism, or cynicism about values. Thus, through remaining hospitable and receptive to values except as they are dogmatic and too arbitrarily held, relativism retains a usefulness which, if followed through consistently, enables it to become at the very least a scientifically impartial interpreter of human values, and sometimes even a referee and mediator among conflicting values. There is, then, this second and more positive role for relativism to exercise in the issues of ideological competition and conflict—one which can lead to an even more constructive usefulness in the interests of peace, so far as peace can be safeguarded intellectually. Cultural relativism, of course more fully and positively developed than at present, can become a very constructive philosophy by way of integrating values and value systems that might otherwise never react to one another, or, if they did, would do so only in opposition, rivalry, and conflict. We can very profitably examine, therefore, at this juncture of human affairs the constructive potentialities of the relativistic position as a possible ideological peacemaker, particularly in the relationships of group cultures and their otherwise antagonistic or incommensurable values.

Paradoxically enough, absolutism in all its varieties—religious, philosophical, political, and cultural—despite the insistent linking together of unity *and* universality, seems able, so far as historical evidence shows, to promote unity only at the cost of universality. For absolutism's way to unity is the way of orthodoxy, which involves authoritarian conformity and subordination. From such premises, dogmatism develops sooner or later, and thereafter, history shows us, come those inevitable schisms which disrupt the parent dogmatism and try to deny it in the name of a new orthodoxy. Relativism, with no arbitrary specifications of unity, no imperious demand for universality, nevertheless enjoins a beneficent neutrality between divergent positions, and, in the case of the contacts of cultures, would in due course promote, step by step, from an initial stage of cultural tolerance, mutual respect, reciprocal exchange, some specific communities of agreement and, finally, with sufficient mutual understanding and confidence, commonality of purpose and action. If in its practical manifestations cultural relativism could promote such results or even attitudes conducive to them, it would be a most fruitful source of such progressive integrations as are so crucially needed in the world today.

Once we fully realize the divisive general effect of fundamentalist ideas and all their institutional incorporations, and understand that orthodox conformity inevitably breeds its opposite—*sectarian disunity*—we reach a position where we can recognize relativism as a safer and saner approach to the objectives of practical unity. What is achieved through relativistic rapprochement is, of course, somewhat different from the goal of the absolutists. It is a fluid and functional unity rather than a fixed and irrevocable one, and its vital norms are equivalence and reciprocity rather than identity or complete agreement. But when we consider the odds against a complete community of culture for mankind, and the unlikelihood of any all-inclusive orthodoxy of human values, one is prepared to accept or even to prefer an attainable concord of understanding and cooperation as over against an unattainable unanimity of institutional beliefs.

Ironically, the very social attribute which man has most in common—his loyalty to his culture and, one might just as well say his inevitable commitment to various culture groups—is the basis of his deepest misunderstandings and a source of his most tragic conflict with his fellow men. When we consider this, we can appreciate the deep-seated desire and the ever-recurrent but Utopian dream of the idealist that somehow a single faith, a common culture, an all-embracing institutional life and its confraternity should some day unite man by merging all these loyalties and culture values. But the day still seems distant, even with almost complete intercommunication within the world's practical grasp. What seems more attainable, realistically, is some reconstruction of the attitudes and rationalizations responsible for this conflict over our separate loyalties.

It is at this point that relativism has its great chance. It may be destined to have its day in the channeling of human progress—not, however, as a mere philosophy or abstract theory of values, though it began as such, but as a new base and technique for our study and understanding of human cultures and as a new way of controlling through education our attitudes toward our various group cultures. Only, then, through having some objective and factual base in the sciences of man and society can cultural relativism implement itself for this task of reconstructing our basic social and cultural loyalties or of lifting them, through some basically new perspective, to a plane of enlarged mutual understanding. For such a task anthropology in the broadest sense must be the guide and adjutant, and the trend toward this new alliance of disciplines, so inevitable in view of the nature of the problem, is already becoming apparent in scholarship generally. As a concrete example we have an increasing segment of it in the deliberations of this Conference.

There never has been a new age without a new scholarship or, to put it more accurately, without a profound realignment of scholarship. And if our times are as cataclysmal as they seem to be, we should reasonably expect today fundamental changes of this sort in ideas and points of view. Through the aid of anthropology, whose aim is to see man objectively and impartially in all his variety, cultural relativism seems capable of opening doors to such new understandings and perspectives as are necessary for the new relationships of a world order and its difficult juxtapositions of many divergent cultures. Only on such a basis can scholarship hope to serve the social situations of the present time. To do so, however, it will be necessary for scholarship to free itself from the provincialisms and partisanships of many of its past traditions. Culture outlooks and philosophies rooted in fanatical religious orthodoxy, or in inflated cultural bias and partisanship, or in overweening national and racial chauvinism, have been outmoded and outflanked by the developments of the age, not to mention their basic theoretical invalidation, which is because they are all subjective and unscientific. All these provincialisms survive considerably, however, but more and more precariously as time goes on. Accordingly, there is crucial importance and scope for well-grounded, rigorously objective relativism.

On such a background, one can more readily see and state the possible uses of cultural relativism as a realistic instrument of social reorientation and cultural enlightenment. As corollaries of its main view of culture, three working principles seem to be derivable for a more objective and scientific understanding of human cultures and for the more reasonable control of their interrelationships. They are:

1. The principle of *cultural equivalence,* under which we would more wisely press the search for functional similarities in our analyses and comparisons of human cultures; thus offsetting our traditional and excessive emphasis upon cultural difference. Such functional equivalences, which we might term *"culture-cognates"* or *"culture-correlates,"* discovered underneath deceptive but superficial institutional divergence, would provide objective but soundly neutral common denominators for intercultural understanding and cooperation;

2. The principle of *cultural reciprocity,* which, by a general recognition of the reciprocal character of all contacts between cultures and of the fact that all modern cultures are highly composite ones, would invalidate the lump estimating of cultures in terms of generalized, *en bloc* assumptions of superiority and inferiority, substituting scientific, point-by-point comparisons with their correspondingly limited, specific, and objectively verifiable superiorities or inferiorities;

3. The principle of *limited cultural convertibility,* that, since culture elements, though widely interchangeable, are so separable, the institutional forms from their values and the values from their institutional forms, the organic selectivity and assimilative capacity of a borrowing culture becomes a limiting criterion for cultural exchange. Conversely, pressure acculturation and the mass transplanting of culture, the stock procedure of groups with traditions of culture "superiority" and dominance, are counterindicated as against both the interests of cultural efficiency and the natural trends of cultural selectivity.

Here, then, we seem to have three objectively grounded principles of culture relations that, if generally carried through, might correct some of our basic culture dogmatism and progressively cure many of our most intolerant and prejudicial culture attitudes and practices.

If they could come into general acceptance, cultural absolutism and its still prevalent presumptions would be basically discredited and perhaps effectively countered. Cultural difference, surely, would be purged of most of its invidiousness, and much cultural divergence would on deeper inspection turn out to be functionally similar. We would be more prone to recognize the legitimate jurisdictions of other cultures as well as to respect the organic integrity of the weaker cultures. Moreover, tolerance and the reciprocities of cultural pluralism within the larger, more complex bodies of culture would become much more matters of course than they are at present, and to the extent we were really influenced by the relativistic point of view, we would all wear our group labels and avow our culture loyalties less provocatively, not to mention the important factor of regarding our culture symbols with less irrationality. Particularly, and most important of all, the proprietary doctrine of culture would be outmoded, as both unreasonable and contrary to fact. Claims of cultural superiority or counter-judgments of cultural inferiority would be specific and carefully circumscribed and would be significant and allowable if substantiated by fair, objective comparison. For I take it, we would not disallow such judgmental valuations as might stem from an objectively scientific criterion of more effective or less effective adaptation. It was only in its initial form that the relativist viewpoint, in disestablishing dogmatic absolutism in cultural valuations, had to be iconoclastic almost to the point of value anarchism. Through functional comparison a much more constructive phase of cultural relativism seems to be developing, promising the discovery of some less arbitrary and more objective norms. Upon them, perhaps we can build sounder intercultural understanding and promote a more equitable collaboration between cultures. The primary fact to be noted is that, however speculative and uncertain a relativistic ethic of culture may be, cultural relativism itself stands on the very firm base of a now rather formidable body of established scientific facts, with the support of an increasing consensus of scientific opinion among the students of human culture.

Nevertheless, there is certainly no warrant for expecting rapid or revolutionary change in traditional human attitudes and viewpoints merely because of the preponderant weight of evidence back of a scientific theory or point of view. Relativism, like any other way of thinking, will have to make headway slowly against intrenched opposition, and gather considerably more reinforcements than it can now muster. We may expect no sudden recanting of our traditional cultural absolutisms and orthodoxies, no more than in the case of similar absolutist doctrines. The one practical hope in this regard seems to be the emergency character of the present world crisis, which may well be more coercive in effect than the logic of reason or the force of scientific facts. It is in the context of the grave practical issues of the present world conflict that the more realistic and wider-horizoned views of human cultures which we have been discussing have their best prospects for a speedier than normal adoption and a more than academic vindication.

Certainly, without having the formal concepts to hand, hundreds of thousands to millions are today acutely aware, as they have never previously been, of the facts of cultural diversity, of the need for less cultural antagonism and conflict, of the desirability of some working agreements between differing creeds and cultures based on reciprocity, and of the probable futility of any world plan cut to the pattern of the old values and principles. Here, it seems, is the challenge and the chance. It is for that reason that one can so heartily concur in the suggestions of Professor Northrop's paper that a value analysis of our basic cultures in broadscale comparison is the philosophical, or rather the scholarly, task of the hour.

Specifically[3] Dr. Northrop calls for this as "philosophy's task with respect to the peace" and proposes:

(1) An analysis of the major cultures of the Western and Eastern worlds designating the basic theoretical assumptions from which the social institutions and practices that they value proceed. (2) The specification of a common single set of assumptions possessed of the greater generality which permits the largest possible number of the resultant diverse, traditional assumptions logically compatible to be retained and acted upon without conflict. (3) The reconstruction of all the traditional assumptions to the extent that this is necessary, in order to bring them more in accord with the nature of things as revealed by contemporary as well as traditional philosophical and scientific knowledge.

A cultural relativist will likely have some doubts and reservations over the practicability of such a synthesis as Professor Northrop's third point proposes, especially if a main objective is a unity and agreement based on an extensive "reconstruction of traditional cultural assumptions." In looking for cultural agreements on a world scale, we shall probably have to content ourselves with agreement of the common-denominator type and with "unity in diversity" discovered in the search for unities of a functional rather than a content character, and therefore of a pragmatic rather than an ideological sort. Indeed, cultural relativism and its approach suggest that mankind is not so much at odds over basic end values as over divergent institutional means and symbols irrationally identified with these basic ends. Although thus uncertain that our basic culture values would reduce so easily or submit as readily to ideological reconstructions as Professor Northrop considers requisite, indeed not regarding such value-content unity as vitally necessary, the relativist position would be in substantial agreement on the need for an objective comparative analysis on a world scale of our major culture values.

In this undertaking cultural relativism would have two important suggestions to make. First, that considerable clarification, with an attendant cultural sanity and harmony, would result from any wide-scale comparison set to discover whatever pragmatic similarities already pertain underneath a variety of divergent value symbols and their traditional rationalizations merely through making manifest such common denominators and basic equivalences. Second, it should be equally obvious that the chances for discovering vital agreements of this sort are infinitely greater on the basis of a functional analysis of our major culture values than through an analytical, merely descriptive one. The main question, however, is neither methodology nor anticipation of the result, but an immediate and collaborative undertaking of what is becoming obvious as one of the most urgent and promiseful tasks yet confronted by the scholarship of our generation in the field of human relations.

One can, of course, foresee, even in advance of such a search for value correlations, one inevitably oncoming content unity among our various cultures, a base denominator of modern science and technology. We can hardly conceive our modern world dispensing with this, whatever its other factionalisms. But even if destined to become the common possession of humanity, science and technology are relatively value neutral, and, since they can be fitted in to such different systems of end values, cannot be relied upon to become deeply influential as unifiers. Indeed, linked to present-day culture feuds and value intolerances, they can quite more easily serve to intensify the conflict as the geographical distance between cultures is shortened and their technological disparities are leveled off. It is, after all, our values and value systems that have divided us, apart from and in many cases over and above our material issues of rivalry and conflict. If we are ever to have less conflict and more unity, it must come about in considerable part from some deep change in our value attitudes and our cultural allegiances. The increasing proximity of cultures in the modern world makes all the more necessary some corrective adjustment of their "psychological distance."

No single factor could serve this end more acceptably and effectively than a relativistic concept of culture, which, by first disestablishing the use of one's own culture as a contrast norm for other cultures, leads through the appreciation of the functional significance of other values in their respective cultures to the eventual discovery and recognition of certain functional common denominators. These culture constants or "culture cognates," as the case might be, would then furnish a base not only for mutual cultural tolerance and appreciation but eventually for effective cultural integration. If discoverable in any large number, they might well constitute a new base for a direct educational development of world-mindedness, a realistic scientific induction into world citizenship. Surely it would be a great gain if we could shift or even supplement our sentimental and moralistic efforts for world-mindedness to an objective educational and scientific basis. As stated by the writer in a previous Conference paper[4]:

For if once this broader relativistic approach could discover beneath the culture differentials of time and place such functional "universals" as actually may be there, these common-denominator values will stand out as pragmatically confirmed by common human experience. Either this observable generality or their comparatively established equivalence would give them status far beyond any "universals" merely asserted by orthodox dogmatisms.

Indeed by some such new and indirect substantiation, we may even be able to reestablish, on a less arbitrary foundation, some of the disestablished certainties among our culture values.

NOTES

1. The papers by F. S. C. Northrop, Charles W. Morris, Bingham Dai, Krishnalal Shridharani, and Clyde Kluckhohn. See *Approaches to World Peace*, ed. Lyman Bryson, L. Finfelstein, R. M. MacIver (New York: Harper & Brothers, 1944).

2. "Pluralism and Intellectual Democracy," *Science, Philosophy and Religion*, Second Symposium, 1942, pp. 196–209.

3. "Philosophy and World Peace," *Approaches to World Peace*, ed. Lyman Bryson, L. Finfelstein, and R. M. MacIver, p. 651 f.

4. "Pluralism and Intellectual Democracy," *Science, Philosophy and Religion*, Second Symposium, 1942, p. 200.

4. A Functional View of Value Ultimates

This full-length article was presented at Columbia University, probably before the Philosophy Club, but it was never published. Locke published philosophy articles on the rare occasions that he was asked to contribute a written article. This article was written, I suspect, as a part of Locke's long-standing effort to secure a teaching position in New York that would allow him to take a year's leave of absence from Howard.

Unlike "Pluralism and Ideological Peace," published in 1947 and written in commemoration of Horace Kallen and honoring cultural pluralism, "A Functional View of Value Ultimates" provides both a sustained argument and indications of Locke's view of social utility. However, it was not finished by Locke for the purpose of publication and should be read with that in mind.

A metaphorical fallacy exists, on Locke's account, when absolutists argue for value ultimates. They take formal values as fixed (truth, beauty, virtue, etc.) when they are in fact always ensconced and encoded in a process of relational meanings. Value ultimates or imperatives are really "system imperatives rather than intrinsic absolutes." Values are functional transpositional systems.

Locke explains that the process of continual transvaluation of values is not only central to what

"A Functional View of Value Ultimates," read at Columbia University, December 13, 1945, unpublished. Printed with the permission of Moorland-Spingarn Research Center, Alain Locke Collection, Howard University.

humans are but has positive consequences. It does not, in effect, leave us in a world without the possibility of criteria for judging or preferring a set of values. Locke contends that changes in values and social norms tend to be progressively corrective. He rejects the possibility of an eternally warranted or fixed set of values or norms. Rather, understanding how values function is a pivotal requirement that should precondition considerations of which regulative normative rules we adopt.

In my opinion, Locke intentionally prefers here, as well as in other articles, a notion of functionalism to depict values rather than a pragmatic depiction. The functionality of values implies for Locke that values are manifest in the operation of material interests or social conventions to accomplish some goal. They are never completely available to us, and a useful method of reasoning may be pragmatic, exegetical, dialectic, or intuitive—that is, no privilege is *a priori* accorded. A pragmatic depiction of values, however, implies that values are tools, foreign instruments, or contrived methods used to accomplish some goal. In this sense, pragmatic values are goods that stand, like a hammer, outside of us, but the notion of functional values allows us to conceive of values as being always integral to our deliberations, actions, and goals. Like one sense of James's and Dewey's understanding of "pragmatism," the word "functional" both depicts what values are and recommends a reasoning modality. However, Locke does not intend "functional" to privilege experimental science as a model of reasoning.

A Functional View of Value Ultimates

Quite patently, the core problem in theory of value is the satisfactory explanation of the formal value ultimates, such as beauty, truth and goodness. Since this has been a perennial question from the very beginning of axiological theorizing, it is a matter of concern, if not of reproach that so little agreement has been reached concerning the nature of the basic value norms. Reasons for this require at least passing consideration. One reason, certainly, is that value theorists have concerned themselves far too much with abstract consideration of their nature as formal norms, and far too little with their specific functional relationships to the values and value situations which they serve as terminal references and evaluative criteria. But in addition, as Urban[1] correctly states, "the field of axiology has been defined largely in relation to ethics." Now not only is ethics traditionally the most categorical and authoritarian of the value fields, leading naturally to an emphasis on solution by definition, but any over-emphasis on the separate consideration of value norms rather than an analysis of their interrelationships leads also, just as inevitably to formalistic analysis, often of the dogmatic variety. I confess at the outset to a preference for a functionalist theory of value, but my brief for a functional analysis of value norms is at least on the methodological side not completely *parti pris,* but is made rather because a functional approach, even should it lead to a non-functionalist theory of value, of necessity treats the value varieties in terms of their interrelationships, guaranteeing a comparative approach and a more realistic type of value analysis.

Indeed, the most illuminating evidence as to the nature of the value genres and their systematic end values promises to come from the examination of parallelisms in their functioning, as well as from case analyses of their occasional overlapping and interchangeability. A functional analysis of values focuses particularly on such phenomena of their selective normativity, also upon the tricky but revelatory phenomena of what Ehrenfels called "value movement" and value change. This wide field of comparative and differential analysis of values should all along have been a major emphasis in value theory, as seems to have been intended by the pioneer axiologists in their demand for a *general* psychology of value. But value formalism has, it seems, deprived of this. Formalism in value theory, moreover, leads so easily to value fundamentalism and its dogmatisms. Many current value theories are in substance extensions of preformulated epistemologies and already adopted metaphysical positions, with a projection of these into a theory of value as a new set of weapons to be used in the traditional warfare of ideologies. On such grounds, it seems wise, therefore, to canvas the possibilities of the functional approach to the problem of value ultimates.

In so doing, we become immediately aware that there are two sets of problems involved which should perhaps not be uncoupled in spite of the risks of lumping problems and confusing the issues involved. Naturally, the normal analytic procedure of philosophers usually separates them as a matter of routine. One set of problems is on the theoretical level, and involves the formal definition of the generic character of the value ultimates: the other set of problems is on the practical level and concerns the active issues of value conflict in our culture and their bearing on the questions of value ultimacy. The functional approach, consistently carried out, is methodologically obligated, I believe, not to uncouple the theoretical from such practical aspects of the value problem, and may eventually find its best leads and most satisfactory solutions coming by way of an insistence on such correlation. Detailed study of the issues of value conflict and the explanation of changing content in even our most stable normative concepts have direct bearing upon the character and scope of our value ultimates. On this point, we must never overlook the significant historical fact that it was Nietzsche's provocative raising of the question of the "transvaluation of values" that inaugurated modern value theory by precipitating the basic question of the ultimacy of our traditional values. But there are also pressing contemporary reasons for this approach in the crucial current problems of value conflict both within and between our contemporary cultures, a situation which seems to verify Nietzsche's diagnosis of our era as a time of unprecedented value crisis.

Value theory was originally expected to provide some basis for the critical and comparative study of our basic values and value systems, but has as yet not fulfilled such expectations, largely, one repeats, on account of its value theory's dominant and chronic formalism. In a time of ideological stress and storm, which is symptomatic of value conflict, any prospect of an adequate value critique should be especially explored and eagerly developed. A functional consideration of values, certainly, heads squarely into such issues and problems, with little chance of avoiding their full impact: that is its good or bad fortune according to its success or failure in handling them. This paper merely attempts to justify the potentialities of such an approach without the further presumption of attempting in constructive outline, an entire functionalist theory of value.

One question, however, must be settled favorably before a functional analysis of the normative element in so-called value "ultimates" can assure itself of safe clearance. That is an adequate answer to the contention of the value realists that functional value analysis can only yield a descriptive account of value assertions and cannot, therefore, account for their normative character or their role in evaluative judgment. The most outspoken form of this argument regards all varieties of value functionalism as merely attentuated forms of the extremist position in value relativism, logical positivism, and reducible to it in final analysis on the presumption that they deny by implication what positivism denies explicitly, *viz.,* the basic normative property of values. An example of such criticism is Urban's quite categorical statement, "It is coming to be seen that there is no middle ground between this positivism and some form of objective axiology," going on to add: "Many, it is true, have sought such a middle ground in pragmatism, with its quasi-objectivity and its instrumental notion of verification. But it is becoming increasingly clear that such a position is untenable." [2]

Such a reduction of the position of all value functionalism to the ultra-relativism of the positivists is arbitrary and unwarranted. Granted that some relativist interpretations of value are so subjective as to be completely atomistic and anarchistic, that is not the case with all. Particularly is this so with a type of analysis whose main objective is to give a consistent account of the relative permanencies of value-modes and their normative criteria *and* the readily observable phenomena of value change and value transposition in a way that they will not contradict one another.

Value content is observably variable and transposable with regard to its value norms. There is no warrant of fact for considering values as fixed permanently to certain normative categories or pegged in position under them or attached intrinsically by nature or "essence" to that mode of valuation to which they may be relevantly referred. Only in our traditional stereotyping of values is this so: in actuality, something in the way they are felt or apprehended establishes their normative relevancy. On this point, it may well turn out that some psychological coerciveness in value feeling or some dispositional role or cue in behavior is an adequate and more verifiable explanation of the relation between the particular value and its referential "ultimate" or norm.

It is, moreover, an oversimplification of the form of relativism under discussion, functional relativism, to say that it merely calls to our attention that what is good today is bad tomorrow [or vice versa]. This interpretation of value is more properly represented by a statement that what is revealed or developed in experience as *better* becomes *the new good*, shifting to the position of normative acceptance or urgency formerly occupied by the older value content. The process continuity of the normative character of values is demonstrated not merely by the substitution of new value content for the old, but even more clearly by the displacement and retroactive devaluing of the old, a procedure which transforms yesterday's good into a relatively bad. That which is felt or judged as relatively better (or truer to the systematic value quality in the case of other types of value than the ethical) is normally preferred and so becomes normatively imperative. When explicit judgment ensues, it is revamped in evaluative thought accordingly.

To my way of construing the situation, it is the retrospective revaluation of the value which, by guaranteeing the stability of the norm and the value system it supports exhibits most clearly the really functional force and character of the normative principle. Paradoxically, in actual practise, it seems to be the progressively corrective character of the value norm more than stability of specific value content which endows our abstract values with normative ultimacy. It is by such a criterion, for example, that we can best explain why a lesser evil becomes a comparative good.

There are, of course, value situations where this functionally normative reaction is lacking, but on close scrutiny they turn out to be situations which even as exceptions prove the rule. For they are situations where the inhibitions and dogmatisms of habit block the corrective revision of the value content. In such cases either the intelligence or feeling or both, intrenched in irrational fixation on the orthodox content, refuses to follow through, and invariably does so by the technique of asserting an inseparable connection between the value form and its value content. I have elsewhere in greater detail[3] attempted to characterize value norms as system values rather than fixed intrinsic values, as process imperatives rather than intrinsic absolutes.

The most effective reply, however, to value realism's rejection of this functionalist interpretation is to challenge the value realist under his presuppositions to explain, in addition to such value change as has just been cited, the numerous observable cases of value transposition. For instance, a demonstration or proof, normally logical in value reverence and criterion, is appraised, because of its virtuosity or style of proof as "neat," "pretty," "elegant" or even "beautiful." Unless this type of value occurrence is illusory or mere metaphorical confusion in the language of value description, it presents an almost unexplainable character to the value realist. If he is consistent with his doctrine of the value type as intrinsic, he must dismiss such situations a mere analogies. But inside acquaintance with the experience shows it to be in the case mentioned to be a genuinely aesthetic value reference both in its valuational and evaluational phases, vested with the characteristic attitudes, feelings and judgment of the aesthetic norm rather than just a metaphorical transfer of aesthetic predicates. It actually becomes an aesthetic value *qua* something admired for its perfection of form and the contemplative satisfaction which this admiration of it yields. Formalizations of values, traditional in attitude association or orthodox in logical evaluation, do stereotype certain content with value references that become typical and characteristic; but there are not only many exceptions in actual valuation but in all specific cases, where the value attitude as experienced or felt is that appropriate to another value-genre, the value reference and judgment as indicated qualitatively by the descriptive predicates, however unorthodox the reference, follow, it seems, the actualities of the value attitude.

On the other hand, the value realist's reasoning, in addition to being an inadequate explanation of the real situation, in its form of thinking would seem to involve another instance of what Reiser aptly calls the "inveterate tendency to make entities out of modes of behavior."[4] Certainly this value objectification upon an intrinsic basis exhibits *usteron proteron* reasoning by reversing the natural order of the value and its content reference, as though the discrimination of the value led to the discovery of the "true" nature of the object, rather than realizing that the valuing of the object in a certain way leads to its apprehension in a certain value context. Ehrenfels has a pithy analysis of such fallaciousness: "Philosophy itself," he says, "at the beginning followed this urge for objectification which transfers the content of the inner experience to the thing itself as absolutely determinant, endeavoring thus to discover that which had *value in itself*, with about as much justification [he shrewdly adds] as one might claim in contending whether the direction toward the north pole or that toward the south pole pointed upwards in itself, or whether the earth by itself was a large or small body."[5] This, I take it, is both an apt description and refutation of the classic fallacy involved in the value absolutist's position. From the functionalist's point of view the basic error lies in regarding the formal value as the cause of the valuation or as an essence of the value object rather than the system value of the mode of valuing, which is sometimes the symbol, sometimes its rationale, but in practise an implementation of the value as apprehended. Of course, to the degree that values are regarded abstractly, they take on a quality of universality and seeming independence, but this is merely a common characteristic of all generalizations. But If we can sufficiently explain the character of value-generals as system norms, functional in value discrimination and comparison, they need not then be unrealistically raised to the status of hypostasized absolutes or perennial essences.

At this point it becomes quite proper to leave behind formal counterargument of opposing views, and turn to the more concrete and congenial consideration of concrete cases, functionally interpreted. Time will permit only a single example from each of the major value-genres, the moral, the logical and the aesthetic, each instance selected to illustrate what we may call the contextual basis of the normative character involved. Each case, involving as it does value change and the displacement of older traditional material by new value content, ought to exhibit the type of relative normativity of the kind we have been delineating, that is, flexible as to material content permitting value change and reconstruction but nonetheless systematic and normatively coercive in its function of value control.

As a case illustrating several important facets of functional relativism in moral values, I choose a profoundly analytic value problem propounded in a play by the Soviet dramatist, Korneichuk, I believe, which deeply impressed me when I saw it some years ago. I think he made out a clear case for the contextual but systematic character of normative value control. He was enabled to do so because he chose a situation involving a complete reversal of value for the same act, but showed how though diametrically opposed one to the other, as between the two systems of values, each was imperatively right in the context of its own appropriate system. By taking an act that most of us find impossible to imagine out of our orthodox context of the greatest of all evils and crimes, Korneichuk dramatically and illuminatingly sets the action and conflict in a setting where the greatest of crimes is not only a virtue but a sacrosanct duty. The act is parricide, and the setting is the changing life of a nomadic Eskimo tribe making their first sustained contact with Western civilization and its moral codes.

Age-old custom, on the very reasonable basis of the peculiar uselessness of the old and feeble in the hazardous life of a nomadic Artic people, has decreed the custom of ritualistic parricide, with the eldest son obligated by custom to push the aged parent off into the sea from an icefloe after a feast in which both the shaman and the aged victim give ritualistic consent. The hero of the play, however, has been away at a Soviet training center and has been exposed to another code in terms of which pardonable parricide has become unpardonable murder, and in addition functionally unnecessary. Returning, he is in general conflict with the tribal values, but has been taught to minimize the impact of the conflict with understanding tolerance and piecemeal reform. But peace cannot be made on that basis with the shaman who represents the unyielding authority of the old system as a whole. The shaman's moment inevitably comes when the time arrives for the father's custom sanctioned death, for at that point the two systems meet in irreconcilable contradiction.

The dramatist has carefully and sympathetically conveyed the imperative logic of the older value system which makes parricide acceptable to the aged parent and a filial duty expected of his son. Though an obsolescent way of life, with its justifying function gone, the old value is presented, correctly, I think, as "right" on its own level, that is, in the mind of the father and the relatives. As he vacillates between the two loyalties, the son's hesitancy and grief over the tragic dilemma emotionally concedes this; at several moments he is pictured as about to perform what to him is a crime but to the others a dutiful favor. But the reappearance of the shaman reinstates the duel between the systems, and it is clear that from that point on the son will never concede in action. The old man, still convinced of the rightness of his going, shocked by his son's hesitancy and yet dimly aware of the new set of values which hinder him, walks off into the sea without benefit of ceremony. The effective dramatization at one and the same time of the respective truths in conflict and of the value system principle as the root of the coercive normativeness of each affords deep insight into the nature of the functional normativity we are discussing. It is an exemplary instance of functional normativity, and one calculated to disprove the value formalist's charge of the non-normative character of the functionalist value interpretation.

The case example for logical values is taken deliberately from scientific theory rather than abstract logic, because although the same principle of systematic consistency is the functioning norm, the scientific example, in addition, will point up the fact that modern scientific theory has fully accepted the relativistic criterion of truth as its normative methodological criterion. It is now a commonplace that science at any given time acknowledges a final truth only in the sense of the most recently accepted consensus of competent experience, and contrary to traditional logic, knows no absolute or irreplaceable truth. Almost any of the larger general theories in science could equally well be taken as illustration of this. But I take the electron theory as most convenient to show in addition to the superiority of the electronic view of the atom as an explanatory concept for the observed behavior of matter, its greater normative range and force as a concept of greater systematic consistency and coverage than the older theory which it has displaced. As von Mach pointed out long ago, we realize that the extension of the system coverage of a theoretical truth is an important factor in its preferability as a theoretical satisfactory and acceptable explanation. As such, the proper interpretation would seem to be to regard this criterion as an evaluative form principle with a normative validity which is functionally based and attested.

But to turn more directly to the problem at hand, no physicist accepting the electronic view would style the older classical theory of the atom as false in its entirety but only in certain of its aspects. Indeed for a long period it was quite satisfactory as a consistent explanation of the nature of matter. However, until radically revised, it was not satisfactory or consistent as an interpretation of matter as energy. The electron theory is, therefore, a *truer* theory of the atom, and I stress truer, because, occupying the same relative position in the systematic analytical explanation of matter, it consistently includes and interprets more observable phenomena than the older atomic theory. For in addition to what it explained before —qualitative description and identification, serial position and relative weight and valence—it now also explains energy structure and energy potential. But the main point is that the new truth incorporates, on the basis of consistency, a good part of the previous theory, although perforce, also in the interest of consistency it has to discard certain other theoretically postulated properties now inconsistent with the enlarged range of known facts. Instrumental logic regards it as important to point out that, though now false, these elements were acceptable and useful in their context and time, and led up to the interpretations we now have substituted for general acceptance.

We should notice that important aspects of the present theory are hypothetical, and are regarded as true because of their systematic value in the explanation of the facts. Some of these items are just as hypothetical as the displaced and discredited elements in the older theory, but their present acceptability is based on the restored consistency, the wider coverage and the greater inclusiveness of the theoretical system as now conceived. The functionally normative character, in contradistinction to a permanent and intrinsic view of the nature of the truth value seems obvious, and this example is typical. A functionally based or relative ultimacy is all that is required, and more than that, at least in scientific procedures is definitely preferable.

Our value judgments in art, though none the less critical today and certainly more technical than ever, are also far from the traditionalism of the older aesthetics. Modern art theory and practise have broken almost completely with the former authoritarian conception of beauty. Indeed, on both the consumer and the productive or creative level, we have actually witnessed in less than a generation the basic criteria of a major value mode going completely relativistic with regard to styles, idioms, art rationales and judgmental evaluation. Creative expression in modern art has particularly operated on radically extended canons of beauty and its appreciation. There are those, I am aware, who will say that art expression today has become so utterly relativistic that there is no longer a standard of beauty left or a valid set of stylistic criteria. But impartial examination of modern art will show rather contrary results. The widening of the variety of styles and aesthetic has actually been accompanied by a deepening of aesthetic taste and a sharpening of critical discrimination.

Certainly normative control has not been lost or sacrificed, as is proved by a double line of evidence. In the first place the appreciation of new forms and varieties has not caused us to lose grasp on our appreciation of the older varieties, the classical heritage of past artistic expression. Indeed, on the contrary, modernist art has never in its best expressions undermined the appreciation of traditional art. In the second place, critical discrimination as tested by genuine knowledge appreciation of the technical aspects of art styles has increased manyfold. Variety, on the whole, has not led to greater confusion, but by actual comparisons, critical taste and judgment have improved. Our current art pluralism is attested by the contemporary tolerance of many mutually incompatible styles, whose growth has been accompanied by a growing liberation of taste from formalism and superficially imposed standards, as concrete examples will show.

The musical formalist or aesthetic authoritarian has to confess his inability to judge the contemporary musical situation and usage. But the modernist, who is a sub-conscious or semi-conscious relativist, finds little or no difficulty in interpreting what has actually happened in modern art. In music, for example, what has the modern composer done? He has changed musical content substantially, but instead of destroying the musical norm has really enlarged its scope. He has not changed, in fact is not able to change the basic attitudinal qualities of musical apprehension nor has he broken down its discriminatory effectiveness. His new forms have developed critical criteria appropriate to their idiom and at the same time not inconsistent with the older criteria after habituation. What the modernist styles have done is really, by conditioning, to enlarge both by bringing them into the orbit of the same favorable aesthetic reaction. The new style and idiom—certainly it is not our hearing but our appreciative apprehension which has improved—has succeeded in bringing into the realm of immediately felt concordance what was previously felt as irregular and cacophonic, and could not, therefore, be apprehended pleasurably and integrated into an aesthetically toned reaction.

A person who cannot, however, synthesize his auditory and emotional experiences on hearing Stravinsky or Hindemith cannot appreciate the musical language of modernist music. He can realize the technical musicianship and also concede its potential musicality for those who can genuinely appreciate it. But that same person can by repeated exposure to such music bring it not only within the range of appreciation but within now enlarged criteria of evaluative judgment, as good, bad or mediocre of its kind. The cacophany by repeated experience has become concordant, meaningful and therefore "beautiful." Now the illuminating aspect of this is that Stravinsky and Hindemith have not to such a matured taste upset the approach to and the appreciation of Mozart and Beethoven; nor for that matter has jazz upset the apprehension of classical musical forms and idioms, except temporarily. One hastens to add good jazz, which has developed for jazz idioms and forms more and more professionalized devotees and rigidly normative criteria of taste and critical musical analysis.

We may cite, quite briefly, the same sequence of results in another phase of art, painting and sculpture. In these forms, too, modernist art at first acquaintance seems a welter of uncoordinated styles and their rival aesthetics. But the anarchy is in large part illusory. Modern art has about solved the problem of art tolerance, by making each style a systematic criterion for itself and whatever is relevant to it. More than that both creative activity and appreciation have broadened base perceptably. Modern art creativity may not be as Alpine as it was in certain periods of the past, but there is undeniably a higher plateau of appreciation and performance.

Incidentally this widening of the range of appreciation and participation is as good an example as we can find of what democratization can mean in a value field. First our exposure to Oriental art with its markedly different idioms and form criteria inaugurated the artistic value revolution we call modernism. The appreciative understanding and creative use of the formerly strange and to us unaesthetic idioms of African and other primitive art followed, and a revolutionary revision of taste and creative outlook was fully on.

Since then, with ever-increasing experimentalism, art forms have been multiplied and taste extended. But here again in this field, as in music, modernistic relativism has not served to invalidate but rather to enhance the appreciation of the classical and traditional expressions of the beautiful.

Certainly this is a good augury for the resolution of certain hitherto irresolvable types of value conflict. I merely throw out the suggestion that through modernism and its enforced but not normatively chaotic relativism we have forged a psychological key for the active and simultaneous appreciation of diverse styles within our own culture, in fact within our own culture period. It seems to serve for the wider but none the less vivid appreciative understanding of alien art forms and idioms, and to give us some insight into their correlated aesthetics. Already through such enlargement we are able to appreciate a good measure of primitive art of all varieties, children's art and the art forms of many cultures that were dead letters to our eyes previously. In an approaching world interchange of culture it is just such widening of taste to a cosmopolitan range and level which seems most desirable, if indeed not imperative. That accents what has previously been mentioned, the functional superiority in explicit terms of improved comprehension of values and their more effective correlation as a direct consequence of relativistic as over against authoritarian approaches to the sets of values involved. If this is extendable to other value fields, and I think it is, we have in this principle of analysis and rearrangement an effective base for resolving large segments of our current value conflicts.

Instrumentalism or functionalism as I prefer to stress it has already pointed out that scientific knowledge operates on the methodological postulates of relativism and the constant revision of a progressively organized body of systematized experience. Art, we have just seen, in its contemporary theory and practise of values has moved in a similar direction, without losing hold on normative criteria that are effective and functional, though not arbitrarily static and absolute. We would do well to remember that both science and art once had doctrines of the finality of beauty and truth, but have been able to abandon them. Absolutism, however, with its corollary of fundamentalism is still fairly generally entrenched in moral theory, in goodly measure still in speculative philosophy and in the orthodox varieties of religious faith and belief. The continuation of the older tradition of absolutism is, of course, closely bound in with the question of the nature of value ultimates and the type of normativeness they are supposed to exercise. This was our starting point. We come back to it to suggest that the more tenable interpretations of value theory as to the actually functioning of value norms aligns value theory on the side of the relativist position. Should that be true, value theory in the next steps of its development may exert the deciding influence among the value disciplines in turning away from absolutism and dogmatism on the one hand and relativism of the revisionist and progressive stripe on the other. Having become accommodated to a progressive truth and an ever-expanding and creatively exploratory quest for beauty, it may be that we shall trend toward a relativistic but not anarchic ethics, world view and religion which will be more functionally correlated with the actualities of life and conduct and more effectively normative without rigidly imposed and dictatorial authority. Our value ultimates from that point of definition and enforcement will no longer be unrealistic as principles and from the cultural point of view provincial tyrants.

NOTES

1. Wilbur Urban, "Axiology," in D. Runes (ed.), *Twentieth Century Philosophy*, p. 54.
2. *Ibid.*, p. 62.
3. Alain Locke, "Values and Imperatives," in Sidney Hook and Horace M. Kallen (eds.), *American Philosophy Today and Tomorrow* (New York: Lee Furman, 1935), p. 313.
4. Oliver L. Reiser, *The Promise of Scientific Humanism: Toward a Unification of Scientific, Religious, Social, and Economic Thought* (New York: D. Piest, 1940), p. 123.
5. C. F. von Ehrenfels, "Werttheorie und Ethik," *Vierteljahrsschrift für wissenschaftliche Philosophie* 17 (1893), p. 87. [In the original Locke noted Volume 1; however, the reference seems to be to Volume 17.]

5. Pluralism and Ideological Peace

This article was published in a commemorative book on Horace Kallen, one of Locke's long-standing friends. Since his days at Oxford with Locke, Kallen had become know for popularizing the term "cultural pluralism" and pursuing rapprochements between ethnic, particularly eastern European, and religious groups, particularly Christians and Jews.

As with his 1942 "Pluralism and Intellectual Democracy" Locke begins by referencing James's epistemological pluralism. In Locke's interpretation of James's pluralism, "it is man himself who is at least in part responsible for the irreducible variety of human experience by making a pluriverse out of the common substratum of experience—the objective universe." As with "Values and Imperatives" (1935) and "Cultural Relativism and Ideological Peace" (1944), absolutes, authoritarianism, and universalism were framed as indefensible positions. Locke pursued a central theme of "Values and Imperatives," that is, "effective mediating principles for situations of basic value divergence and conflict." It is the lack of these that limits the use of James's anarchistic pluralism on Locke's account. Locke recommends a set of attitudes (parity, tolerance, reciprocity) he believes to be functional for the negation of absolutism, and value relativism (many-sided truth) as their theoretical ground.

"Pluralism and Ideological Peace," *Freedom and Experience: Essays Presented to Horace M. Kallen*, ed. Sidney Hook and Milton R. Knovitz (New York: New School for Social Research and Cornell University Press, 1947), pp. 63–69.

Pluralism and Ideological Peace

Ever since William James's ardent and creative advocacy of it, pluralism has involved, explicitly or by implication, an antiauthoritarian principle. This is because James carried the pluralistic position definitely and perhaps permanently beyond the traditional metaphysical pluralism based on the recognition of a plurality of principles or elements to the discovery and vindication of a psychological pluralism stemming from a plurality of values and viewpoints. In this view it is man himself who is at least in part responsible for the irreducible variety of human experience by making a pluriverse out of the common substratum of experience—the objective universe. Except for agreement on the hard core of experience susceptible of empirical validation, ideological agreement in terms of values such as is envisaged by monism and absolutism is, accordingly, not to be expected. It is the potentialities of such value pluralism, with its still only partially developed corollaries of cultural pluralism, that need to be explored as a possible and favorable foundation for wide-scale ideological peace. For the complete implementation of the pluralistic philosophy it is not sufficient merely to disestablish authoritarianism and its absolutes; a more positive and constructive development of pluralism can and should establish some effective mediating principles for situations of basic value divergence and conflict.

Some realistic basis for ideological peace is certainly an imperative need today, and that need is for more than a pro tempore truce; a real intellectual and spiritual disarmament is indicated by the ideological tensions of our present-day world crisis. Admitting that ideas originally became weapons merely as rationalizations of other conflicts of interest, and that there still remain many nonideological factors of potential strife and discord, it is still true that in our time ideological divergence has become a primary basis of hostility and is so potent a possible source of strife that more than ever now "ideas are weapons." The present situation, then, calls for some permanently conceded basis of ideological neutrality or reciprocity in the context of which our differences over values can be regarded as natural, inevitable, and mutually acceptable. It is ironical to talk of "civilization" without as yet having acquired ideological civility—a necessary ingredient of civilized intercourse and co-operation, especially now that we are committed to contact and communication on a world scale.

Of course, such intellectual tolerance and courtesy cannot be effectively arrived at by cynical indifference or by proclaiming value anarchy, but only through the recognition of the importance of value systems on a "live and let live" basis. For this we need a realistic but sympathetic understanding of the bases of our value differences, and their root causes—some of them temperamental, more of them experiential, still more, of cultural derivation. After outlawing orthodoxy, the next step is to legitimate and interpret diversity, and then, if possible, to discover some "harmony in contrariety," some commonality in divergence.

In spite of the leveling off of many present differences under the impact of science, technology, and increased intercommunication, we cannot in any reasonably near future envisage any substantial lessening of the differences in our basic value systems, either philosophical or cultural. The only viable alternative seems, therefore, not to expect to change others but to change our attitudes toward them, and to seek rapprochement not by the eradication of such differences as there are but by schooling ourselves not to make so much of the differences. These differences, since they are as real and hard as "facts" should be accepted as unemotionally and objectively as we accept fact. F. S. C. Northrop, who so brilliantly and suggestively has attempted to bridge the great ideological divide between the Occident and the Orient, is quite right in calling this pluralistic and relativistic approach "realism with respect to ideals."

A genuine realism in this respect must take into account . . . the ideological beliefs to which any people has been conditioned by its traditional education, political propaganda, artistic creations, and religious ceremonies. These traditional ideological factors embodied in the institutions and emotions of the people are just as much part of the *de facto* situation as are the pestilences, the climate, the ethnology, or the course of pig iron prices in the market place.[1]

This type of understanding, it seems to me, begins in a basic recognition of value pluralism, converts itself to value relativism as its only consistent interpretation, and then passes over into a ready and willing admission of both cultural relativism and pluralism. In practice, this ideological orientation concedes reciprocity and requires mutual respect and noninterference. It pivots on the principle that the affirmation of one's own world of values does not of necessity involve the denial or deprecation of someone else's. The obvious analogy with a basic democratic viewpoint will immediately suggest itself; in fact there seems to be an affinity, historical and ideological, between pluralism and democracy, as has been frequently observed. Only this is an extension of democracy beyond individuals and individual rights to the equal recognition of the parity and inalienable rights of corporate ways of life. Cultural parity and reciprocity we have yet in large part to learn, for where our values are concerned, most of us, even those who have abandoned philosophical absolutism, still hold on to remnants of absolutistic thinking. How slowly does this ancient obsession retreat from the concept of an absolute God to that of an absolute reason, to that of an absolute morality, to linger on entrenched in the last-stand theories of an absolute state and an absolute culture!

But we can build no vital tolerance and mutual understanding on such relics of absolutistic thinking. How aptly Toynbee describes our prevalent cultural monism in this searching passage:

We are no longer conscious of the presence in the world of other societies of equal standing; and that we regard our society as being identical with "civilized" mankind and the peoples outside its pale as being mere "natives" of territories which they inhabit on sufferance, but which are morally as well as practically at our disposal, by the higher right of our assumed monopoly of civilization, whenever we choose to take possession. Conversely, we regard the internal divisions of our society—the national parts into which this society has come to be articulated—as the grand divisions of mankind, and classify the members of the human race as Frenchmen, Englishmen, Germans, and so on, without remembering that these are merely subdivisions of a single group within the human family.[2]

This cultural absolutism of ours is, of course, today under heavy pressure, a double pressure of declining and semibankrupt imperialism and surprisingly strong counterassertive challenge from Asiatic, Moslem, and even African culture groups that for so long a time have been its rather helpless victims. But though shocked out of its traditional complacency and retreating step by step on the basis of tactical expediency, there is as yet no general disestablishment of the core idea in our mass thinking, no profound conversion of our basic value attitudes. Expediency rather than renunciation seems to dictate whatever changes are taking place. But to their great credit, pluralists and relativists like Toynbee and others have long since conceded the principle and have wholeheartedly recanted this arrogant and long-standing bigotry of Western culture. They alone, through having done so, are fully equipped to face the present world crisis with understanding and equanimity. To that extent pluralist thinking has opened out to them in advance the progressive vistas of the new intercultural internationalism and given them passports of world citizenship good for safe ideological conduct anywhere.

Interestingly enough, Northrop[3] discovers an analogous relativistic strain in Oriental thought, one that is, in his estimation, of surprising strength and long standing, since it stems from the heart of Buddhist philosophy. Much older and deeper-rooted then than our Occidental pluralism, it accounts, Northrop thinks, for Buddhism's wide tolerance and effective catholicity. In its more enlightened followers, he says, Buddhist teaching has "a fundamental and characteristic open-mindedness, in fact a positive welcoming of religious and philosophical doctrines other than its own, with an attendant tolerance that has enabled Buddhism to infiltrate almost the whole range of Eastern cultures without disrupting them or losing its own characteristic identity." In documenting this acceptance of a doctrine of many-sided truth, Northrop quotes a Buddhist scripture as prescribing for the perfect disciple these maxims, among others:

To read a large number of books on the various religions and philosophies; to listen to many learned doctors professing many different doctrines; to experiment oneself with a number of methods; to choose a doctrine among the many one has studied and discard the others; . . . to consider with perfect equanimity and detachment the conflicting opinions and various manifestations of the activity of beings; to understand that such is the nature of things, the inevitable mode of action of each entity, and remaining always serene, to look upon the world as a man standing on the highest mountain of the country looks at the valleys and the lesser summits spread out below him.[4]

It may well be, as Northrop thinks, that we have mistaken as mystical indifference and disdain what basically is a humane and realistic relativism motivated by a profound and nonaggressive respect for difference and the right to differ.

Be that as it may, it is important and encouraging to recognize that, however differently based and cued, both Western and Oriental thought do contain humane pluralistic viewpoints which can join forces for intercultural tolerance and ideological peace. Only on some such basis can any wide-scale rapprochement of cultures be undertaken. One can appreciate the deep-seated desire and the ever-recurrent but Utopian dream of the idealist that somehow a single faith, a common culture, an all-embracing institutional life and its confraternity should some day unite man by merging all his loyalties and culture values. But even with almost complete intercommunication within practical grasp, that day seems distant, especially since we have as great need for cultural pluralism in a single unit of society as in a nation as large and composite as our own. What seems more attainable, realistically, is some reconstruction of those attitudes and rationalizations responsible for bitter and irreconcilable conflict over our separate loyalties and value divergencies. The pluralist way to unity seems by far the most practicable.

Indeed, as the present writer has said previously,

it may well be that at this point relativism has its great historical chance. It may be destined to have its day in the channeling of human progress, not, however, as a mere philosophy or abstract theory, though it began as such, but as a new base and technique for the study and understanding of human cultures and a new way of controlling through education our attitudes toward various group cultures, beginning with our own. For only through having some objective and factual base in the sciences of man and society, can cultural relativism implement itself for this task of reconstructing our basic social and cultural loyalties by lifting them, through some radically new perspective, to a plane of enlarged mutual understanding.[5]

Cultural outlooks and philosophies rooted in fanatical religious orthodoxy or in inflated cultural bias and partisanship, or in overweening national and racial chauvinism have been outflanked and outmoded by the developments of the present age. Nevertheless, they survive considerably, though more precariously as their provincialisms become more and more obvious. For that very reason they cling all the more tenaciously to the only psychological attitude which can give them support and succor—the mind-set of fundamentalism and orthodoxy. We know all too well, and sorrowfully, how this mind-set constitutes the working base for all those absolutistic dogmatisms that rationalize orthodoxy. In so doing, it fortifies with convictions of finality and self-righteousness the countless crusades for conformity which provide the moral and intellectual sanctions not only for war but for most other irreconcilable group conflicts. If pluralism and relativism can nip in the psychological bud the passion for arbitrary unity and conformity, they already have functioned effectively as ideological peacemakers. And successful in this first and necessary step, they can often later provide favorable ground for the subsequent rapprochement and integration of value systems. But where, as in many instances, values cannot be mediated, they can at least be impartially and sympathetically interpreted, which is almost as important. For with greater mutual understanding, there can only be less motivation for forced unification. Just as in the democratic philosophy, the obvious limit of one's personal rights is where they begin to infringe similar rights of others, so in this value domain mutual respect and reciprocity, based on nonaggression and nondisparagement, can alone be regarded as justifiable.

Paradoxically enough, absolutism in all its varieties—religious, philosophical, political, and cultural—despite the insistent linking together of unity and universality, seems able, so far as historical evidence shows, to promote unity only at the expense of universality. For absolutism's way to unity, being the way of orthodoxy, involves authoritarian conformity and subordination. From such premises dogmatism develops sooner or later, and thereafter, history shows us, come those inevitable schisms which disrupt the parent dogmatism and deny it in the name of a new orthodoxy. Once we fully realize the divisive general effect of fundamentalist ideas and all their institutional incorporations and understand that orthodox conformity inevitably breeds its opposite—sectarian disunity—we reach a position where we can recognize relativism as a safer and saner approach to the objectives of practical unity.

What is achieved through relativistic rapprochement is, of course, somewhat different from the goal of the absolutists. It is a fluid and functional unity rather than a fixed and irrevocable one, and its vital norms are equivalence and reciprocity rather than identity or complete agreement. But when we consider the present lack of any overarching synthesis and the unlikelihood of any all-inclusive orthodoxy of human values, we are prepared to accept or even to prefer an attainable concord of understanding and co-operation in lieu of an unattainable unanimity.

Horace Kallen, whom we honor in this volume, himself a pioneer and creative advocate of pluralism, has very aptly described the type of philosophy that can furnish the ideological framework for what he calls "the structure of a lasting peace."

Such a philosophy will be pluralist and temporalist, its morality will live and let live, it will acknowledge the equal claim of every event to survive and attain excellence, and it will distinguish consequences, not set norms. The unities it validates consequently will be instrumental ones: its attitude toward problems will be tentative and experimental, it will dispute all finalities and doubt all foregone conclusions; its rule will be Nature's: *solvitur ambulando.*

NOTES

1. F. S. C. Northrop, *The Meeting of East and West* (New York: Macmillan, 1946), p. 479.

2. Arnold Toynbee, *The Study of History* (London: Oxford University Press, 1934), pp. 31–32.

3. Northrop, *The Meeting of East and West*, p. 355.

4. Ibid., p. 356.

5. Alain Locke, "Cultural Relativism and Ideological Peace," *Approaches to World Peace*, ed. Lyman Bryson, L. Finkelstein, R. M. MacIver (New York: Harper & Brothers, 1944), p. 612.

6. Good Reading

Entitled "Good Reading: Penguin Edition," this article is undated, and I have been unable to locate a publication, if there is one, to which it corresponds. Because Locke mentions Bergson and Dewey, and because of the character of the typescript, "Good Reading" was probably written sometime between 1935 and 1947. In "Good Reading," Locke justifies and explains the benefits of reading philosophy. In so doing, he gives us a picture of who he regards as important philosophers and an understanding of both philosophy's contextuality and universality. Professional philosophy, for example, seeks technical answers to a host of traditional questions, albeit questions of universal interest. Philosophy thus constitutes personal expressions of belief and provides a map of a culture's historicity as its members search to discover a pattern of meaning and truth in the universe. Locke's description of philosophy provides an indication of his appreciation for systems of thought. Philosophy's utility in correcting our normally fragmented view of life is applauded. The utility of philosophy's historicity is considered by Locke.

"Good Reading," undated, unpublished. Printed with the permission of Moorland-Spingarn Research Center, Alain Locke Collection, Howard University.

Good Reading

Philosophy is reading that is both stimulating and profitable, though seldom is it easy reading: indeed, by reason of its difficult objectives, it cannot be easy. Like mountain climbing, it undertakes hard and hazardous but challenging tasks, which become exhilarating because of their difficulties, fascinating because of their daring, but proportionately rewarding because of the wide outlooks and rare insights which surmounting them affords. In philosophy's case, the task is that of scanning the terrain and horizons of human experience from such exploratory heights of reason as alone, it seems, can yield a panoramic view of man and his place in the universe. Shunned by many for its difficulties, philosophy is also often blamed for its cold abstraction and lofty detachment from the immediate actualities of life, but here again, these are but the price of philosophy's final benefits and satisfactions. For philosophy's comprehensive perspectives dictate this characteristic calm and disinterested distance corrects the distortions of ordinary close, familiar but fragmentary views of life.

Throughout the ages and in spite of varying approaches, philosophical thinking has aimed essentially at the same basic objective —a panoramic world view or life view. Whether concerned with the relationship of man's mind to the outer worlds of nature and society or to his inner world of ideas, values and ideals, or with contriving a common rationale for both, the philosopher searches for some integral and integrating view of things in terms of which they become more relatedly understandable. Consequently, the philosopher is not concerned, like the scientist, with details primarily, but with overall relationships. This is why, in all its many varieties, philosophy has maintained a vital and essential unity of objective, a common consensus about what are its basic problems, no matter how much it has differed controversially over the specific answers.

Being thus essentially systematic, philosophy, even in its detailed and technical analyses, works toward a system of interpretation, for some meaningful synthesis of knowledge and experience. Scientific knowledge, on the whole, rests on detailed and specific truths, and as it grows deploys in all directions in search of them. Philosophy, on the other hand, even when using scientific knowledge as a base, is committed, like religion and art, to discovering some pattern or mosaic of meaning which can be comprehended not merely as a compartmentalized collection of truths but as a composite and illuminating picture of *the* truth. So philosophical systems, for the most part, have the creative quality of framed intellectual landscapes, and confront us as significant panoramas of meaning, skillfully composed or happily discovered. And when science likewise fits its findings into a significant mosaic, it, too, becomes a scientific philosophy.

Sometimes the unifying factor in a philosophy is the integrating force of a great mind or personality; sometimes, instead, it is the epitomized rationale of an age or phase of human culture. But whether expressing a personal synthesis or the systematized rationalization of a whole way of life, philosophies are best understood by the layman as such representative reflections of the lineaments of a personality or an age, which is what, in the last analysis, most of them really are. Professional philosophers may approach and understand them differently, as expressive of what T. V. Smith has called "philosophy's high degree of continuity,"—that is to say, as a succession of professional answers to certain technical questions involved in the theory of mind, knowledge or reality, certain theories as to the nature of society, morality, beauty, truth and man's destiny.

But even in such technical aspects, formal philosophy either sharpens the tools or quarries the building blocks that finally combine to construct an edifice of ideas whose architecture expresses some historically or culturally representative life or world view.

The reading of philosophy in historical perspective can thus become an entertaining and enlightening tour of the progressive development of our basic values and ideas. As we follow their path through the changing scenery of our culture, we can clearly recognize the continuous role and function of philosophy as sometimes the guide to life and sometimes merely the trail that shows the paths man's mind has taken. But in both cases, we meet the great thinkers at junction points and signposts on the main highways of this intellectual journey, marking off the completion of a stage of the way, or signaling a new turn in the road, or revealing, in their controversial divergence, the dilemmas that have confronted mankind at this or that stage of cultural history.

As followers of the progress of philosophical thought, we must resolve to take the hazards of the journey, like those of any road, pleasant and smooth in places, rugged and tortuous in others. Fortunately the greatest thinkers, however technical in details, have meaning for the amateur as well as the professional student. Occasionally, too, they have the gift of style added to the gift of wisdom, and like Plato, Lucretius, Dante, Voltaire, Rousseau, Emerson, Nietzsche, James or Santayana, are poet-philosophers who invest their ideas with artistic as well as intellectual illumination. But then there must also be concern and respect for those who speak the equally important prose of wisdom,—the Aristotles, Aquinas, Spinozas, Leibnizs, Kants, Hegels, Spencers, Bergsons, and Deweys.

The beginner happily can commence with the clear paths and broad perspectives of the Greco-Roman synthesis,—the classic works of Plato, Aristotle, Epictetus and Marcus Aurelius, and if he wishes to be scholarly, those of Lucretius and Plotinus. Then with classical humanism behind him, he can thread the narrower foothill paths of neo-Platonism and early Christian thought, with a glimpse at least of the mystic citadel of St. Augustine's Plato-inspired *City of God*. One may skip the technicalities of Scholasticism, but still will need to ponder the imposing world view of Aquinas, that great medieval synthesis whose prose Dante poetized in *The Divine Comedy*. And so, on and on, through the syntheses of Renaissance humanism in Bacon and Erasmus, seventeenth-century rationalism in Descartes, Spinoza and Leibniz, the mechanistic empiricisms of Hobbes, Locke, Newton and La Mettrie, the humane rationalism of the Enlightenment that culminated in Voltaire and Kant, nineteenth-century naturalism and evolutionism, down to our own twentieth-century realism and pragmatism.

Though better understood that way, it is, however, not necessary to retrace twenty or more centuries to understand the thought of our time. One can begin with contemporary thought and its problems and trace them back to their roots in the past. But if it is philosophic insight we seek, we cannot content ourselves with the flat projection map of mere historical information. Some integrating continuity, some panoramic dimension is essential to place before the mind's eye, like a relief map, a moving, living landscape giving a dynamic understanding of the actualities of life and culture. Philosophy may be harder to construct and more difficult to follow, but when it succeeds, it does do just that [provide an integrating continuity and panoramic dimension]. Only through re-living the problems of man can we learn truly to appreciate their living; only by sharing the thoughts of an age can we really come to understand it.

7. Value

"Value" is filed in the Alain Locke Collection in front of "Values and Imperatives." At first glance, it would appear to be notes taken for the preparation of "Values and Imperatives." However, upon close reading I found that it is too unlike "Values and Imperatives" to be simply notes. The author's references, the main thesis, the design of the argument, and the article's structure all differ from "Values and Imperatives." Because Dewey is not mentioned by Locke until "Values and Imperatives" and because Dewey was not sufficiently prominent in Locke's works prior to the 1930s, I doubt that "Values" was written prior to 1935. However, there is little evidence that it was written much later, except for the discussion of Christian Freiherr von Ehrenfels. Locke focuses significant attention on Ehrenfels in his dissertation (1917), in "A Functional View of Value Ultimates" (1945), and again in "Value." If Dewey and Ehrenfels can be taken as guides, then "Value" was written between 1935 and 1947, the period that roughly parallels Locke's mature interest in philosophy and value theory. "Value" is placed here, however, not because of my speculation on the date of its authorship but because it stands as a summation of Locke's views on the nature of values and valuation.

"Value" is reminiscent of Marx's *Theses on Feuerbach* because it is directed at foundational notions underlying the works of Plato, Spinoza, Kant, Hegel, R. H. Lotze, Munsterberg, F. E. Beneke,

"Value," undated, unpublished. Printed with the permission of Moorland-Spingarn Research Center, Alain Locke Collection, Howard University.

Albrecht Ritschl, Royce, James, Dewey, Nietzsche, Meinong, and Ehrenfels. It is structured like Ludwig Wittgenstein's *Tractatus Logico-philosophicus* and the *Philosophical Investigations*. Each issue Locke addresses is numbered, the first issue is reinforced by the last, and each issue has relevant notions for the one preceding and following.

"Value" can be read as a synthesis by Locke of Ehrenfels, Meinong, James, and Urban on the nature of values, cast in a Lockean transvaluation. "Value" begins as a survey of the historical issues surrounding the role of values and knowledge. The survey provides the mechanism by which Locke encases his argument. It is an extensive presentation of Locke's philosophic views and a sustained argument of fine points.

The latter part of Section 3 begins Locke's synthesis of what values are in terms of his summation of what all previous explications had to contribute. In Section 4, Locke rejects the traditional distinction between facts and values and relies, in a Jamesian fashion, on the importance of experience in shaping what counts as our realities. He critiques the view in Section 5 that values adhere in the world in a way that makes existence teleological. Kantian methods of justification and the search for self-proving claims are rejected in Section 6. (One way to read Locke's use of "valid" here is "justification.") Locke discusses the way "facts" can be constituted by values in Section 7. In concert with Dewey and Nietzsche, Locke holds in Section 8 that the cognitive process of valuing is by necessity a continual process of transvaluation. Locke concludes in Section 9 by providing a definition of values, a summation of previous points, and the nature of values: "Values therefore are not to be regarded as gratuitous additions to reality, made out of the superfluity of human perversity, but as its highest qualities and the culminating point of its [reality's] significance for us."

Value

1. The Nature of Value.—Value is one of the last of the great philosophic topics to have received recognition, and even now the *Encyclopaedia Britannica* has an article only on economic value. Its discovery was probably the greatest philosophic achievement of the 19th century, but opinions on the subject are not yet crystallized, and it is still one of the growing points of philosophy and one which seems likely to overshadow older issues. Reflexion at present commonly starts from the antithesis of 'fact' and 'value' and the difference between the standpoints of 'description' and 'appreciation.' It is widely held that consciousness of value differs in kind from consciousness of fact. It is posterior to the latter, and represents a reaction upon fact. It is an attitude assumed towards fact, a weighing of fact in relation to an agent, and his feelings, desires, interests, purposes, needs, and acts; and it expresses his appreciation (approbation) or reprobation (depreciation) of it in this relation. It follows (1) that a certain subjectivity, or, better, a relation to personality, is inherent in all values; (2) that value arises out of the mind's practical attitude, when it reacts upon stimulation, and that for a purely theoretic or contemplative view no values would exist; (3) that values are something super-added upon the other qualities of objects by the mind, in order to express their relation to its purpose and acts, and do not inhere in objects *per se*. Indeed they seem to be even more subjective, variable, and personal than the 'secondary' qualities of objects, and hence are often called 'tertiary' qualities. Nevertheless they are also objectified and projected into objects, when these are regarded as valuable objectively and *per se*, or when the 'validity' of actual valuations and of existing values is called in question. Hence 'superpersonal' or 'over-individual' and even 'eternal' and 'absolute' values are recognized by many philosophers. Moreover, the genesis of values and their relations to the objects of desire to which they refer, to the value-feelings which accompany them, and the *valuation-processes* and value-judgments by which they are reached, instigate a number of psychological inquiries, while their validity raises the deepest questions of epistemology, metaphysics, and religion. All the questions raised moreover, are complex and contentious, and have had a history which is not easy to unravel.

2. The History of the Notion.—Historically the importance of the problem of value has been recognized very slowly, gradually, and grudgingly, and, moreover, its philosophic history is obscure; no early philosophy having made it central, or even expressly considered it. In the light of subsequent developments, however, we may trace its emergence to the Platonic doctrine (in *Republic* VI) of the idea of good. When Plato conceived the Good as the culmination of the Ideal world and as the principle which was to unify, systematize, and organize all the other 'forms,' he was really putting 'value' above 'being,' conceiving it as the supreme principle of explanation, and expressing the same thought as Lotze, when he declared that the beginning of metaphysics lies in ethics. For he was proposing to view all being teleologically, and to make its relation to a 'good' or end (an ethical notion) essential to its being. This was to affirm not only the objective validity of the 'tertiary' qualities, but also their supremacy over the others. Plato, however, did not himself develop this line of reflexion, nor succeed in inducing philosophers in general to investigate the problem of values. To the more naturalistic they seemed all too human to be attributed to ultimate reality. Spinoza's wholesale repudiation of their objectivity, at the end of book I of his *Ethics*, is typical in this respect. The modern developments of the subject proceed from Kant, who, however, came upon it rather incidentally at the end of his philosophic career, and apprehended its significance very imperfectly. Kant's philosophizing had ended in the theoretic *impasse* that certain vitally essential beliefs (in God, freedom, and immortality) could not be scientifically justified. Yet they had to be presupposed, he believed, for purposes of action; that is, to carry on life it was necessary to act *as if* they were true. He devised therefore the notion of a practical postulate, which was to be practically imperative without being theoretically cogent, attaching it to the Moral Law of unconditional obligation, and endowing it with objects of 'faith,' which were to be carefully distinguished from objects of knowledge. He thus established (1) a dualism between faith and knowledge which had obvious interest for theology, and (2) a supremacy of the practical over the theoretic reason, which was more fruitful, because less naive, than Plato's. The latter result tended to raise 'values' above 'facts,' though the former at first masked this consequence, and it took subsequent philosophy a long

time to overcome the Kantian dualism. Both, however, were prolific of further developments, divergent from the main line of post-
Kantian speculation, which was too intellectualistic to notice that,
just as the existence of fact must be conditioned for us by our knowledge, so our knowledge must in turn be conditioned by our interests
and the prospective value of the objects of our cognitive endeavors.
For a long time the investigation of value was carried on only in
Germany, and even there progress was slow. The first (probably)
to see that here was a new problem was F. E. Beneke (1798–1854),
the only empirical psychologist among the German philosophers of
his time, and hence a victim of Hegel's intolerance. Already in his
Grundlegung zur Physik der Sitten (1821) he sees that, if the science
of morals is practical, the notion of value lies at the root of it. He lays
it down that the value which we attribute to a thing is determined
by the pleasure which it has excited in us, and he makes the whole
of ethics depend on feelings of value. In his *Grundlinien des natur-
lichen Systems der praktischen Philosophie* (1837–1840) he makes
it more explicit that valuations arise in the mind as reactions upon
stimulations and depressions produced by the things of the external world, distinguishes between subjective valuation (*Wertgebung*),
and traces the growth of 'dispositions' to value and to desire. R. H.
Lotze (1817–1881) revived the Platonic idea that good ranks above
being, wanting metaphysics to show that what *ought* to be conditions what is (*Metaphysik* of 1841), and that 'Nature is directed to
the accomplishment of Good,' and interpreted the 'ontological' proof
of the existence of God as meaning that the totality of value cannot be utterly divorced from existence. In the endeavor to vindicate
value he had the sympathy of his theological colleague at Gottingen,
Albrecht Ritschl (1822–1889), who agrees with him that the facts of
concrete experience are the source of our general notions, and not, as
Platonism has always held, pale reflexions of the latter. Hence personal experience is not deducible from metaphysics, but *vice versa*.
Ritschl, however, started rather from the Kantian dualism of faith
and knowledge and tried to differentiate them still further. Faith he
equipped with distinct objects, those of religion—an independent
method, which it shared with ethics and aesthetics—distinct from
that of metaphysics and science, and formulated in value-judgments,
different in kind from theoretical judgments, though equally capable

of validity and certainty. It was therefore to misconstrue the essential meaning of religious affirmations to take them as expressions of theoretic insight rather than of moral trust. It is mainly to Ritschl that is due the current antithesis between value-judgments and judgments of fact, and the attempt to regard the sciences as different in kind according as they use the one or the other. Ritschl, however, recognized that this separation could not be really carried through. He observes:

> All continuous cognition of the things which excite sensation is not only accompanied but also guided by feeling [pleasure-pain, as indicative of value for self, by way of enhancement or inhibition and] in so far as attention is necessary to attain the end of knowledge, will becomes the vehicle of the purpose of exact cognition; the proximate motive of will, however, is feeling, as expressing that a thing or an activity is worth desiring. . . . Value-judgments therefore are what determine all connected knowledge of the world, even when it is carried out in the most objective fashion. Attention during scientific observation . . . always declares that such knowledge has a value for him who exercises it.

This seems to render all theoretic judgments dependent on, and subordinate to, value-judgments; but Ritschl distinguishes between concomitant and independent value-judgments. In the sciences value-judgments accompany the theoretic, whereas "independent value-judgments are all cognitions of moral ends or impediments thereto in so far as they excite moral pleasure or displeasure, or otherwise set the will in motion to appropriate goods or to ward off evils." The religions also are composed of such independent value judgments expressing man's attitude towards the world. From Ritschl's position it was easy to pass to that of W. Windelband (1848–1915), who, while sharply distinguishing between judgments and evaluations or judgments about judgments (*Beurteilungen*), emphasized that the latter are involved in every judgment in that it affirms or denies, approves or disapproves. Logic, therefore, becomes a science of values, a third normative science, along with ethics and aesthetics, and like them aims at the discovery of universally valid 'norms.' Philosophy becomes the critical study of the universally valid values; their recognition is its duty and its aim. Windelband was followed by H. Rickert and H. Munsterberg (1863–1916). The Austrian schools of C. Von Ehrenfels (1859–1932) and

A. Meinong (1853–1920) devote themselves to the discussion of objects and sorts of values, and their relation to desire and will, the laws of valuation-process, and the accompanying feelings; and apply to all values the economic law of marginal utility. The rise of pessimism and the influence of Schopenhauer (1788–1860), by raising the question of the value of life as a whole, emphasized the importance of values. F. W. Nietzsche (1844–1900) effectively drew attention to the transformations of values, and set himself, before he went mad, to bring about a 'transvaluation' (*Umwertung*) of all the accepted values. Josiah Royce (1855–1916) acclimatized the distinction between appreciation and description in the English-speaking world with his *Spirit of Modern Philosophy* (1892), and since then there has been a good deal of (rather unsystematic) discussion of the problems of value, especially in America, though the intellectualistic bias of the dominant 'idealism' has been unfavorable to it. The pragmatists, however, were glad to recognize the presence of valuations in cognitive processes, as a proof of the fictitious nature of 'pure' thought and 'absolute' truth. They emphasize the human purposive and personal character of value, tend to regard all values as relative, primarily in the particular situation which is valued, and declare the existence and efficacy of values to be plain, empirical facts.

3. Sorts and criteria of value.—As the result of this historical development it is generally admitted that distinct species of value exist, though there is no agreement as to what they are. However, it is clear that several sciences have been specialized to study them. Thus (1) *Economic* value has long been recognized as a fundamental notion of political economy, which, ever since Adam Smith, has divided it into value in use, that is, the utility of objects for human purposes, or, as J. S. Mill said, their "capacity to satisfy a desire or serve a purpose," and value in exchange, that is, their power to induce or compel people to pay (other valuables) for the use of them. The former is simply teleological value, which refers to the relation of means and end; the latter arises when an object is not only useful but also difficult to procure, and is the special concern of economics (*q.v.*). (2) That *ethics* deals with values is also agreed, though there is much dispute as to what the specific ethical values are and how they are related. (3) *Aesthetic* values are also beyond dispute. (4) *Pleasure* must be regarded as a positive and *pain* (unpleasantness) as

a negative value, since even the most ascetic do not really succeed in holding that pleasure is, or in denying that pain is, as such bad. The opposite doctrine, that all values are ultimately reducible to pleasure-pain, is commoner, but need not disturb the classification of values. For, even if the question whether objects are valuable because they give pleasure or give pleasure because they are desired (valued) were decided in favor of the former alternative, it would still be true that the other values are at least relatively independent. Consciousness of value does not directly imply consciousness of pleasure-pain, nor vary concomitantly with it; for example, in conscious wrongdoing an ethical value which is felt not as pleasant, but as painful, is nevertheless recognized; similarly the aesthetic value of a work of art may be recognized, which is yet declared to give no pleasure and to leave the spectator 'cold.' (5) It has been mentioned that, according to the school of Ritschl, the objects of the *religious* consciousness are really values, and affirmations about them are essentially value judgments. And, though other theologians dissent from it, this view gets considerable support both from the psychology of religion, which interprets religious beliefs as expressions of spiritual needs, and from every theological admission that faith, as well as reason, is operative in the apprehension of religious truth. (6) There are good reasons for recognizing the distinctiveness of *biological* or *survival*-values. For they are capable of objective scientific study, and cannot be simply represented, as Herbert Spencer thought, by the hedonic values. Pleasures are not always conducive to life, nor are all pains evil. The relations of survival to pleasure-pain are complex; so are its relations to the ethical values, as is vividly brought out by the ethics of pessimism. Moreover, the survival-values enter into all other values: the value of every being, belief, and institution is affected by its survival-value between the limits of such a high degree of positive value as to entail complete extinction and universal reprobation. (7) Several schools of philosophy hold that logic is the science of cognitive values, and that truth is the positive, error the negative, value; and this treatment is often implied also where it is not avowed. It would seem to be borne out by the far-reaching analogy between logic, ethics, and aesthetics as 'normative' sciences, and proved by the conformity of logic with the criteria generally used to distinguish values.

As criteria two primary oppositions appear to be used: (1) That between existence and value, the 'is' and the 'ought.' Even though there are in man natural tendencies to approve of what has succeeded in establishing itself, and to bring into being what is considered worthy of being—that is, both to realize ideals and to idealize the actual—there remains a considerable discrepancy between the existent and the valuable. It cannot (ordinarily) be argued that because a thing exists, it is valuable, or that, because it is valuable it must exist. What is need not be what ought to be, nor need what ought to be exist. Hence the laws of a science of values are not natural uniformities, but 'norms,' that is, precepts or imperatives; they formulate not what actually does happen, but what 'ought' to happen 'normally,' that is, if the persons concerned recognize and submit to the order proper to the subject. (2) Values appear to be positive and negative. As they express the attitude of a subject to an object, they indicate the acceptance or rejection, pursuit or avoidance, of the former, the attractiveness or repulsiveness of the latter. They occur therefore in couples of antithetical predicates, both admitting of degrees of intensity. Hence values may compensate, cancel, or neutralize each other, and the final value of an object may vary according to the balance between its positive and negative value, or become practically nil. A state of consciousness which is 'neutral' and an object of which is 'indifferent' are cases of such zero values. (3) All values are disputable. They involve a relation to a valuer whose valuation need not be correct, and need not be accepted. The allegation of a value, therefore, is not equivalent to its validity. All values are to be understood as primarily claims to value, which may be allowed, disallowed, or reversed, when other values are considered. In some cases such reversal is normal: thus: if A and B are enemies or have opposite interests, what is 'good' for A is normally 'bad' for B, and *vice versa*. With the aid of these criteria the following kinds of value can now be enumerated. (1) Hedonic values are the pleasant (positive) and the unpleasant or painful (negative). (2) Aesthetic values are the beautiful (positive) and the ugly (negative); also the attractive-repulsive, the fitting-improper, the noble-vulgar, the elegant-coarse, and many others. (3) Utility values are the good (positive) and the bad (negative); also the useful-useless. These last, though they properly have reference to the relation of means and ends ('the good'), naturally pass over into ethics, when this science is conceived 'teleologically,' that is, as the science of the final end or supreme good. (4) Other ethical values relative to other conceptions of ethics, are marked by the oppositions of 'good' and 'evil,' 'right' and 'wrong,' 'ought' and 'ought not.' 'Good' and 'bad' seem sometimes to be used absolutely in ethics, but this usage hardly proves the existence of 'absolute values.' On closer inspection, the meaning is seen to be good or bad for the ethical end, however that is conceived. (5) Religious conceptions reveal their character as values by the frequency of such dualistic antitheses as God-devil, salvation-damnation, election-reprobation, holy-sinful, sacred-profane; also by the frequency with which religious arguments turn out to be postulates of faith. (6) Logic falls into line with the values 'true' and 'false,' 'truth' and 'error.' These also claim to be absolute; but whether what is believed true is so may be disputed, just as whether what is believed good or right, or beautiful, or valuable, or conducive to survival actually has the value which it claims. Even what is felt as pleasant is not always conceded to be a 'true' pleasure, nor is every 'imaginary' pain said to be 'real.' This illustrates also a further confirmation of the whole doctrine, that the various value-predicates are freely transferable from one species of value to another.

4. Value and Fact.—The recognition of logic as a science of values entails a radical revision of the antitheses between fact and value, existence and 'value,' the 'theoretic' and the 'practical.' If all 'truths' are values, there can be no absolute separation of the practical, the sphere of value, from the theoretic, the sphere of facts. Facts, being the objects of truths, must all imply values, and it must be vain to search for any existence which is wholly free from valuations. Now this is precisely what history shows. (1) The search for 'true reality' in pure and unadulterated 'fact' uncontaminated by any work of the mind, in an unconditional datum which has merely to be recognized, has always been in vain. Only the moral to be drawn is not, as idealism supposes, that reality is the work of 'pure thought.' The thought which cannot be rooted out is a valuing thought, which is aiming at ends and selecting means, and accepting, rejecting, and variously manipulating the data presented to it in the whole process of 'recognizing' reality. Thus the absolute antithesis between fact and value collapses, because facts without value cannot be found. (2) The very

fact that it is considered so desirable to find it proves that it is impossible to do so. For the importance attributed to the discovery of fact, and the eulogistic sense in which 'reality' is opposed to 'appearance' or 'illusion' are, in fact, values. This comes out especially in doctrines about the 'degrees of reality,' which are plainly of value, or about the distinction between 'reality' and 'existence.' (3) It is not psychologically possible to reach any 'fact' except by a process permeated throughout by values, *viz.*, a purposive endeavor to attain an end ('good') by a choice of the 'right' means, which implies selective attention, preferences for what seems valuable, and the influence of concomitant value-feelings and of a variety of prejudices and forms of bias. (4) Lastly, it seems a conclusive logical reason for holding that every 'fact' alleged must contain a latent value, that it claims not only to be 'true' but also implicitly to be better than any other judgment it was possible to make under the circumstances. Its maker was probably aware of this, and consciously preferred it to all alternatives that occurred to him; but, even where he did not think of any, they remain logically conceivable, and hence the actual judgment is only justifiable by its logical claim to be the best. Hence the value-relation and attitude can never be eradicated from even the merest and most stubborn 'fact.'

Nor, conversely, can a recognition of fact be wholly eliminated from knowledge. Pure value exists as little as pure fact. It would be pure fancy or sheer postulation, and neither fancies nor postulates are elaborated without regards to fact. They are made to be realized, and when they are recognized as impossible their value is destroyed or impaired. It is said to be 'no use' to postulate the impossible or to cherish utterly unrealizable ideals. This recognition of fact, however, is always relative to the existing state of knowledge, and may be modified as knowledge grows. Knowers are often conscious of this, and assume their facts for the purpose of an inquiry or a science, hypothetically and experimentally. Hence it is not to be supposed that what is taken as fact and formally is 'fact' must remain so. It may turn out to be only a methodologically convenient 'fiction.' In general it may be concluded that since values inhere in all the 'facts' that are recognized as such, they are themselves facts, and that the antithesis between values and facts cannot be made absolute. Values are not simply fortuitous and gratuitous and should be eliminated by strict science, but are essential to cognitive process and compatible with any sort and degree of objectivity. Facts too are always reactions—upon prior facts—and are generated by their evaluation; and, moreover, these prior facts may have been merely hypothetical constructs recommended by their prospective value.

5. Value and existence.—It would seem to follow from relations between value and fact that value cannot be denied existence in any world that can exist for man, and this in several senses. (1) They are operative in and on human minds, and find expression in human acts and embodiment in human institutions; (2) they can occur in, and relative to, any universe of diction, however fanciful; (3) hence also in ideals and fictions, both of which are sometimes said to be incapable of real existence, and cited as objections to the connection of values with existence. But both must be so related to real existence as to be applicable to it and to conduce to its successful manipulation. Otherwise they become false ideals and futile fictions. Also an ideal which is recognized as impossible appears to lose *pro tanto* its obligatoriness and power of attraction. 'Ultra posse nemo obligatur.' Whether it is possible to infer the existence of a valuable object from a recognition of its value alone is a question of great importance for religion. For the objects of the religious consciousness appear to be largely or wholly of this kind, and the religious 'proofs' of their existence to be ultimately such inferences. They are, moreover, stubbornly persisted in, in spite of the protests of common sense against their validity, and have an important function also in the other sciences, in which they are not recognized so openly, but masquerade as 'axioms' and '*a priori*' truths. In discussing in its generality this inference from value to existence, we should remember that all values are initially claims, which may fail of validation; hence it will hardly seem valid to rest the reality of the valuable objects on what may be an unsound claim, *viz.*, on the demand for them alone, unsupported and unconfirmed by experience. Logically we are to start with nothing but postulates. It may be legitimate to take them as methodological principles, but even then, they must be regarded as hypotheses to be assumed experimentally, until they have adequately approved and verified themselves by their applications to the actual problems which they concern. For example, it may be legitimate to extract from the actual pursuit of ends and of

happiness by men the methodological assumptions that all things are to be regarded as tending towards a supreme all-embracing end and towards universal happiness (that is, everlasting and unalloyed pleasure unaccompanied by pain). . . . To justify such inferences two further assumptions would seem to be required, *viz.* that the whole of reality is conformable with human nature and bound to satisfy its demands. Now these assumptions, traditionally described as the axiom of the ultimate rationality of existence, are evidently themselves nothing but values for which existence is postulated, and, if they are to be admitted as axiomatic truths on their own assurance, it is difficult to see what limits can be set to the postulation of objects of desire. Even as it is, methodological postulates are given great, and perhaps undue, facilities in verifying themselves, because, so long as they work at all, their failures can always be ascribed to the imperfection of our knowledge, and so are not counted against them. Thus nothing short of total failure to predict the course of events need lead us to abandon the postulate of their 'casual connection.' Hence the testing of a value-postulate always, in a sense, presupposes its truth, though not in any sense that makes this presupposition alone a sufficient reason for regarding it as absolutely true; still it is better to get a postulated value confirmed by experience than to accept the mere recognition of value as an adequate guarantee of its existence. What kinds and amounts of experimental confirmation are to be considered adequate to verify the existence of postulated objects of value will naturally depend on the specific subject matter, and, as in addition, the various values sought and got need to be in harmony with each other, and some may prefer one sort and others another, and as, moreover, the relevance of some of the values found to the existences to be proved may be called in question, opinions will probably long continue to differ on these matters.

6. Value and validity.—It follows from the above that the transition from value to validity is by no means a matter of course, though this is often assumed, both as regards ethical and as regards logical values. In both cases the motive is the difficulty of validating value-claims, which is a long, and indeed theoretically an unending, process. Hence the temptation to allege absolute and self-proving values which are independent of their working in experience. The absolute

values, alleged however, are only formal claims, as comes out very clearly in Kant's account of the absolute value of personality and of the 'law' of duty. The declaration that everybody should be treated as an end in himself is merely a recognition of the formal claim that every person makes to be so treated (even though he never is so treated and apparently could not be, in the actual order of things), which may serve as a definition of personality; while the moral 'law' that duty should be unconditionally fulfilled, is merely a paraphrase of the obligatoriness of the ought-value; in neither case is any light thrown on the questions how, concretely, anyone should be treated, or what, concretely, his 'duties' are. Similarly every judgment formally claims to be true, absolutely and unconditionally, and, as it mentions no restrictions to its claim, it may be said to be so; but, as this is so, however false a judgment turns out to be, it establishes no presumption in favor of its real truth. Thus it is quite possible, and indeed necessary, to enquire whether the values claimed are really possessed, and to question the validity of the values actually recognized. This indeed is one of the chief occupations of a critical philosophy. It means that the problem of value occurs also in the sphere of values; the antithesis of 'ought' and 'is,' which was supposed to differentiate value and fact, arises again over the value of values, when they are taken as facts for the purpose of assessing their value. The explanation perhaps is that error and failure are possible in all human operations, and hence also in the estimation of values. The values which are claimed are subject to revision and correction, and if it is decided that they are, but ought not to be, they can be called either 'false' or 'wrong'; for it is intrinsically as legitimate to use the value-predicates of logic as those of ethics to describe their failure. The difficulty of determining the precise connection between value and validity is, however, largely due to the obscurity of the notion of validity itself. We are accustomed to regard validity at first as an absolute and (theoretically) unquestionable degree of value and to illustrate it from the ideal validity of logic and ethics. On examination, however, this sense of validity appears to be merely formal, and to be nugatory or null as a guarantee of real value. For in both these sciences the valid and the valuable fall apart. Neither is the valuable necessarily valid, nor is the valid necessarily valuable. Every moral order makes extensive use of inferior moral motives; every science uses probable but invalid reasonings. Whether the ideal validity is ever reached, or would be valuable if it were, seems more than doubtful. Hence it seems proper to reduce the meaning of validity to a high or generally recognized and practically indisputable degree of value, and to make value determine validity, and not validity value.

7. Value and valuation.—If value is conferred upon an object by a personal attitude towards it, it is clear that all objects can be valued by being included in a valuation-process. Many objects, however, are so variously valued according to circumstances, or are so really important enough to be valued at all, that they are conceived as neutral or indifferent *per se*. So it is only if an object is constantly valued in a particular way that its value adheres to it and it comes to seem intrinsically valuable. For it then emancipates itself from the personal valuation and makes its valuation look like a mere recognition of an already existing value. Value acquires objectivity in other ways also. Thus the personal reaction expressed in a value-judgment carries a formal claim to universality, since every one initially regards himself as the measure of all things, until he is instructed by the dissent of others. This claim therefore maintains itself only while it is not disputed, and should not be taken as more than methodological. By the comparison of value-judgments it appears that different persons value very differently; hence many value-judgments being in dispute are regarded as 'merely subjective.' About others, many or all are found to agree, and these may thereby acquire every degree of 'objectivity.' Thus objects which have obtained social recognition as valuable come to rank as objective values. A value that has risen to be objective may then maintain itself without continuing to be valued, and even though, under the circumstances, its value may have been converted into the opposite. Thus, once a literary work is ranked as a 'classic,' its value remains uncontested, even though few care for it or even read it, except for examination purposes; and King Midas no doubt continued to think gold most valuable in spite of his inability to digest it. It cannot always be assumed therefore that, because a value is current and is recognized, it is fully functional, any more than it is right. There are then plenty of objective values, which any valuer encounters and has to recognize as given. But they may nevertheless all be conceived as products of valuation-

processes, and as presupposing prior value-judgments. For when the valuation of an object has been repeated and has grown familiar, the conscious and reflective value-judgment becomes superfluous, and an immediate apprehension of value results, just as immediate perception supersedes judgment about familiar objects of cognition. In other cases, it is true, this process does not occur in the history of the individual, but it can be traced in that of the race, whose achievements the individual inherits. An object may, for example, be apprehended as pleasant, beautiful or right, without a judgment or process of valuation; but the immediacy of its value-claim is no bar to any inquiry into why it is so valued, how it has come to be so, and whether it ought to be so, and really is as beautiful, right, or pleasant as it seems to be. Hence the values which are psychically data, and psychologically immediate, may always be logically mediated and made objects of valuation-processes and explicit value-judgments. They then function as facts to be evaluated.

8. Transvaluations.—The process of reflective reconsideration of given values continually leads to changes in their status. Hence 'transvaluations' must be regarded as normal and entirely legitimate occurrences in every sphere of values, though they are not every-where as socially prominent as in the annual changes of the fashions.

As Dewey says, "All valuation is in some degree a revaluation. Nietzsche would probably not have made so much of a sensation, but he would have been within the limits of wisdom, if he confined himself to the assertion that all judgment, in the degree in which it is critically intelligent, is a transvaluation of prior values."

One sufficient reason for this is that, strictly speaking, it is not psychologically possible to repeat a valuation. The second time the valuation has lost its novelty, and the delight of discovery is gone; it is acquiring familiarity and beginning to breed contempt or indifference; or again it is growing easier, and the resistance to it is diminishing, as habituation renders it less repugnant. Moreover, valuations necessarily vary according to the changes in the organic needs which condition them. His tenth penny bun will neither taste as good nor be valued as highly by a hungry boy as his first. No doubt these changes in value are little noticed because many of them are slight, unimportant, and ephemeral; but they would anyhow be obscured by the general bias in favor of stability. Unless it is discounted, it will hardly be recognized that stable values are exceptions rather than the rule. They bulk large because they are attended to and selected. Their stability is always more or less a construction for methodological purposes, like the extraction of stable objects out of the flux of happenings. It is always to some extent a fiction, because it is never absolute, and because there are no eternal values, none that endure unchanged and untransformed by new valuations forever, unless it be life itself, so long as that lasts. It may even become a dangerous illusion, if its character is not understood, and it is made an obstacle to salutary and necessary changes. In such changes the old values always condemn the new, and *vice versa,* often with tragic results. Transvaluations are the stuff out of which heroes and martyrs of 'reform' or 'loyalty' are made, at every step in human progress. The question of what is the right value is unanswerable for the time being, because it is precisely the question which is being fought out. But we can predict that such changes will always be opposed, for there is always a conservative and a progressive party with respect to any change. These party attitudes are essentially valuations, as any one can discover for himself, if he is open-minded, and also distracted enough to have a 'cross-bench mind' and to feel the force of both the opposite contentions. Nor are these the only conflicts which may lead to a change of values. Every society, and nearly every soul, is full of conflicts between opposing valuations, and any variation in their relative strengths may entail a change in values. The chief agency which blinds us to these transvaluations is the stability of words; for these change their form much less rapidly than their meaning.

9. Conclusions.—The above survey of the problems of value may be regarded as confirming most of the preliminary points noticed in #1. The philosophic importance of the subject has been attested by the great variety and universal prevalence of values. The provisional definition of value as essentially a personal attitude, as a recognition of the supremacy of the category of personality, has maintained itself and proved a clue to the labyrinth of values. It also renders somewhat nugatory the psychological debates of the schools of Meinong and Ehrenfels as to whether values are rooted in feeling, will or desire. For a personal attitude is a concern of the whole man and not

of psychological abstractions. If, however, it is thought necessary to pick one among such psychological phrases, it is probably best to say that value is a personal attitude, of welcome or the reverse, towards an object of interest. For few are likely to dispute that 'interests' are relative to personality. This relativity, however, is not to be regarded as importing any objectionable subjectivity into values, just because it proves to be the source also of their objectivity. For it turns out that all objects are pervaded by values and constituted for man by valuations, and hence their avowed values may just as rightfully belong to them as the values latent in their other qualities. Accordingly the opposition between value and fact breaks down. 'Facts' are themselves values, values established in the endeavor to analyze out the factor of givenness contained in experience, and presupposing purposive manipulation of apparent 'facts.' They are thus 'made' things, though they are not made out of nothing, but out of previously recognized facts which are subjected to criticism to determine what they 'really are.' Values are also acts in so far as they presuppose valuations, purposive manipulations of date, and judgments; also in that they have prospective reference to action, and are intended to guide it. Accordingly the belief that values belong to the practical side of life is well founded, and even truer than it seems; for in ultimate analysis, logic also is a science of values. Its 'theoretic' values presuppose purposes, selections, choices, and judgments which are acts and do not differ in kind from those which are openly 'practical.' It is clear also that the notion of value as something gratuitously superadded upon fact must be modified, if it is interpreted as meaning that values are something unreal, artificial, and optional. Reality in its fullness contains and exhibits values, and they are ejected from it only by an effort of abstraction, which is relative to certain restricted purposes, and is never quite successful. Values therefore are not to be regarded as gratuitous additions to reality, made out of the superfluity of human perversity, but as its highest qualities and the culminating points of its significance for us.

II. Valuation: Commentaries and Reviews

8. The Orientation of Hope

Locke was increasingly drawing attention in the 1930s to the compatibility of universality in art and its manifestation through particularities of specific cultures. He was also extolling optimism in the face of domination and admonishing hope for a better future although America was mired in misguided materialism and religious bigotry. "The Orientation of Hope" is a definitive expression of Locke's belief in the Bahá'í faith and its focus on the universal principles definitive of spiritual faiths. Locke expresses several ideas concerning the way valuations may be changed to accomplish a more peaceful world through the practical manifestation of universalities. Locke encourages his reader to learn the language of the "common man." So doing, he implies, will enhance communication, argue against disillusionment, and aid in the creation of what H. G. Wells termed an "imperative new world order."

"The Orientation of Hope," reprinted by permission from *The Bahá'í World: A Biennial International Record, Volume IV, 1930–1932*, comp. National Spiritual Assembly of the Bahá'ís of the United States and Canada (New York: Bahá'í Publishing Committee, 1933), 527–528.

The Orientation of Hope

As the clouds darken over our chaotic world, all of us—even those who still cherish the dream and hope of a new world order of peace, righteousness and justice, must face the question of where to focus our expectations, where to orient our hopes. To do otherwise is merely to hug an ideal to our bosoms in childish consolation and passive fatalism—a reaction only too human, but not worthy of the possessors of a virile and truly prophetic spiritual revelation. If we fall victims to the twilight mood and the monastic flight from reality, are we not really false friends and even spiritual traitors to the universal idea? Must we not as true Bahá'í believers in these times embrace our principles more positively, more realistically, and point everywhere possible our assertion of the teachings with a direct challenge?

In fact, for those of us who are truly dawn-minded, the present twilight hour, this dusk of disillusionment is auspicious. It is the occasion and opportunity of convincing many who were sceptical because they could not see the impending failure of the old order, but who now almost without exception are in a questioning and thoroughly disillusioned mood. Especially does it seem to me to be the opportunity to bring the Bahá'í principles again forcefully to the attention of statesmen and men of practical affairs, who now may in all likelihood be in their period of greatest receptivity, having turned to so many plans and remedies to little or no avail. Is it not reasonably clear to us that now is the time for a world-wide, confident and determined offensive of peaceful propaganda for the basic principles of the Cause of brotherhood, peace and social justice?

I have one humble suggestion: that without forgetting the language in terms of which we ourselves have learned the principles, we shall take pains to learn and speak a language which the practical-minded man of affairs, and the realistic common man can and will understand. The message must be translated to terms and ideas and practical issues of the present-day world and its problems and dilemmas, or, I am afraid, much of the advantage of this marvelous seed-time will be lost.

Too often previously, we have been confronted with that characteristic and almost pardonable distrust of the average man for the "panacea type of solution," his interest in only one segment of the problem. Today even the man in the street is becoming keenly convinced of the fundamental and widescale character of the difficulties underlying the present crisis. In a recent article, H. G. Wells has this to say: "It is becoming plain to us that the disaster of the Great War and our present social and economic disorder are not isolated misfortunes, but broad aspects of a now profound disharmony in the conditions of human life. A huge release of human energy through invention and discovery drives us on inexorably toward the establishment of a new type of society in which the production and distribution of necessities will be the easy task of a diminishing moiety of the population, while research, new enterprise, new extensions and elaborations of living, the conquest not simply of material but of moral and intellectual power and of beauty, vitality and happiness become the occupation of an ever increasing multitude. . . . We cannot go back. Retrogression to less progressive conditions seems more difficult and dangerous now than a revolutionary advance. Either we must go on to this new state of disciplined plenty or lapse into chaotic and violent barbarism."

And of this that he calls "an imperative new world order," Mr. Wells has this interesting and challenging thing to say: "I doubt if it is in the capacity of any single human being to lead our race around this difficult corner. . . . The carry-over from the catastrophic phase of today to the new world state of freedom and abundant life must, I believe, be the work of a gathering, growing number of men inspired by a common apprehension of the needs and possibilities of the case. I am thinking of a wide, unorganized growth of understanding. . . . When that understanding develops commanding force, the new world will be made accessible, and not before."

I have cited this quotation as a representative sample of the drift of intelligent thought today upon the whole world situation. Its tone and trend show clearly just that groping toward universal and spiritual principles and forces which alone can save us. More clearly still, it reveals the demand for a social ideal of religious appeal and intensity, but at the same time sane, practical and progressive. This despair and disillusionment of the present, this bankruptcy of materialism must be seized upon constructively and positively as a God-given opportunity for teaching men where the true principles and hopes of a new and universal human order really can be found. And to do that powerfully, effectively, the Bahá'í teaching needs an inspired extension of the potent realism of 'Abdu'l-Bahá by which he crowned and fulfilled the basic idealism of Bahá'u'lláh.

9. Unity through Diversity

Locke considered the following a social dilemma: "we feel and hope in the direction of universality, but still think and act particularistically." In his 1935 "Values and Imperatives" article and later works, this dilemma reappeared, if not as axiomatically given in the human situation, as a seemingly relentless problematic. Locke credits Royce with appreciating the problem of loyalty as group self-interestedness. The possibility of cross-cultural unity, mediated by the principle of reciprocity, is the basis of unity through diversity.

There is, for Locke, a "spiritual equivalence" between various religious faiths. He locates recognition of this within Bahá'í history, but considers its origin less important than its adoption. The acceptance of spiritual equivalence, Locke suggests, is a positive good that can be beneficial in limiting sectarian conflict.

"Unity through Diversity: A Bahá'í Principle," reprinted by permission from *The Bahá'í World: A Biennial International Record, Volume V, 1932–1934*, comp. National Spiritual Assembly of the Bahá'ís of the United States and Canada (New York: Bahá'í Publishing Committee, 1936), 372–374.

Unity Through Diversity: A Bahá'í Principle

There is one great spiritual advantage in the tidal series of negative upsets and breakdowns in the contemporary world and that is the ever-accumulative realization of the need for a complete reconstruction of life. Even among the unintellectual classes and in the most partisan circles the idea of reform and radical change meets no effective resistance, where but a short while ago, any suggestion of change would have met both emotional and doctrinal resistance to a serious degree. And although there is still a considerable amount of surviving partisanship in the notion of specific cures and panaceas, each based on some over-emphasis on some special view or theory or formula, in many cases,—perhaps the majority, there has come the recognition that superficial and local change are alike insufficient, and that to cure or affect modern ills, any remedy seriously proposed must be fundamental and not superficial, and wide-scale or universal rather than local or provincial. And so the most usual sanctions of contemporary thinking even for partisan and sectarian causes are the words "universal," "international," "human." Ten years ago, national, racial, or some equivalent circumscribed loyalty and interest would have been unquestioningly assumed, and agitated almost without apology as axiomatic. I regard this change, although as yet a negative gain, as both one of the most significant and positive steps forward that humanity has taken,—or rather,—has been forced to take.

In this dilemma of doubt and frantic search, many are the gods and principles invoked, and doubtless a few of the many will turn out historically to have had saving grace. For certainly no pure principle can of itself do more than motivate or sanction; mankind is not saved by declarations and professions of faith, but by works and ideas. However, in the doing and the acting, there is always the important factor of the orientation and attitude which are so vital, and often the initial aspect of a new way of life. In this connection, I think, it is of the utmost importance to recognize as an influential factor in the contemporary situation a common trend toward universalism. Even though it is not yet accepted as a general principle, as a general desire and an ideal goal, the demand for universality is beyond doubt the most characteristic modern thing in the realm of spiritual values, and in the world of the mind that reflects this realm.

But when we come to the statement of this generally desired universality, we fall foul of countless nostrums, and welter again in the particularisms that we have inherited from tradition and our factional and denominationalized world. Here, then, is the present dilemma;—we feel and hope in the direction of universality, but still think and act particularistically. And in many ways and connections, it seems that we must. Is there no solution to this typical but tragic situation?

It is just at this juncture that the idea of unity in diversity seems to me to become relevant, and to offer a spiritual common denominator of both ideal and practical efficacy. What the contemporary mind stands greatly in need of is the divorce of the association of uniformity with the notion of the universal, and the substitution of the notion of equivalence. Sameness in difference may be a difficult concept for us,—it is. But the difficulty is historical and traditional, and is the specific blight and malady of the modern and Western mind. I take it for granted that the desire and effort to reach universality in the characteristic modern and Western way would be fatal if possible, and is fortunately impossible in practice. Only in the chastisement of defeat will it be recognized how unnecessary and hopeless the association of the two concepts really is. Spiritual unity is never achieved by an exacting demand for conformity or through any program of imposed agreement. In fact, the demands of such an attitude are self-defeating. What we need to learn most is how to discover unity and spiritual equivalence underneath the differences which at present so disunite and sunder us, and how to establish some basic spiritual reciprocity on the principle of unity in diversity.

This principle is basic in the Bahá'í teaching. It may lead us to another dangerous partisanship to assert it as exclusively. Bahá'í; but there is no escaping the historical evidences of its early advocacy and its uncompromising adoption by the Bahá'í prophets and teachers. But it is not the time for insisting on this side of the claim; the intelligent, loyal Bahá'í should stress not the source, but the importance of the idea, and rejoice not in the originality and uniqueness of the principle but rather in its prevalence and practicality. The idea has to be translated into every important province of modern life and thought, and in many of these must seem to be independently derived and justified. Suffice it, if the trend and net result are in the same general and progressive direction and serve to bring some values and behaviour nearer to the main ideal. Through the realization of this, and the welcome acceptance of all possible collaboration, a spiritual leadership and influence can be exerted that is otherwise impossible. And no narrow cultism, however pious and loyal, can accomplish this. The purity of Bahá'í principles must be gauged by their universality on this practical plane. Do they fraternize and fuse with all their kindred expressions? Are they happy in the collaborations that advocate other sanctions but advance toward the same spiritual goal? Can they reduce themselves to the vital common denominators necessary to mediate between other partisan loyalties?

We should not be over-optimistic. The classical statements of this and other basic Bahá'í teachings like the oneness of humanity are on the lips and tongues of many, but almost every specific program enlisting the practical activities of men today still has in it dangerous elements of sectarianism. And to the old sectarianisms that we could possibly regard as having had their day, there is constantly being added new ones that are very righteous in the view of their adherents. Oppressed classes and races cannot be told that their counterclaims forced from them by the natural reactions and resistance to suppression and restriction should yield in the early hours of their infancy to broader and less specific loyalties. These new nationalisms and other causes will not listen immediately to such caution or impose upon themselves voluntarily such unprecedented sacrifices. Let us take specific instances. Can anyone with a fair-minded sense of things, give wholesale condemnation to the partisanships of Indian Nationalism, or Chinese integrity and independence, or Negro and proletarian self-assertion after generations of persecution and restriction? Scarcely,—and certainly not at all unless the older partisanships that have aroused them repent, relax, and finally abdicate their claims and presumptions.

On questions like these we reach the crux of the problem, and seem to face a renewal and intensification of national, class and racial strife. Is there no remedy?

In my view, there is but one practical way to the ideal plane on which a cessation or abatement of the age-old struggle can be anticipated with any degree of warrant. And that is in the line of not asking a direct espousal of universalism at the expense of the natural ambitions and group interests concerned; but rather to ask on the basis of reciprocity a restriction of these movements to their own natural boundaries, areas and interests. Josiah Royce, one of the greatest of the American philosophers saw this problem more clearly than any other Western thinker, and worked out his admirable principle of loyalty, which is nothing more or less than a vindication of the principle of unity in diversity carried out to a practical degree of spiritual reciprocity.

Of course, it will be a long time yet before the mind of the average man can see and be willing to recognize the equivalence of value between his own loyalties and those of all other groups, and when he will be able to assert them without infringement of similar causes and loyalties. But when the realization comes from hard necessity that the only alternative policy is suicidal, perhaps we can count on a radical reversal of what still seems to be the dominant and ineradicable human failing and propensity to continue the tragic narrow self-assertiveness of the human past.

In starting with the unequivocal assertion of equivalence and reciprocity between religions, the Bahá'í teaching has touched one of the trunk-nerves of the whole situation. But it seems that this principle needs to be carried into the social and cultural fields, because there the support and adherence of the most vigorous and intellectual elements in most societies can be enlisted. Translated into more secular terms, a greater practical range will be opened up for the application and final vindication of the Bahá'í principles. Only the narrowly orthodox will feel any loss of spirituality in this, and the truly religious-minded person will see in it a positive multiplication of spiritual power, directly proportional to the breadth and variety of the interests touched and motivated. The Bahá'í teaching proposed a religion social and modern in its objectives; and so the challenge comes directly home to every Bahá'í believer to carry the universal dimension of tolerance and spiritual reciprocity into every particular cause and sectarianism that he can reach. His function there is to share the loyalties of the group, but upon a different plane and with a higher perspective. He must partake of partisanship in order to work toward its transformation, and help keep it within the bounds of constructive and controlled self-assertion.

Each period of a faith imposes a special new problem. Is it too much to assume that for us the problem of this particular critical decade is just this task of transposing the traditional Bahá'í reciprocity between religions into the social and cultural denominationalisms of nation, race and class, and vindicating anew upon this plane the precious legacy of the inspired teachings of 'Abdu'l-Bahá and Bahá'u'lláh? Certainly that is my reverent conviction and my humble suggestion.

10. Santayana

In "Santayana" Locke expresses again his attitude toward pragmatism. It had "grown old and smugly complacent." Arguments against modes of domination, whether pragmatist or not, were appealing to Locke. Although Santayana's aristocratic attitudes and conservative politics are rejected, Santayana's critique of domination and authoritarianism, as human inclinations to be forever guarded against, and Santayana's inclusion of his own views as contextually shaped, receive Locke's support.

Locke highlights the features of Santayana's *Dominations and Powers* that he considers defensible. Many of these features in the book, for example, a "flexible detachment," are important facets of Locke's approach to religion, philosophy, and value change.

"Santayana," review of *Dominations and Powers*, by George Santayana (New York: Charles Scribner's, 1951), in *Key Reporter* 16:4 (1951): 4–5.

Santayana

Review of DOMINATIONS AND POWERS,
by George Santayana

In his prime in the first decade of the century, George Santayana made a characteristic and important contribution to philosophical thinking. In his lucid, casual way he did nearly as much as the crusading, over-zealous William James to overthrow the genteel tradition of that day—supermundane idealism. Now at the close of a phenomenally long career, with undiminished virtuosity he tilts a skillful lance against the present incumbent, naturalistic pragmatism, now itself grown old and smugly complacent. In its stead he would set up as the present goal of the life of reason a humanistic relativism that views itself, history, and the world scene in calm and urbane historical and cultural detachment. Today's saving grace, Santayana believes, lies in a resourceful skepticism.

Many will contend that we cannot, especially in a time of great political crisis, afford any such intellectual luxury. Santayana recognizes the logic but also the tragedy of an age which must perforce identify itself militantly with civilization. But he warns against what he thinks might well turn out to be a fatal illusion. History should have taught us better her lesson of endless change and shifting emphasis, so that while we struggle for dominance and self-preservation, we can divorce our minds from our wills and see ourselves under the aspect of eternity.

Some readers, no doubt, will interpret this as the detachment of pampered withdrawal, thinking of Santayana through the stereotype of the ivory-tower esthete. But on the contrary, closer reading will disclose that Santayana bases his position on a wide and shrewd scrutiny of man and his history, recommending flexible detachment as a weapon and strategy of survival. Societies and cultures, like animals and plants, are creatures of specific time and place. They survive through adaptive change and by virtue of their natural boundaries. Wisdom with regard to human societies therefore dictates the recognition of pluralism in culture, relativism in mores and morals, functionalism in institutions, and moderation and temporizing in objectives and powers. In such a context of tentative and experimental flexibility human values have more chance for realization than in one of rigid self-righteousness and provincial absolutism.

With Socratic serenity and ironic delight, it is pointed out that the perfect and the stable society are both as unattainable as the immortal or ubiquitous organism. Consequently, Santayana finds as the basic principle for political life a "live and let live" policy, with tolerance and liberty the basic because the most functional virtues. Even those who cannot accept his general thesis will welcome these corollaries, for one of Santayana's few firm convictions is an uncompromising condemnation of authoritarianism, religious and secular. But here again he would not have us make fetishes even of freedom, lest fanaticism creep in to destroy the vitality of the progressive search for it. Each society, each culture, and every sub-phase of them must have the privilege of taking its own way to salvation.

In spite of the reasonableness of his general position, many readers will find themselves in sharp disagreement with some of Santayana's obviously temperamental quips and biases. His strictures on this or that, especially such subjects as the prospects of present-day Europe, the viability of the United Nations, the fitness of the industrial democracies, all of them of a decidedly pessimistic cast, reflect the chronic bias of an aristocratic, highly critical temperament. There can be no valid accusation of partisanship, since other periods of history as well as ours run the same gauntlet of his hard scrutiny and caustic comment. Emotionally unwelcome, they provide a stimulating and salutary tonic. It is the part of wisdom on occasion not to offer us what we want but what we need. And surely there is today special need for the balancing and corrective sanity of not taking ourselves and our time over-seriously, for both in time and space we are only a fraction of humanity.

Although the general mood of this book is that of detached disillusionment, there are scattered throughout it very constructive implications. Central among them is the oft-repeated caution that the road to domination is the road to mass suicide. There is evident approval of the self-contained type of culture, modified by a quizzical sadness because far too many societies choose to overstep their proper bounds and try to swallow more than they can assimilate. This warning not to make trade export of one's civilization seems a special caution directed at the United States in its present position in an erupting world. The East, it is hinted, must not only have its day, but is more likely both to take and give more without coercion and duress. Such sage observations are rarely made as overt moralizing which, fortunately, is alien to the best side of Santayana's temperament, but are delicately implied as in a beautifully written fable. For above all else, this is the swan-song of a placid mind and a poised spirit. Style and perspective are constantly paramount objectives, as indeed in previous works, but here they are presented with a polished perfection that instead of registering decline and impairment, exhibits, if anything, greater intellectual and stylistic mastery than ever before.

Modestly and consistently Santayana imputes no finality to his reactions and opinions. This would be a fatal flaw. But instead he says very explicitly: "It is sheer conceit in a contemporary neutral or in a later historian to pose as a superior and impartial spirit; for his spark of spirit is no less subject to passions and accidental interests than those that he presumes to understand and criticize." Such selfinclusion adds a Socratic dimension to his thinking and, whether one agrees or disagrees with his conclusions, puts Santayana among the greatest thinkers of our time.

11. Moral Imperatives for World Order

On Tuesday morning, June 20th, Locke's discussion of "Race: American Paradox and Dilemma" focussed on the apparent conflict between America's self-concept as a model democracy and the reality of undue racial and ethnic prejudice. World War II seemed nearly ended, and discussions of what attitude Americans should have toward Russia, China, the Axis powers, and a weak League of Nations dominated conference discussions. But on the mild Wednesday evening of June 21, Locke abandoned his role as representative of the Negro race's place in the world order as well as discussion of the character of group conflict. Unlike other participants, Locke addressed moral features that should over arch future world order in "Moral Imperatives for World Order." In so doing, he linked idealism, realism, and his views of loyalty, identity, and change. The "process of evolution by progressive enlargement of values" is a route for the potential cooperation between national, cultural, and religious loyalties. Contrary to a Christian doctrine that there exists only one route to salvation, Locke holds that true universality requires a different view of spiritual brotherhood—one compatible with world peace.

"Moral Imperatives for World Order," *Summary of Proceedings*, Institute of International Relations, Mills College, Oakland, California, June 18–28, 1944, pp. 19–20.

Locke at Oxford University, Hertford College, as a Rhodes Scholar, 1908.
Locke also attended courses at the University of Berlin, 1910–1912. Re-
printed by permission of Moorland-Spingarn Research Center, Alain Locke
Collection, Howard University.

Oxford University Cosmopolitan Club dinner, 1908. Noted persons associated with the club that promoted ideas of collective identity were D. B. Burckhardt of Norway; Satya V. Mukerjea of India; H. El Alaily, president of the Egyptian Society of England; Pixley Ka Isaka Seme, a South African who helped form the South African Native National Congress; Har Dayal, India, noted Indian nationalist and Marxist. At another dinner for Thanksgiving 1907 held by Americans to honor Rhodes Scholars, Horace Kallen boycotted the dinner because Locke was not invited, as was the preference of southern American Rhodes Scholars. Reprinted by permission of Moorland-Spingarn Research Center, Alain Locke Collection, Howard University.

William Stuart Nelson, Alain Locke, and Ralph Bunche (l. to r.), probably in the 1930's. Reprinted by permission of Moorland-Spingarn Research Center, Howard University.

Alain Locke, Eleanor Roosevelt, [Charles] Prescott, and Joseph Drew (l. to r.), probably between 1942 and 1945. Reprinted by permission of Moorland-Spingarn Research Center, Howard University.

Town Hall Meeting of the Air, June 1942. Moderator: George Denny; discussants: Mordecai W. Johnson, Alain Locke (standing), Doxey A. Wilkerson, and Leon A. Ransom; topic: "Is there a basis for spiritual unity in the world today?" Robert McNeil Photo. Reprinted by permission of Moorland-Spingarn Research Center, Howard University.

Alain Locke (seated) and Paul Robeson, probably in late 1940's. Reprinted by permission of Moorland-Spingarn Research Center, Howard University.

Fourth annual Adult Education Conference, 1941, at Atlanta University. *Left to right, front row:* first three are unknown delegates, Leonora Williams, Hampton Institute; M. C. Nunn, Arkansas College; Lyman Bryson, CBS director of education and organizer for Conferences on Science, Philosophy and Religion; Crystal Bird Fauset, race relations, OCD; Stanley Braithwaite; Alain Locke, Howard University; Major Campbell Johnson, Selective Service; unknown delegate. *Second row:* W. H. Brown, Atlanta University; J. E. Bowen, North Carolina CCC; Walter N. Ridley, Virginia State College; C. A. Crocker, Negro Organization Society; Morse A. Cartwright, Columbia University; J. P. Morton, Mississippi State College; Samuel A. Madden, Virginia State College; Ralph Jones, Sr., state adult education supervisor, Baton Rouge, La.; William M. Cooper, Hampton Institute; L. O. Lewis, Morehouse College. *Third row:* unknown delegate; B. R. Brazeal, Morehouse College; unknown delegate; Moss A. Kendrix, NYA administrator for Georgia; W. A. Robinson, Atlanta University; L. O. Lewis, Atlanta University; J. H. Daves, TVA; W. R. Chivers, Morehouse College; P. L. Whatley, Georgia, NYA. Reprinted by permission of Moorland-Spingarn Research Center, Howard University.

Portrait of Alain Locke by Betsy Graves, in late 1940's. Graves toured the United States with her portraits of famous Negroes in that decade. Portrait currently held by the National Portrait Gallery, Smithsonian Institution, Washington, D.C. Photo courtesy of Schromberg Center for Research in Black Culture, The New York Public Library, Astor, Lenox and Tilden Foundations.

Moral Imperatives for World Order

Realism and idealism should be combined in striking for a world order. Skeletal ideals of universal human brotherhood have been in the world a long time and we are further from tribal savagery and its tribalism because of these ideals. But they are but partial expressions of what we hope to make them mean and what today's world crisis demands.

Loyalty to corporate unity is a necessary loyalty to something larger than the individual in order to unite men. However, the traditional ideas and values associated with human group loyalties are now hopelessly inadequate as a foundation for a larger society and impose limitations on a more comprehensive human society. In the transformation of these values we need something bigger and more understanding.

These basic corporate ideas concern (1) the nation as a political corporate idea, (2) the race as a cultural corporate idea, and (3) the sect as a spiritual corporate idea. These larger loyalties, however, are and have been seeds of conflict and division among men everywhere —loyalties that were originally meant to bring people together. How can we give them up? One great and fundamental way of giving up something that is vital is to find a way to transform or enlarge it.

Nationality now means irresponsible national sovereignty. We must give up some of this arbitrary sovereignty in order to prevent war, to get fellowship among nations, to erase conflict boundaries which are potential battlelines. We must work for enlargement of all our loyalties, but most particularly this one,—of the sovereign self-judging politically expansive nation.

This process of evolution by progressive enlargement of values can be illustrated by the stages reported Biblically when sacrifice to God meant the sacrifice of a human being. This was changed to the substitution of an animal in the place of a man. Fundamentalists must have said if we give this up, that will be the end of sacrifices; but instead, there was more meaning to the act and then the next stage took sacrifice to the still more meaningful level of "an offering of a pure and contrite heart."

We must consider race not in the fascist, blood-clan sense, which also is tribal and fetishist, but consider race as a common culture and brotherhood. Cultural superiority of one race is only an expression of arbitrary loyalty to that which is our own. Confraternity of culture will have to be put forward as what race can mean, and as an ideal of the parity of races and cultures.

We must in the third place consider religion as having many ways leading to salvation. The idea that there is only one true way of salvation with all other ways leading to damnation is a tragic limitation to the Christianity, which professes the fatherhood of God and the brotherhood of man. How foolish in the eyes of foreigners are our competitive blind, sectarian missionaries! If the Confucian expression of a Commandment means the same as the Christian expression, then it is the truth also and should so be recognized. It is in this way alone that Christianity or any other enlightened religion can vindicate its claims to Universality; and so bring about moral and spiritual brotherhood.

The moral imperatives of a new world order are an internationally limited idea of national sovereignty, a non-monopolistic and culturally tolerant concept of race and religious loyalties freed of sectarian bigotry.

12. Philosophy Alive

The *Cleavage in Our Culture* is a collection of articles in memory of Max Otto. It supports, for Locke, a case against essentialists' views of human nature and a case for seeing human nature as a part of an always changing universe. He supports Otto's functionalist approach to philosophy and his rejection of narrow professional technocratic dialogue. Otto was a fellow cultural pluralist and humanist. He was also instrumental in opening the doors of the University of Wisconsin to blacks desiring to study philosophy. Locke suggests "interpreting life mainly in terms of process, function, cumulative adjustment, and integration rather than in terms of essence, absolute values, preordained purpose and design." Scientific humanism's affinity for such interpretive approaches is, for Locke, a major advantage over idealistic rationalism.

"Philosophy Alive," review of *The Cleavage in Our Culture: Studies in Scientific Humanism in Honor of Max Otto*, ed. Frederick H. Burkhardt (Boston: Beacon Press, 1952), in *The Progressive* 17 (February 1953): 41–43. Copyright © 1953, The Progressive, Inc. Reprinted by permission from The Progressive, Madison, WI 53703.

Philosophy Alive

It is rare indeed when a volume of academic tribute is as completely in key with the personality, character, and philosophy of the man it honors as is this brilliant group of essays in honor of Max Otto. Only the happiest combination of circumstances could have made it so. Responsible in the first instance was careful planning and editing to coordinate a most thoughtful and devoted collaboration of a dozen friends and colleagues. This has produced a book with an exceptional unity of theme and cumulative effect.

But behind and beneath that, and basic to it all, was Max Otto's own nearly fifty years of intellectual activity and the singular consistency with which he has maintained and matured in scholarship, teaching, and social action his own progressive principles and all their moral and social corollaries. So, although the contributions range widely over a number of disciplines besides philosophy proper, the authors have been enabled, by focussing their thinking in terms of Otto's life interest in scientific humanism, to project a whole movement, to emphasize its constructive general trends, and thus present it more completely than ever before as a challenging and promising contemporary interpretation of life.

The various contributors make an impressive roll-call of the chief exponents of scientific humanism stretching over more than two generations of this important school of American thought. Philosophy proper is represented by Boyd H. Bode, whose lead-essay sets the general theme; the late John Dewey with an incisive paper on the special differentials of the "modern" philosophy, of double significance as his valedictory utterance; Horace M. Kallen with a trenchant and closely reasoned exposition of the functional doctrine of truth, and George Geiger with a cogent plea for a realistically integrated science of ethics.

The late Horace S. Fries, lamentably cut off at the height of his powers, has stepped over the philosophical borderline in a most constructive essay on social planning based on Max Otto's concept of "creative bargaining."

Others follow with pioneering suggestions of the implications of the new humanism for other disciplines—E. C. Lindeman for social philosophy, Norman Cameron for social psychology and psychiatry,

Arnold Dresden for the social sciences, and C. E. Ayres for economic theory; A. Eustace Haydon and Harold Taylor defend the case for functionally realistic theories of religion and education. George Sellery concludes with a restrained but deeply perceptive biographical sketch of Otto.

All of these men, more than half of whom at one time or another were Otto's colleagues at the University of Wisconsin, have sensed the sort of tribute that would be most appropriate and acceptable to their friend. Instead, therefore, of the traditional laurel wreath celebrating the past and merely detailing Max Otto's long and valuable contributions to scientific humanism, they have more wisely chosen to plant, so to speak, in his name a seed-garden that promises a rich perennial yield as it sprouts new growth and generates new vitality for the movement itself.

Their consensus can be briefly stated: it is their confident belief in and optimistic advocacy of a pragmatically functional type of philosophy, to serve as a guide to life and living rather than what Dewey calls "busy work for a few professionals" refining the techniques and polishing the tools of rational analysis. The methodological path to this, they think, is to extend the scientific method and temper beyond the domain of science in the narrower sense to all other intellectual domains.

Even fifty years after their movement's start with Charles Peirce and William James, they consider it still a young contender that has not yet reached its prime, and considering the centuries of dominance of the older rationalisms, whose chronic dualisms they seek to resolve, this optimistic perspective is plausible and perhaps warranted.

Certainly this book makes a strong, readable case for a philosophy interpreting life mainly in terms of process, function, cumulative adjustment and integration rather than in terms of essence, absolute values, preordained purpose and design. Harold Taylor aptly characterizes this as a "new philosophy which accepts human nature as a part of a growing and changing universe," stating succinctly the main issue which scientific humanism poses over against traditional idealistic rationalism.

13. Values That Matter

Ralph B. Perry was Locke's dissertation advisor at Harvard. The review of Perry's *Values that Matter* is among Locke's last book reviews before his death. The review is a friendly discussion of Perry's contributions and a reaffirmation of the importance Locke placed on values as the constituting foundation of our ideations. It marks Locke's last published statement about an American philosopher that figured in his life personally and with whom he held some philosophic affinity. Locke reaffirms his hope for valuation processes that will allow co-loyalties to exist within a peaceful world.

"Values that Matter," review of *Realms of Value*, by Ralph B. Perry (Cambridge, Mass.: Harvard University Press, 1954), in *Key Reporter* 19:3 (1954): 4.

Values That Matter

The realm of value—or as Professor Perry pluralistically and more wisely says, "Realms" of value—is one of the most important and most baffling of the provinces of philosophy. Its importance as a primary point of contact between thought and actual living is seldom given proper emphasis in either professional or lay thinking. The reasons are many, among them our chronic inclination to take values for granted. But on the professional philosopher rests also an ample share of blame. Not only have the older philosophies turned their backs on the vital link between values and life, pursuing their abstractions into transcendental absolutes of idealistic metaphysics, but many, if not most, of more recent philosophies—realism and positivism—have likewise gone astray by pressing their value analyses into a disembodied stratosphere of transcendental mathematics. It is both a notable and welcome exception to encounter an analysis of value that, without loss of scholarly depth, examines values in the vital context of their actual functioning, and as in the case of *Realms of Value*, yields cumulative insight into the role of values in motivating and sustaining human behavior and in providing sanctions—rational and rationalized—for our civilization.

Professor Perry's book is a leisurely revision of his "Gifford Lectures" of 1946–1947 and 1947–1948, and it marks the climax of a lifelong specialization that began with *The Moral Economy* and includes the definitive *The General Theory of Value*. Like William James, Professor Perry gives full weight to the practical and creative controls of ideas and ideals. In this Jamesian approach, which he has not only maintained but matured, Professor Perry has a viewpoint ideally suited to the task of analyzing the basic values of Western civilization. This huge task, it can be reported, has been accomplished in urbane and integrated fashion, with a singular absence of dogmatism. By carefully maintaining the historical approach, he has obviated all need for the specious generalizations and overall rationale that cripple so many other systematic studies of values. A consistent realism has also aided materially, and the prudent pluralism already mentioned has safeguarded against such likely pitfalls as the illusion of automatic progress or involvement in the blind provincialisms of our own culture. As an end result, we are the richer for an enlightening review, easily comprehensible by the layman, of the way in which civilized man has worked out effective and progressively inclusive integrations of his human interests and their supporting values. This review is a notable achievement.

Although *Realms of Value* offers no solutions and no formulae of progress, it is far from being a colorless and non-committal study. Here and there are quiet, firm hints of constructive insights and saner goals. No careful reader will come away with his provincialisms or partisanships untempered, nor is he likely to persist in the conviction that values are absolute, sacrosanct and automatically universal. He may have shed any previous notions that values are best professed or understood in their original perspectives, or most sanely practiced in their traditional loyalties and sanctions. In the light of what the history of value development and conflict alike indicate, he will be more prone to consider humanity's best hope to be the discovery and implementation, through reason and experience, of more and more generic underlying values toward which future co-loyalties and collaboration can be directed.

III. Identity and Plurality

14. The Problem of Race Classification

In this article, Locke explores the treatment of anthropologically defined racial groups as codeterminant with groups of people socially identified as a race. Locke centers on a problematic that is germane to David Hume's *Treatise on Human Nature*, which he implies is at the base of *The Racial History of Man* by Roland Dixon, namely, the "tendency to identify cultural aptitudes with ability to survive." This identification is to be constantly "discounted and combatted." Moreover, identifying abstract racial types with actual social races underlies the fallacy of the "block conception of race."

"The Problem of Race Classification," *Opportunity* 1 (1923), 261–264. Reprinted by permission of The National Urban League.

The Problem of Race Classification

The proper study of mankind is man, but we must add, even tho it breaks the beauty of the epigram—*if properly studied*. And no human science comes more under the discount of this reservation than anthropology, of which we may warrantably say that it has yet to establish its basic units and categories. The problem of anthropology today is not the problem of facts but of proper criteria for the facts; the entire scientific status and future of the consideration of man's group characters rests upon a decisive demonstration of what factors are really indicative of race, retrieving the science from the increasing confusion and cross-classification that the arbitrary selection of such criteria has inevitably brought about. The only other alternative is to abandon as altogether unscientific the conception of physical race groups as basic in anthropology; and throw the category of race into the discard as another of the many popular misconceptions detrimentally foisted upon science.

So when we find as pretentious a treatise as Professor Dixon's "The Racial History of Man"[1] prefaced by the declaration: "I have attempted to approach the whole racial problem '*de novo*'", there arises instantly and pardonably the hope that a Daniel has arisen among anthropologists. Professor Dixon faces the crouching dilemmas of his science squarely, unflinchingly: "The physical anthropologists are not by any means yet agreed as to what are the true criteria of race, and there is considerable doubt as to the real correlation of the various characteristics." And again (p. 87): "The present status of the whole question of race is, therefore, somewhat confused and uncertain. For not only is there wide divergence of opinion between different investigators in regard to the number, distribution, and origin of races, owing to the varying criteria which each adopts, but a certain hesitancy to face the larger problems boldly and without prejudice is apparent." Any attempt, such as this, to be fundamentally critical and at the same time comprehensive is noteworthy in a day when the specialized descriptive monograph seems to have become the refuge of the cautious anthropologist.

Confronting the problem with the confidence of a fresh start, Professor Dixon takes, for better or worse, the path of a "radical simplification of the criteria", relying almost exclusively upon three cranial measurements,—the cephalic, altitudinal, and nasal indices. These he regards most scientific because available to bring into the field of comparison skeletal data of all periods, including prehistoric remains, and because he believes them to be practically unmodifiable by environmental conditions and, therefore, accurately indicative of the racial heredity. It is only fair to Professor Dixon to state that in terms of the possible variations of these three indices, he constructs eight primary types—combinations, and nineteen cross-blends, which he treats as sufficiently descriptive of the actual combinations of these characters in the individual as to be truly descriptive, even tho arbitrarily and almost mathematically arrived at.

Professor Boas, in a trenchantly severe review of the book,[2] has taken exception to these artificial types of Professor Dixon's, and has insisted that as strict median averages, they ignore the Mendelian principles of type variation, and do not fit the most elastic possibilities of racial cross-breeding and intermixture. While recognizing the force of this criticism brought forward by Dr. Boas, the present reviewer is willing to grant Professor Dixon his premises, however contrary to fact, for the sake of what is to be gained from a critical consideration of his conclusions. For an analysis of these brings us to the very crux of the anthropological problem. Moreover, any investigator who attempts a rigorous analysis on a comprehensive scale,—and that Professor Dixon undeniably does,—is entitled to very serious hearing: the ground hypotheses in this science are very much in need of fundamental testing. Indeed Professor Dixon has produced a book to which a majority of his colleagues will take exception, not so much because he challenges on many points the current consensus of anthropological opinion, but because by the rigorousness of his procedure, he has brought the methods of physical anthropology face to face with its crucial dilemmas. If we are not seriously mistaken, the book will have a decided influence, tho a negative one, by serving as a sort of *reductio ad absurdum* test of the purely anatomical approach to the questions of human classification. No book brings us more clearly face to face with the issue between physical and biological anthropology, between the strictly anatomical and the more general morphological approach.

The paradox of Professor Dixon's book is that recognizing so clearly that the criteria of race-type which he chooses cannot be expected to conform with descriptive accuracy to the "natural race-groups", he nevertheless persists in treating them in his conclusions as historical strains or actual races, with definite cultural traits and heredity, and responsible for characteristic effects and influences throughout human history. There is a flagrant inconsistency involved in treating these abstract race-types as equivalent to actual sub-species or natural and cultural race-groups. No one can possibly be cited to better effect against this procedure than Professor Dixon himself. "If by the term 'race' we mean to describe actually existing groups of people, as I think we should, then our types are certainly not races, since, with few exceptions, there are no groups of men who actually represent them." These types are "but scantily represented among the world's peoples, the vast majority of whom present not the characteristics of our pure types, but of blends between them" (p. 502). Again, (p. 501): "It is extremely probable that the real criteria of race are rather complex and that various external features of pigmentation, hair-form, etc., together with many structural and metrical factors are involved. . . . In other words, we cannot point to any group of criteria and say these are inherently connected and form a true racial standard." And finally (p. 503): "Moreover, from this point of view a race is not a permanent entity, something static; on the contrary, it is dynamic, and is slowly developing and changing as the result of fresh increments of one or another of its original constituents or of some new one."

Yet having cautioned the reader (p. 401) to regard the terms "Proto-Negroid, Mediterranean, etc., as merely convenient (although perhaps misleading) names for a series of purely arbitrary types which might just as well be denominated by numbers or letters of the alphabet," Professor Dixon in glaring contradiction himself proceeds to treat these same abstract, almost hypothetical, types as "real" races, blithely confident that they have played recognizable historical roles and exhibited characteristic cultural capacities. It is true that he halts himself on the very verge of extreme Nordicism by saying (p. 516) "To no one race or type, however, can the palm be thus arrogantly assigned—rather to the product of the blending of these types which seem of all the most gifted—the Mediterranean-Caspian and the Alpine." And again we read (p. 519): "That neither the Proto-Australoid nor Proto-Negroid peoples by themselves have ever attained to greatness does not mean that they have not contributed anything to the progress of the human race. The elements of both, which seem to have been incorporated into the complex of the Baltic peoples, or in larger measure into that of the population of northern India, doubtless brought qualities the value of which has been considerable, if difficult to analyze and appraise." But from such occasional reefs of resurgent fairness, he plunges headlong into seas of eulogistic appraisal of the "favored races." According to Professor Dixon, the sudden advance in culture which marks the early Dynastic period in Egypt (pp. 186–7) is supposedly due to the leavening influence of the higher cultural capacities of the Mediterranean type; a thin stream of Alpine blood trickling into the Nile Valley, associated with the Caspian, suggests the explanation for the cultural development of the period of the Middle Kingdom (pp. 188–9) and from that point on, one might imagine the course of civilization to follow in the footsteps of these people. "With strong admixture of Alpine elements we have the development of the great Middle American civilization, and the less advanced but still striking cultures of the Cliff-Dwelling and Pueblo peoples of the Southwest. In South America, again, it was among peoples primarily of Alpine type that most of the higher cultural developments of Peru took place, the coastal tribes as well as the Inca being of this type." And finally this passage (p. 514 f.) which amounts to a sweepstake claim to civilization: "Thus Babylonian civilization grew out of the blending of the supposedly Alpine Sumerian with the Mediterranean-Caspian Semetic peoples who seem long to have been in occupation of the Mesopotamian plains; in Greece, before the florescence of Hellenic culture, the earlier Mediterranean population was reinforced by the immigration of the probably Alpine Dorians; Rome rose to greatness only after the older Mediterranean-Caspian people of Latium had been half-dominated by Alpines coming southward from the valley of the Po and the region where the older Etruscan culture had its center. In the East, Chinese civilization had its rise in an area where strong Caspian elements were absorbed by the incoming Alpine folk; lastly, the marvellous development of modern European civilization has occurred in that region in which Alpine, Mediterranean and Caspian have been more completely and evenly fused than elsewhere in the world." Thus one more anthropologist goes over to the idols of the tribes. Professor Dixon would have us accept as scientific race-types that in one context are abstract nouns of classification, and in another, represent concrete historical stocks or breeds; that on one hand have no determinable physiognomic or structural stability, and exhibit almost limitless variability of their physical components, yet on the other, maintain sufficiently characteristic cultural traits and capacities as to have everywhere in all environments appreciably similar effects upon civilization. With such types something or someone must be victimized: they breed, so to speak, their own characteristic illusions.

If Professor Dixon had really contemplated from the beginning such conclusions about the cultural role and capacities of races, he should have confronted first the problem,—as anthropology eventually must,—of discovering some criteria of true race, of finding some clue to the inter-connection between physical character, and group-behavior, psychological and cultural traits. Unless this is done,—until this is done, anthropology cannot reliably or warrantably extend its classifications into the field of ethnic differential and cultural characteristics. Or else the heredity formula will have to be abandoned, and anthropologists go over entirely to the ranks of the environmentalists. One need only call attention in this regard to the fact that on Professor Dixon's own criteria and comparison, the relationships of cephalic indices link peoples as different in physiognomic and cultural type as the Proto-Australoid and the Mediterranean —whereas the Proto-Australoid and the Proto-Negroid, linked culturally and geographically, exhibit quite the greatest divergence in cranial indices of any of the eight primary types. So except as there is some definite clue to the correlation of the many factors in question, there seems no alternative to giving up the concrete descriptive reference of the physical race-types in anthropology, regarding them, as Professor Keller[3] suggests, "merely as those imaginary forms about which the peoples of the earth can be assembled with the nearest approach to exhaustiveness, orderliness and sequence." Then for the history of the rise and diffusion of human culture, we would divorce the idea of race in the physical sense from "culture-group" or race with respect to ethnic traits. This independent start on an ethnological and archeological basis would, of course, give us ethnic or culture groups of little or no inherent connection with the physical race-groups. Pretty much this same mode of analysis, making admittedly an exception, Professor Dixon (p. 175 pf.) metes out to the Jews, regarding them more as a culture-group than a race. "It is probable," he says, "that the majority of all the Jews of today are 'Semites' only in speech, and that their true (racial or physical) ancestry goes back not so much to Palestine and Arabia as to the uplands of Anatolia and Armenia, the Caucasus and the steppes of Central Asia— and their nearest relatives are still to be found in those areas today." With wider cultural diversities and relatively more disparate cultural variability, the fallacy of the block conception of race as applied to the Negro peoples is even more unscientific. We cannot change this popular error, at least in respect to physical components, to Professor Dixon, who is never more insistent upon the composite character of living stocks than when dealing with African peoples. But we must point out nevertheless that ethnologically Professor Dixon is not so consistent, but "lumps" this group of peoples unfairly with respect to their cultural capacities and attainments. For the way is very open to this as long as one assumes that blood as mixture acts as a "cultural leaven" and not merely as an activating agent, and that it always works from so-called "higher" to so-called "lower" instead of on a reciprocal basis.

But the prime object of this review is to point out the situation with respect to the fundamental criteria in anthropology, and to call attention to a promising but neglected field, from which may very possibly be wrested a scientific determination of whatever connection may actually exist between these variously disputed basic factors. While the line and field of investigation seem on casual analysis to be of primary concern to the biological school of anthropologists, the results of its thoro-going investigation would be of fundamental importance for the physical anthropologists. Yet both schools have quite abandoned the scientific investigation of the active present-generation inter-breeding of diverse racial stocks, as instanced in the inter-mixture of the Negro with Nordic stocks in America to the unsound charlatan or the casually and exotically curious.[4] Meanwhile in what must be pronounced for this very same reason a half-hearted attack on these crucial vital problems, biological anthropologists have resorted from time to time for working hypotheses to the far-fetched field of animal genetics. It is not too much to claim for the field of investigation suggested that there, if anywhere, the problem of the correlation of the physical criteria of races is to be discovered, and perhaps also the main line of evidence for the solution of the question as between the direct and the indirect inheritance of cultural traits.

It is useless to argue that because the scale of ultimate operation is the whole vast range of the life history of the human species, such factors as are admittedly common for both long and short-term change and development cannot be profitably investigated within the restricted field of short-term observation available. Indeed with respect to their morphological connection with one another, and the question of their physiological correlation or independent variability, they can only be approached in this way. Enough evidence has already scientifically gone to waste in seven or eight generations of the history of the Negro stocks in America, to have solved the questions of the relative fixity or variability as well as the determinate correlation of these important moot factors, without a determination of which race classification in anthropology cannot hope to establish itself upon either an exact or a truly descriptive basis.

Intensive anthropometric study of race hybrids, especially of cases where these are widely diverse parental types, is one of the most important of the few research fields that yet remain comparatively untouched. The recent investigations of Frets[5] of the progeny of parents of sharply contrasted cranial types (dolio and brachycephalic), reported by Dixon as distinctly indicating the development of the meso-cephalic or medial forms, are as a matter of fact highly tentative, and need to be widely supplemented in scope and in the criteria investigated. The advantages of the investigation of a problem of this sort with Negro and non-Negroid stocks, with very evident variation in the correlative factors of skin-pigmentation and hair-texture, ought to be quite apparent. But the possibilities of the field are so intriguing that one may be pardoned for specifying more definitely a few of them: the confirmation or revision of the Frets' hypothesis, the question of the relative variability of head-form, skin-pigmentation and hair-texture, the question whether there are differences in the degree of change or preferential lines of dominant heredity along any of these lines as between the same qualities in the maternal strain or in the paternal strain, and most important of all, extensive and concrete observational investigation of the hypothesis advanced by Sir Arthur Keith in his "Differentiation of Mankind into Racial Types," that physical anthropological characters and structural changes of the human type are incident upon physiological, especially glandular processes. There is not one of these questions that, in spite of the importance of its being settled, is not yet purely tentative and hypothetical, and yet where the evidence stares, science has looked away. Each generation of science, even our own, has had its characteristic taboos, and this, we fear, has been one of them. So that after all, it is not the interests of the special field, but rather the general interests of anthropology and some of its most comprehensive and basic problems that seem to be here concerned.

One of the very points that must remain purely hypothetical, pending investigation of the sort this article suggests, is a peculiar, almost startling, theory of Professor Dixon's (p. 490) suggesting Negroid and non-Negroid branches of what he regards as essentially the same race-type. A reversible process of "bleaching-out" and "darkening" under pronounced climatic and prolonged dietary change is thus assumed—an assumption natural enough to have been advanced earlier, but as yet scientifically unestablished. "The Palae Alpine type presents us with a problem comparable in many ways to that which we have already met with in the case of the Proto-Negroid type, where a Negroid and a non-Negroid form appear to exist, similar in cranial characteristics, but differing in pigmentation and type of hair. The conditions here are, however, just reversed from those in the Proto-Negroid, for, whereas in that instance the majority of living members of the type are Negroid and the minority non-Negroid in the Palae-Alpine the vast majority present no trace of Negroid pigmentation and hair, these being found only among the numerically insignificant Negrito peoples." While in the particular instance, this hypothesis stands or falls on the confirmation or disproof of Professor Dixon's thesis about the stability of the cranial characters, the suggestion that the progressiveness from blond to brunette coloration have worked in both directions seems in itself to be of greater plausibility than the usual assumption of a one-way process. When we begin once to realize that on the mixing palette of nature, "darkened" white races and "whitened" dark races, the present-day significances of color will have scientifically evaporated.

It is interesting to note in passing that as to a very definite derivation of many of the elements of the Pre-Columban American cultures together with considerable blood-intermixture from African sources and stocks in Professor Dixon's view, there appears to be conclusive evidence. Thus reinforced from an entirely different line of analysis, the singular coincidence with the conclusions of Professor Leo Wiener, as worked out in his "Discovery of America" on strictly philological evidence and with similar views advanced by Professor G. Elliot Smith in his "Early Migrations of Culture" should shortly have the effect of establishing a consensus of opinion and securing general acceptance of the view. But both the latter investigators are more generous and in all probability more scientific in the interpretation they put upon the situation. Unlike Professor Dixon, they regard cultural contacts of such types as reciprocal in effect and as establishing in the majority of instances a composite culture. But with Professor Dixon, there seems to be an insistent assumption,—which indeed in his conclusions about culture amounts to an underlying fallacy, that the cultural dominant has coincided throughout history with the physical dominant. But surely it ought to be evident that it is not always the race which survives in physical characteristics that has counted most or that survives culturally. This tendency toward identifying cultural aptitudes with ability to survive has constantly to be discounted and combatted.

The feature of the treatise likely to receive most attention from technical anthropologists is the rather unusual position in reverting to the polygenic theory of human origins. The monogenic theory had become so generally held that in this respect the book may not even succeed in effectively re-opening the question. But Professor Dixon has opened more issues than he has closed, and the general effect will be to direct attention to the more fundamental ground questions of anthropology. Like Hume's treatise, the book propounds profounder questions at the end than those it started out to settle, and in this way, perhaps not too intentionally, it may exert a very important influence in current anthropological effort. Certainly the quite successful attempt to restore the comprehensive scope of the classical days of anthropology is to be welcomed, for there are few, perhaps no other, special sciences with so general a bearing and influence. History and the science of human society cannot be put upon a strictly scientific and comparative basis until a sounder and broader anthropology has been achieved.

NOTES

1. Roland Dixon, *The Racial History of Man* (New York: Charles Scribner's Sons, 1923).

2. *The New York Times Book Review*, April 1, 1923, p. 13.

3. A. G. Keller, *Race Distinctions* (New Haven, Conn.: Yale University Press, 1909).

4. A notable exception in Davenport's "Heredity of Skin Color in Negro-White Crosses" (Carnegie Institution Publication No. 188).

5. G. Frets, "The Heredity of Human Head Form" (The Hague, 1920).

15. The Ethics of Culture

The "Ethics of Culture" is a published speech
originally delivered to a freshman lecture course at
Howard University. It explicates the importance of
conversation and manner as cultural appointments,
the development of which are necessary for a people
to attain greatness. Locke is acutely aware of the
way Afro-Americans are subject to being judged
by whites. An individual black person's mode of
being and the mode of being of black people as a
group were commonly judged identically. Locke's
elitism takes the form of admonishing students to be
advance guards and models. This article also helps
situate Locke's self-perception as an aesthete and an
indication of the regard that he held for Du Bois'
view of the Talented Tenth (that is, that the talented
members of the black race should be the race's
representatives to whites and models to be emulated
by the rest of the race).

It should be remembered in reading this article
that in the 1920s "ethics" entailed judgments of
customs, manners, habits of speech, and dress codes
and not simply, as is now commonly the case, general
principles regulating institutional arrangements and
the limits of personal expressions. The concepts of
culture, duty, personality, and group responsibilities
are thus considered ethical concepts.

"The Ethics of Culture," *Howard University Record* 17 (1923),
178–185. Reprinted with the permission of Moorland-Spingarn Research Center, Alain Locke Collection, Howard University.

The Ethics of Culture

I am to speak to you on the ethics of culture. Because I teach the one and try to practice the other, it may perhaps be pardonable for me to think of them together, but I hope at least not to leave you without the conviction that the two are in a very vital and immediate way connected. In my judgment, the highest intellectual duty is the duty to be cultured. Ethics and culture are usually thought out of connection with each other—as, in fact, at the very opposite poles. Particularly for our country, and the type of education which generally prevails, is this so. Quite unfortunately, it seems, duty toward the beautiful and the cultural is very generally ignored, and certainly, beauty as a motive has been taken out of morality, so that we confront beautiless duty and dutiless beauty. In an issue like this, it behooves education to try to restore the lapsing ideals of humanism, and to center more vitally in education the duty to be cultured.

It follows if there is any duty with respect to culture, that it is one of those that can only be self-imposed. No one can make you cultured, few will care whether you are or are not, for I admit that the world of today primarily demands efficiency—and further the only reward my experience can offer you for it is the heightened self-satisfaction which being or becoming cultured brings. There is, or ought to be, a story of a lad to whom some rather abstract duty was being interpreted who is said to have said, "If I only owe it to myself, why then I really don't owe it at all." Not only do I admit that culture is a duty of this sort, but I claim that this is its chief appeal and justification. The greatest challenge to the moral will is in the absence of external compulsion. This implies, young ladies and gentlemen, that I recognize your perfect right not to be cultured, if you do not really want to be, as one of those inalienable natural-born privileges which so-called "practical minded," "ordinary" Americans delight to claim and exercise. As a touch-stone for the real desire and a sincere motive, the advocates of culture would not have it otherwise.

The way in which duty comes to be involved in culture is this: culture begins in education where compulsion leaves off, whether it is the practical spur of necessity or the artificial rod of the school-master. I speak to a group that has already chosen to be educated. I congratulate you upon that choice. Though you have so chosen for many motives and with very diverse reasons and purposes, I fear that education for most of you means, in last practical analysis, the necessary hardship that is involved in preparing to earn a better living, perhaps an easier living. It is just such narrowing and truncating of the conception of education that the ideals and motives of culture are effective to remove or prevent. Education should not be so narrowly construed, for in the best sense, and indeed in the most practical sense, it means not only the fitting of the man to earn his living, but to live and to live well. It is just this latter and higher function of education, the art of living well, or, if I may so express it, of living up to the best, that the word *culture* connotes and represents. Let me offer you, if I may, a touch-stone for this idea, a sure test of its presence. Whenever and wherever there is carried into education the purpose and motive of knowing better than the practical necessities of the situation demand, whenever the pursuit of knowledge is engaged in for its own sake and for the inner satisfaction it can give, culture and the motives of culture are present. I sense immediately that you may have quite other and perhaps more authoritative notions of culture in mind. Culture has been variously and beautifully defined. But I cannot accept for the purpose I have in view even that famous definition of Matthew Arnold's. "Culture is the best that has been thought and known in the world," since it emphasizes the external rather than the internal factors of culture. Rather is it the capacity for understanding the best and most representative forms of human expression, and of expressing oneself, if not in similar creativeness, at least in appreciative reactions and in progressively responsive refinement of tastes and interests. Culture proceeds from personality to personality. To paraphrase Bacon, it is that, and only that, which can be inwardly assimilated. It follows, then, that, like wisdom, it is that which cannot be taught, but can only be learned. But here is the appeal of it, it is the self-administered part of your education, that which represents your personal index of absorption and your personal coefficient of effort.

As faulty as is the tendency to externalize culture, there is still greater error in over-intellectualizing it. Defining this aspect of education, we focus it, I think, too much merely in the mind, and project it too far into the abstract and formal. We must constantly realize that without experience, and without a medium for the absorption and transfer of experience, the mind could not develop or be developed. Culture safeguards the educative process at these two points, and stands for the training of the sensibilities and the expressional activities. Mentioning the former as the neglected aspect of American education, former President Eliot contends that, since it is the business of the senses to serve the mind, it is reciprocally the duty of the mind to serve the senses. He means that properly to train the mind involves the proper training of the sensibilities, and that, without a refinement of the channels through which our experience reaches us, the mind cannot reach its highest development. We too often expect our senses to serve us and render nothing back to them in exchange. As a result they do not serve us half so well as they might: coarse channels make for sluggish response, hampered impetus, wastage of effort. The man of culture is the man of trained sensibilities, whose mind expresses itself in keenness of discrimination and, therefore, in cultivated interests and tastes. The level of mentality may be crowded higher for a special effort or a special pursuit, but in the long run it cannot rise much higher than the level of tastes. It is for this reason that we warrantably judge culture by manners, tastes, and the fineness of discrimination of a person's interests. The stamp of culture is, therefore, no conventional pattern, and has no stock value: it is the mold and die of a refined and completely developed personality. It is the art medallion, not the common coin.

On this very point, so necessary for the correct estimation of culture, most of the popular mistakes and misconceptions about culture enter in. Democracy and utilitarianism suspect tastes because they cannot be standardized. And if I should not find you over-interested in culture or over-sympathetic toward its ideals, it is because of these same prejudices of puritanism and materialism, which, though still typically American, are fortunately no longer representatively so. Yet it is necessary to examine and refute some of these prevalent misconceptions about culture. You have heard and will still hear culture derided as *artificial, superficial, useless, selfish, over-refined*, and *exclusive*. Let us make inquiry into the reasons for such attitudes. It is not the part of loyal advocacy to shirk the blow and attack of such criticism behind the bastions of dilettantism. Culture has its active adversaries in present-day life, indeed the normal tendencies of life today are not in the direction either of breadth or height of culture. The defense of culture is a modern chivalry, though of some hazard and proportional glory.

The criticism of culture as artificial first concerns us. In the mistaken name of naturalism, culture is charged with producing artificiality destructive of the fine original naturalness of human nature. One might as well indict civilization as a whole on this point; it, too, is artificial. But perhaps just a peculiar degree of artificiality is inveighed against—to which our response must be that it is just that very painful intermediate stage between lack of culture and wholesomeness of culture which it is the object of further culture to remove. All arts have their awkward stages: culture itself is its own cure for this. Closely associated, and touched by the same reasoning, is the argument that culture is superficial. Here we encounter the bad effect of a process undertaken in the wrong order. If the polished surface is, so to speak, the last coat of a consistently developed personality, it lends its final added charm to the total worth and effect. If, on the contrary, beginning with the superficial as well as ending with the superficial, it should be merely a veneer, then is it indeed both culturally false and artistically deceptive. No true advocacy of an ideal involves the defense or extenuation of its defective embodiments. Rather on the contrary, culture must constantly be self-critical and discriminating, and deplore its spurious counterfeits and shallow imitations.

More pardonable, especially for our age, is the charge of uselessness. Here we need not so much the corrective of values as that of perspective. For we only need to appreciate the perennial and imperishable qualities of the products of culture to see the fallacy in such depreciation. Fortified in ideas and ideals, culture centers about the great human constants, which, though not rigidly unchangeable, are nevertheless almost as durable as those great physical constants of which science makes so much. Indeed, if we count in the progressive changes of science through discovery, these are the more constant— the most constant then of all the things in human experience. Moreover, there is their superior representativeness by which posterity judges each and every phase of human development. Through their culture products are men most adequately represented; and by their culture-fruits are they known and rated. As we widen our view from the standpoint of momentary and partial judgment, this fact becomes only too obvious.

I take seriously, and would have you, also, the charge that culture is selfish. Being unnecessarily so is to be unduly so. Yet there is a necessary internal focusing of culture because true culture must begin with self-culture. Personality, and to a limited extent character also, are integral parts of the equation. In the earlier stages of the development of culture there is pardonable concentration upon self-cultivation. Spiritual capital must be accumulated; indeed, too early spending of the meager resources of culture at an early stage results in that shallow and specious variety which means sham and pretense at the start, bankruptcy and humiliation at the finish. Do not begin to spend your mental substance prematurely. You are justified in serious self-concern and earnest self-consideration at the stage of education. And, moreover, culture, even when it is rich and mature, gives only by sharing, and moves more by magnetic attraction than by transfer of material or energy. Like light, to which it is so often compared, it radiates, and operates effectively only through being self-sufficiently maintained at its central source. Culture polarizes in self-hood.

Finally we meet the criticism of exclusiveness, over-selectness, perhaps even the extreme of snobbery. Culture, I fear, will have to plead guilty to a certain degree of this: it cannot fulfill its function otherwise. Excellence and the best can never reside in the average. Culture must develop an elite that must maintain itself upon the basis of standards that can move forward but never backwards. In the pursuit of culture one must detach himself from the crowd. Your chief handicap in this matter as young people of today is the psychology and "pull" of the crowd. Culturally speaking, they and their point of view define vulgarity. As Professor Palmer says, "Is this not what we mean by the vulgar man? His manners are not an expression of himself, but of somebody else. Other men have obliterated him." There is no individuality in being ordinary: it is the boast of sub-mediocrity. Who in the end wishes to own that composite of everybody's average qualities, so likely to be below our own par? Culture's par is always the best: one cannot be somebody with everybody's traits. If to be cultured is a duty, it is here that that element is most prominent, for it takes courage to stand out from the crowd. One must, therefore, pay a moral as well as an intellectual price for culture. It consists in this: "Dare to be different—stand out!" I know how difficult this advice will be to carry out: America's chief social crime, in spite of her boasted freedoms, is the psychology of the herd, the tyranny of the average and mediocre; in other words, the limitations upon cultural personality. Strive to overcome this for your own sake and, as Cicero would say, "for the welfare of the Republic."

I am spending too much time, I fear, in pointing out what culture is when I would rather point out the way to its attainment. I must not trespass, however, upon the provinces of my colleagues who are to interpret culture more specifically to you in terms of the art of English speech, the fine arts, and music. I content myself with the defense of culture in general, and with the opportunity it gives of explaining its two most basic aspects—the great amateur arts of personal expression—conversation and manners. These personal arts are as important as the fine arts; in my judgment, they are their foundation. For culture without personal culture is sterile —it is that insincere and hypocritical profession of the love of the beautiful which so often discredits culture in the eyes of the many. But with the products of the fine arts translating themselves back into personal refinement and cultivated sensibilities, culture realizes itself in the fullest sense, performs its true educative function and becomes a part of the vital art of living. We too often estimate culture materialistically by what has been called "the vulgar test of production." On the contrary, culture depends primarily upon the power of refined consumption and effective assimilation; it consists essentially in being cultured. Whoever would achieve this must recognize that life itself is an art, perhaps the finest of the fine arts—because it is the composite blend of them all.

However, to say this is not to commit the man of culture to hopeless dilettantism, and make him a Jack of the arts. Especially for you, who for the most part work toward very practical professional objectives and who lack as Americans of our time even a modicum of leisure, would this be impossible. But it is not necessary to trouble much about this, for, even were it possible, it would not be desirable. There are, of course, subjects which are primarily "cultural" and subjects which are not, but I am not one of those who bewail altogether the departure from the old-fashioned classical program of education and the waning appeal of the traditional "humanities." Science, penetratingly studied, can yield as much and more culture than the humanities mechanically studied. It lies, I think, more in the point of view and the degree of intrinsic interest rather than in the special subject-matter or tradition of a subject. Nevertheless, to be sure of culture, the average student should elect some of the cultural studies; and, more important still, in his outside diversions, should cultivate a steady and active interest in one of the arts, aiming thereby to bring his mind under the quickening influence of cultural ideas and values. Not all of us can attain to creative productiveness and skill in the arts, though each of us has probably some latent artistic temperament, if it only expresses itself in love and day-dreaming. But each of us can, with a different degree of concentration according to his temperament, cultivate an intelligent appreciation of at least one of the great human arts, literature, painting, sculpture, music or what not. And if we achieve a high level of cultivated taste in one art it will affect our judgment and interest and response with respect to others.

May I at this point emphasize a peculiarly practical reason? In any community, in any nation, in any group, the level of cultural productiveness cannot rise much higher than the level of cultural consumption, cannot much outdistance the prevalent limits of taste. This is the reason why our country has not as yet come to the fore in the production of culture-goods. And as Americans we all share this handicap of the low average of cultural tastes. As educated Americans, we share also and particularly the responsibility for helping raise this average. A brilliant Englishman once characterized America as a place where everything had a price, but nothing a value, referring to the typical preference for practical and utilitarian points of view. There is a special need for a correction of this on your part. As a race group we are at the critical stage where we are releasing creative artistic talent in excess of our group ability to understand and support it. Those of us who have been concerned about our progress in the things of culture have now begun to fear as the greatest handicap the discouraging, stultifying effect upon our artistic talent of lack of appreciation from the group which it represents. The cultural par, we repeat, is always the best: and a group which expects to be judged by its best must live up to its best so that that may be truly representative. Here is our present dilemma. If the standard of cultural tastes is not rapidly raised in the generation which you represent, the natural affinities of appreciation and response will drain off, like cream, the richest products of the group, and leave the mass without the enriching quality of its finest ingredients. This is already happening: I need not cite the painful individual instances. The only remedy is the more rapid development and diffusion of culture among us.

It follows from this that it is not creditable nor your duty to allow yourselves to be toned down to the low level of average tastes. Some of you, many of you, I hope, will be making your life's work in sections of this country and among groups that are fittingly characterized as "Saharas of culture," that know culture neither by taste nor sight. You betray your education, however, and forego the influence which as educated persons you should always exert in any community if you succumb to these influences and subside to the mediocre level of the vulgar crowd. Moreover, you will find that, like knowledge or technical skill, culture to be maintained must be constantly practiced. Just as we saw that culture was not a question of one set of subjects, but an attitude which may be carried into all, so also we must realize that it is not a matter of certain moments and situations, but the characteristic and constant reaction of a developed personality. The ideal culture is representative of the entire personality even in the slightest detail.

I recall an incident of visiting with a friend a celebrated art connoisseur for his expert judgment upon a painting. He examined with a knife and a pocket magnifying glass a corner of the canvas. I perhaps thought for a moment he was searching for a signature, but it was not the signature corner. Without further scrutiny, however, he gave us his judgment: "Gentlemen, it is not a Holbein." The master painter puts himself into every inch of his canvas, and can be told by the characteristic details as reliably, more reliably even than by general outlines. Culture likewise is every inch representative of the whole personality when it is truly perfected. This summing up of the whole in every part is the practical test which I want you to hold before yourselves in matters of culture. Among cultivated people you will be judged more by your manner of speech and deportment than by any other credentials. They are meant to bear out your training and your heritage, and more reliably than your diplomas or your pedigree will they represent you or betray you. Manners are thus the key to personal relations, as expression is the key to intellectual intercourse. One meets that element in others which is most responsively tuned to a similar element in ourselves. The best fruits of culture, then, are the responses it elicits from our human environment. And should the environment be limited or unfavorable, then, instead of compromising with it, true culture opens the treasuries of art and literature, and lives on that inheritance.

Finally I must add a word about that aspect of culture which claims that it takes several generations to produce and make the truly cultured gentleman. Exclusive, culture may and must be, but seclusive culture is obsolete. Not all that are well-born are well-bred, and it is better to be well-bred. Indeed, one cannot rest satisfied at any stage of culture: it has to be earned and re-earned, though it returns with greater increment each time. As Goethe says, "What thou hast inherited from the fathers, labor for, in order to possess it." Thus culture is inbred—but we ourselves are its parents. With all of the possible and hoped for spread of democracy, we may say that excellence of this sort will always survive. Indeed, when all the other aristocracies have fallen, the aristocracy of talent and intellect will still stand. In fact, one suspects that eventually the most civilized way of being superior will be to excel in culture.

This much, then, of the ideals of humanism must survive; the goal of education is self-culture, and one must hold it essential even for knowledge's own sake that it be transmuted into character and personality. It must have been the essential meaning of Socrates' favorite dictum—"Know thyself"—that to know, one must be a developed personality. The capacity for deep understanding is proportional to the degree of self-knowledge, and by finding and expressing one's true self, one somehow discovers the common denominator of the universe. Education without culture, therefore, ignores an important half of the final standard, "a scholar and a gentleman," which, lest it seem obsolete, let me cite in those fine modern words which former President Eliot used in conferring the arts degree. "I hereby admit you to the honorable fellowship of educated men." Culture is thus education's passport to converse and association with the best.

Moreover, personal representativeness and group achievement are in this respect identical. Ultimately a people is judged by its capacity to contribute to culture. It is to be hoped that as we progressively acquire in this energetic democracy the common means of modern civilization, we shall justify ourselves more and more, individually and collectively, by the use of them to produce culture-goods and representative types of culture. And this, so peculiarly desirable under the present handicap of social disparagement and disesteem, must be for more than personal reasons the ambition and the achievement of our educated classes. If, as we all know, we must look to education largely to win our way, we must look largely to culture to win our just reward and recognition. It is, therefore, under these circumstances something more than your personal duty to be cultured—it is one of your most direct responsibilities to your fellows, one of your most effective opportunities for group service. In presenting this defense of the ideals and aims of culture, it is my ardent hope that the Howard degree may come increasingly to stand for such things—and especially the vintage of 1926.

16. The Concept of Race as Applied to Social Culture

The foundation for this article was "Race Contacts and Inter-Racial Relations: A Study in the Theory and Practice of Race," Syllabus, 1915–1916, prepared under the auspices of the Howard Social Science Club and the NAACP. It was the basis for a new course that the university rejected.

Locke attacks a host of social evolutionists, including Tylor, Morgan, and Spencer. His thesis is that race and culture are two distinct variables, often correlated, but not causally connected. Nor do they form an organic unity. "Race" is not an unchanging biological category but an anthropological tool and a social myth with significant explanatory value and problematics. Cultural idioms, styles, and temperaments are also variables subject to historical change. Contrary to R. H. Lowie's view, however, Locke holds that there are important relationships between social race and culture.

"The Concept of Race as Applied to Social Culture," *Howard Review* 1 (1924), 290–299. Reprinted with the permission of Moorland-Spingarn Research Center, Alain Locke Collection, Howard University.

The Concept of Race as Applied to Social Culture

In dealing with race and culture we undoubtedly confront two of the most inevitable but at the same time most unsatisfactory concepts involved in the broad-scale consideration of man and society. There is the general presumption and feeling that they have some quite vital and relevant connection, but as to the nature of this or even as to the scientific meaning of the individual concepts there is the greatest diversity of scientific opinion and theory. An analytic study of their highly variable meanings, confining this even to the more or less strictly scientific versions, would constitute two important and highly desirable treatises. But what we are here attempting is something quite more immediate and practical from the point of view of the use of these terms in the social sciences, and quite capable perhaps, if the analysis be successful, of settling some of these complexly controversial differences as to meaning by a process of elimination, namely an examination into their supposed relationship one to the other. For it seems that in the erroneous assumption of fixed relationships between the two, most of the serious difficulties and confusions lie. It will be our contention that far from being constants, these important aspects of human society are variables, and in the majority of instances not even paired variables, and that though they have at all times significant and definite relationships, they nevertheless are in no determinate way organically or causally connected. And if this should be so, whole masses of elaborately constructed social theory and cultural philosophizing fall with the destruction of a common basic assumption, that has been taken as a common foundation for otherwise highly divergent and even antagonistic theorizing. This position, differing from that of the school of interpretation which denies all significant connection between racial and cultural factors,[1] does not deny that race stands for significant social characters and culture-traits or represents in given historical contexts characteristic differentiations of culture-type. However, it does insist against the assumption of any such constancy, historical or intrinsic, as would make it possible to posit an organic connection between them and to argue on such grounds the determination of one by the other.

But the unwarranted assumption of race as a determinant of culture is still very current, and contemporary discussion, especially in ethnology, is still primarily concerned with the destructive criticism of this inveterate and chronic notion. We would by no means minimize the success and scientific service of such criticism as that of Boas in the field of anthropology and "race psychology," of Flinders-Petrie in archeology, of Finot, Babington, Hertz, and von Zollschan in social and political theory, and of Lowie and Wissler in ethnology,[2] in saying that as yet, however, we seem to be only at a transitional stage in the scientific consideration of the relationship of race to culture. In some revised and reconstructed form, we may anticipate the continued even if restricted use of these terms as more or less necessary and basic concepts that cannot be eliminated altogether, but that must nevertheless be so safe-guarded in this continued use as not to give further currency to the invalidated assumptions concerning them. It is too early to assume that there is no significant connection between race and culture because of the manifestly false and arbitrary linkage which has previously been asserted.

In the interval between these two stages of the discussion, as one might normally expect, there is considerable tendency to continue the corollaries of the older view even where the main position and hypothesis has been abandoned. Goldenweiser[3] is therefore quite justified in his insistence upon linking up these corollaries with the position of classical social evolutionism which gave them such vogue and standing, and disestablishing both by the same line of argument. For although this notion of race as a prime determining factor in culture was historically established by the theory and influence of de Gobineau,[4] its scientific justification has been associated with the doctrines of the strictly evolutionary interpretation of culture, especially with the influence of the social evolutionism of Spencer. The primary scientific use of this fixed linkage between race and culture was to justify the classical evolutionary scheme of a series of stepped stages in an historical progression of cultural development. In this connection it has been the analogue in the theory of society of the heredity factor in the biological field, and its stock notions of *race capacity* and *racial heredity* have had approximately the same phases of acceptance, repudiation, and revision. In their "classical" form they are now equally discredited by several lines of detailed evidence where the historical succession of stages does not coincide with those posited as the ground basis of the supposedly universal process of development,[5] and by the more intensive and objective study of primitive cultures which has shown how insidiously their consideration in the light of such evolutionary schemes has distorted their concrete facts and values. There is considerable warrant therefore for the position that wishes to exclude all further misinterpretation by a complete disassociation of the concept of race from the concept of culture.

This is the position of Lowie[6] who concludes after a brilliant and rigorous examination as to the inter-connection between culture and race that not only are cultural changes "manifestly independent of the racial factor," but that no race has permanent or even uniform alignment with reference to culture-type or cultural stages. His position, though one of the closest reasoned of any, is the most iconoclastic with respect to the assumption of any significant relation between race and culture, as may be estimated from the following passage:

With great confidence we can say that since the same race at different times or in different subdivisions at the same time represents vastly different cultural stages, there is obviously no direct proportional between culture and race and if great changes of culture can occur without any change of race whatsoever, we are justified in considering it probable that a relatively minute change of hereditary ability might produce enormous differences.

But the extreme cultural relativism of Lowie leaves an open question as to the association of certain ethnic groups with definite culture-traits and culture types under circumstances where there is evidently a greater persistence of certain strains and characteristics in their culture than of other factors. The stability of such factors and their resistance to direct historical modification marks out the province of that aspect of the problem of race which is distinctly ethnological and which the revised notion of ethnic race must cover. It seems quite clear that no adequate explanation can be expected from the factors and principles of anthropological race distinctions. In the light of the most recent and accepted investigations any attempt to explain one in terms of the other must be regarded as pseudoscientific. Nevertheless though there is lacking for the present any demonstrable explanation, there are certain ethnic traits the peculiarly stable and stock character of which must be interpreted as ethnically characteristic. They are in no sense absolutely permanent, the best psychological evidence as yet gives us no reason for construing them as inherent, yet they are factors not without an integral relationship one to the other not satisfactorily explained as mere historical combinations. Indeed it seems difficult and in some cases impossible to discover common historical factors to account for their relative constancy. Few challenge the specific factuality of these peculiarly resistant combinations of group traits.

As Sapir[7] aptly says,

Here, as so often, the precise knowledge of the scientist lags somewhat behind the more naive but more powerful insights of non-professional experience and impression. To deny to the genius of a people an ultimate psychological significance and to refer it to the specific historical development of that people is not, after all is said and done, to analyze it out of existence. It remains true that large groups of people everywhere tend to think and to act in accordance with established and all but instinctive forms, which are in a large measure peculiar to it.

The point that seems to be important to note and stress is that we do not need to deny the existence of these characteristic racial molds in denying that they are rooted in "inherent hereditary traits either of a biological or a psychological nature."

If, instead of the anthropological, the ethnic characters had been more in the focus of scientific attention, there probably would have resulted a much more scientific and tenable doctrine of the relationship of race to culture. Race would have been regarded as primarily a matter of social heredity, and its distinctions due to the selective psychological "set" of established cultural reactions. There is a social determination involved in this which quite more rationally interprets and explains the relative stability or so-called permanency that the old theorists were trying to account for on the basis of fixed anthropological characters and factors. To quote again from Sapir:[8]

The current assumption that the so-called 'genius' of a people is ultimately reducible to certain inherent heredity traits of a biological and psychological nature does not, for the most part, bear very serious examination. Frequently enough, what is assumed to be an innate racial characteristic turns out on closer study to be the resultant of purely historical causes. A mode of thinking, a distinctive type of reaction, gets itself established in the course of a complex historical development as typical, as normal; it serves then as a model for the working over of new elements of civilization.

The best consensus of opinion then seems to be that race is a fact in the social or ethnic sense, that it has been very erroneously associated with race in the physical sense and is therefore not scientifically commensurate with factors or conditions which explain or have produced physical race characters and differentiation, that it has a vital and significant relation to social culture, and that it must be explained in terms of social and historical causes such as have caused similar differentiations of culture-type as pertain in lesser degree between nations, tribes, classes, and even family strains. Most authorities are now reconciled to two things,—first, the necessity of a thorough-going redefinition of the nature of race, and second, the independent definition of race in the ethnic or social sense together with the independent investigation of its differences and their causes apart from the investigation of the factors and differentiae of physical race. Of course eventually there may be some interesting correlation possible at the conclusion of these two lines of investigation, but up to the present they seem only to have needlessly handicapped and complicated one another and to have brought comparative ethnology and comparative anthropology both to a deadlock of confusion because of their incompatible points of view and incommensurable values. It is undoubtedly this necessity of a new start that Wissler[9] has in mind when he says, "So it is obvious that the relation between culture and race is a subject of more than passing interest, and though as yet not seriously investigated, the time is near at hand when its solution must be sought, if life is to be understood rationally and socially." Similarly we find Flinders-Petrie[10] in his address before the British Association saying "The definition of the nature of race is the most requisite element for any clear ideas about man," and then veering over to the strictly social definition of race by adding, "The only meaning a race can have is a group of persons whose type has become unified by their rate of assimilation and affection by their conditions exceeding the rate of change produced by foreign elements." Evidently the thought here is that blood intermixture is only one of the conducive conditions to cultural assimilation and absorption and that therefore *culture-type* or *social race* is the important fact and concept. Race in the vital and basic sense is simply and primarily the culture-heredity, and that in its blendings and differentiations is properly analyzed on the basis of conformity to or variance from culture-type.

Gault,[11] discussing Stevenson's study, *Socio-Anthropometry: An Inter-racial Critique*, and several studies of Indian cross-breeds, all of which draw conclusions that differences are due to blood-race factors, says:

There is always the possibility that the Indian of mixed blood owes a degree of his superiority (we should say 'difference') to the *social* stimuli of one or the other parent from earliest infancy: stimuli that from the beginning have induced a level of reactions that otherwise would have been lacking, and have built up personality complexes that are next to original nature as respects substantiality.

Thus even in instances where physical assimilation is the condition responsible for cultural assimilation, the latter takes place in terms of social factors. Divorced then by every line of objectively considered evidence from the anthropological notion and criteria of race with which its distinctions rarely if ever coincide, ethnic race or what Gault calls "sociologic type" becomes the most scientifically tenable and useful concept.

Instead therefore of regarding culture as expressive of race, race by this interpretation is regarded as itself a culture product. Goldenweiser[12] puts the matter this way; he says:

Enough has been said to show that the view generally held of the relation between race and culture may well be reversed. According to the prevailing view, man is many and civilization one, meaning by this that the races differ significantly in potential ability and that only one, the white race, could have and has achieved civilization. The reverse view, forced upon the ethnologist and the historian by a more critical and open-minded survey of the facts, reads thus: *man is one, civilizations are many,* meaning by this that the races do not differ significantly in psychological endowment, that the variety of possible civilizations is great and of actual ones, considerable, and that many civilizations other than ours have achieved things of genuine and unique worth.

Perhaps the revolutionary significance of this can only be realized when we see it applied to specific descriptive analysis as in the case of Rivers'[13] use of the term race solely in a sense which means the people who had such and such culture-traits, whose customs dominated this or that period and set the pattern upon which a certain culture-type was developed.

Nothing seems more likely than that there will gradually develop out of this new and more objective analysis of culture a series of relatively divergent and basic culture-types, for each of which perhaps some more or less organic principle of development or evolution can be worked out, so that we may eventually get a standard of value for relative culture grading. Meanwhile we must grant the logic of the position of Lowie which is that the most objective study at present gives no warrant for the relative scientific grading of cultures. Meanwhile each culture must be treated as specific and as highly composite, and each ethnic group as the peculiar resultant of its own social history. This is what we mean then by this reversal of emphasis, that instead of the race explaining the cultural condition, the cultural conditions must explain the race traits, and that instead of artificially extracted units representing race types, the newer scientific approach demands that we deal with concrete culture-types which as often as not are composite racially speaking, and have only an artificial ethnic unity of historical derivation and manufacture.

Confident that this is the correct scientific conception of culture and its most warrantable scientific basis of approach and study, we return to the consideration of whether or not by such interpretation the concept of race is not entirely relegated from serious consideration in connection with it. So considerable is the shift of emphasis and meaning that at times it does seem that the best procedure would be to substitute for the term *race* the term *culture-group*. But what has become absolutely disqualified for the explanation of culture groups taken as totalities becomes in a much more scientific and verifiable way a main factor of explanation of its various cultural components. Race accounts for a great many of the specific elements of the cultural heredity, and the sense of race may itself be regarded as one of the operative factors in culture since it determines the stressed values which become the conscious symbols and tradition of the culture. Such stressed values are themselves factors in the process of culture making, and account primarily for the persistence and resistance of culture-traits. For these determine what is the dominant pattern in any given culture, and it is toward these dominants as social norms that social conformation converges and according to which it eventually establishes the type. It is with respect to such principles of determination that the newer psychology of race must be worked out instead of with reference to assumed innate traits and capacities. The type itself may have been established by accident or fortuitous combinations of historical circumstances, but re-enforced by the sense of race as perhaps the most intense of the feelings of commonality, it becomes an accepted, preferred and highly resistant culture complex that seems to be and often is self-perpetuating.

Race operates as tradition, as preferred traits and values, and when these things change culturally speaking ethnic remoulding is taking place. Race then, so far as the ethnologist is concerned, seems to lie in that peculiar selective preference for certain culture-traits and resistance to certain others which is characteristic of all types and levels of social organization. And instead of decreasing as a result of contacts this sense and its accumulative results seems on the whole to increase, so that we get accumulative effect. It intensifies therefore with contacts and increases with the increasing complexity of the culture elements in any particular area. A diversity of cultural types temporarily at least accentuates the racial stresses involved, so that even when a fusion eventuates it takes place under the conditions determined by the resistance developed and the relative strength of the several cultural components.

Indeed, the evidence shows most cultures to be highly composite. Sometimes there seems to be a race relatively pure physically with a considerably mixed culture, sometimes, perhaps more frequently, a highly mixed race with a relatively fused culture. But in the large majority of cases the culture is only to be explained as the resultant of the meeting and reciprocal influence of several culture strains, several ethnic contributions. Such facts nullify two of the most prevalent popular and scientific fallacies, the ascription of a total culture to any one ethnic strain, and the interpretation of culture in terms of the intrinsic rather than the fusion values of its various constituent elements. Especially does this newer view insist upon the disassociation of the claims of political dominance and cultural productivity, and combat the traditional view that all or even the best elements of a culture are the contribution of the ethnic group which in a mixed culture has political dominance and is in dynastic control. Already a number of such politically proprietary claims have been disallowed and disestablished by the more intensive and objectively comparative study of culture-traits. Such procedure promises to redeem the fields of discussion which till recently have been so vitiated by racial and national bias that some ethnologists have been led to conclude the impossibility of the scientific evaluation of cultures. After all, the failure to maintain objective standards, relevant values, and parity of values ought not be taken as evidence that this is not possible. So great is the tendency to lapse back into the former positions of bias, that the rigid maintenance of objective description as the sole aim of the ethnologist may, however, be fully warranted for the time being.

But races may, and must eventually be compared with respect to their relative and characteristic abilities and tendencies with respect to cultural origins, cultural assimilation, cultural survival, and their concrete institutional contributions. But in every case absolute objective parity of condition and values must be maintained. An instance in point is Lowie's [14] own illustration in a discussion of the relative rating of cultures on the basis of cultural originality and assimilation. He says: "If the Japanese deserve no credit for having appropriated our culture, we must also carefully eliminate from that culture all elements not demonstrably due to the creative genius of our race before laying claim to the residue as our distinctive product." This seems simple enough to be axiomatic, yet as a principle of comparison one can find in treatise after treatise a score of breaches for every single observance of what ought to be a fundamental procedure. Irrelevant evaluation and invidious comparisons that do not even make the pretense of establishing either parity or equivalence of values abound, yet it is not to be corrected by excluding values, but rather through insistence upon the only properly scientific criteria—intrinsic values for the interpretation of any culture, and strictly commensurate or equivalent values as a basis of comparisons between them.

The chief source of error in the evaluation of cultures can be traced as the same source already described as responsible for the prevalent errors in the description of cultures. It is incumbent upon us to see clearly why the evolutionary formula has led in both these instances to such unsoundness of interpretation. It would seem that by putting all types and varieties into the same series, and this is the crux of the straight evolutionary point of view, the error of assuming basic common factors and commensurate values has almost irretrievably been made. Not that such factors may not exist, but that they are not to be discovered except from the point of view of a more objective and detailed comparison than has in most cases been attempted. Since the days of the Indo-Germanic myth, and its twin fancy the Aryan hypothesis, the desire and suppressed objective in many investigations has been to build a social pyramid of straight line progressive stages, and subtle variations of this point of view have been introducing error upon error into the interpretation of cultures, especially primitive and alien cultures which have naturally borne the brunt of the scheme through having been distorted and pinched into alignment with the pre-conceived formula.[15] We have a clear and succinct statement of the responsibility in this regard in the following passage:[16]

The earlier anthropologists and sociologists, swayed by the biological theories of evolution, posited parallel development in every people, following upon innate psychological tendencies. Complete systems, with stages of development culminating in our own particular type of civilization, were posited by such early writers as Morgan, Spencer, Tylor and others. However, it has been found that the other cultural mechanism, that of diffusion, constituted a grave stumbling block to this a priori scheme of stage development, and it is now known that independent origins of inventions are infinitely more rare than was believed, and that they are conditioned not by innate psychological tendencies, but by the cultural milieu in which they occur.

Gradually it has become apparent that the procedure of using primitive cultures as the stock arguments and illustrations for societal evolution has disorganized the organic unity of these cultures, and merely used certain aspects of them as illustrating a comparative series which even if it were correct for the institution in question from which the accentuated culture-elements were taken, would not place correctly in scale as totalities the cultures respectively in question.

It follows then that the work of correction will have to begin at the very point where originally the errors and distortions have been introduced, namely, the more carefully objective study and organic interpretation of primitive cultures. This would be necessary from the purely corrective point of view, even if it were not also true as Wissler[17] says that "our clearest insight into the mechanisms of culture is attained when we examine the more primitive marginal cultures of the world." After the application of the reconstructed notion of race as social in manifestation and derivation, this would seem to be the most important and promising revision of idea and method in the entire field of our discussion. As a straight methodological question then we get the following as the only correct and acceptable procedure in the study of any given culture—first, its analytic and complete description in terms of its own culture-elements, second, its organic interpretation in terms of its own intrinsic values as a vital mode of living, combined if possible with an historical account of its development and derivation, and then finally and not till then its assignment to culture-type and interpretation as a stage of culture. Almost any culture so treated will be found to be radically different both in description and evaluation from that account which would have been given it if immediately submitted on first analysis to the general scale and to universal comparison. Let us call this the *principle of organic interpretation* and the other the *principle of cultural relativity,* and conclude that in combination with the dynamic and social interpretation of race, the three are the methodological foundation and platform of the newer science of social culture. Especially in connection with the concept of race are all of the biased and partisan points of view and scales of evaluation obviated by such procedure so that it becomes possible to continue the term scientifically and usefully in the context of discussion to which it is most relevant, but into which until recently it has introduced primarily serious errors both of fact and of value.

NOTES

1. R. H. Lowie, *Culture and Ethnology*, Chap. II, 1923.
2. Franz Boas, *The Mind of Primitive Man*, (1911); W. M. Flinders-Petrie, *Race and Civilization* (Proc. Brit. Assoc., 1895); Jean Finot, *Race Prejudice* (Trans. 1907); W. D. Babington, *Fallacies of Race Theories*; Hertz, *Moderne Rassentheorien*; I. von Zollschan, *Das Rassenproblem* (Vienna, 1912).
3. A. Goldenweiser, *Early Civilization*, Chap. I. pp. 14–15.
4. de Gobineau, *Essai sur l'inegalite des races humains* (Paris, 1854).
5. [The reference is probably to R. H. Lowie, *Culture and Ethnology.*]
6. R. H. Lowie, *Culture and Ethnology*, p. 41.
7. E. Sapir, "Culture, Genuine and Spurious." *American Journal of Sociology* 29, p. 406.
8. *Ibid.*, pp. 405–406.
9. Wissler, C., *Man and Culture* (1923).

10. Flinders-Petrie, *Race and Civilization* (Proc. Brit. Assoc., 1895).

11. Gault, R. H., *Social Psychology* (New York, 1923), p. 104.

12. Goldenweiser, *Early Civilization*, p. 14.

13. Compare Rivers, W. H., *Psychology and Ethnology* (London, 1926).

14. Lowie, *Culture and Ethnology*, pp. 32–33.

15. Compare Goldenweiser, Chap. I and p. 125.

16. Herskovits and Willey, "The Cultural Approach to Sociology," *American Journal of Sociology* 29, p. 195.

17. Wissler, *Man and Culture*, p. 286.

17. The Contribution of Race to Culture

The question this article answers is whether the
advantages of cultural differentiations are possible
without the disadvantages of chauvinism and
prejudice. By "internationalism" Locke means a world
that prioritizes what humans have in common. This
would mean for Locke the end of the subjugation of
cultural peculiarities in the service of industrialization,
routinization of work, and the according of not
only status but legitimacy to the cultural modalities
of ruling classes. Locke justifies his promotion of
African peoples' cultural idioms and social interests
and provides us with his conception of civilization
and the relation of social race to culture. This article
provides the characteristic argument Locke tenders in
future articles on the same topic such as "The Negro's
Contribution to American Art and Literature," *Annals
of the Academy of Political and Social Science* 140
(1928), 234–247. Of particular note is his "The
Negro's Contribution to American Culture," *Journal
of Negro Education* 8 (July 1939), 521–529, which
argues against abandoning appreciation of racial
particularities in favor of a color-blind universalism.

"The Contribution of Race to Culture," *The Student World* 23
(1930), 349–353.

The Contribution of Race to Culture

The proposition that race is an essential factor in the growth and development of culture, and expresses culturally that phenomenon of variation and progressive differentiation so apparently vital on the plane of the development of organic nature, faces a pacifist and an internationalist with a terrific dilemma, and a consequently difficult choice. Even so, granted that race has been such a factor in human history, would you today deliberately help perpetuate its idioms at the cost of so much more inevitable sectarianism, chauvinistic prejudice, schism and strife? It amounts to this, then, can we have the advantages of cultural differences without their obvious historical disadvantages? For we must remember that national and racial prejudices have been all through history concurrent with such traditional differences, and have grown up from the roots of the engendered feelings of proprietorship and pride.

History has made this question a grave dilemma. Or rather the chauvinistic interpretation of history,—which is orthodox. Theoretically the question can be straddled; but practically it is time to front-face the sharp paradoxes of the situation, even at the risk of being impaled. The issue is particularly unavoidable in our day when we have side by side with our conscious and growing internationalism a resurgence everywhere of the spirit of nationalism and the principle of the autonomy and self-determination of national and racial groups. We have carried the principle into the inner boundaries of many nations, and have aroused expectant and clamorous minorities, where before there were repressed and almost suffocated minor groups.

Personally I belong to such a minority, and have had some part in the revival of its suppressed hopes; but if I thought it irreconcilable with the future development of internationalism and the approach toward universalism to foster the racial sense, stimulate the racial consciousness and help revive the lapsing racial tradition, I would count myself a dangerous reactionary, and be ashamed of what I still think is a worthy and constructive cause.

The answer to this dilemma, in my opinion, lies behind one very elemental historical fact, long ignored and oft-forgotten. There is and always has been an almost limitless natural reciprocity between cultures. Civilization, for all its claims of distinctiveness, is a vast amalgum of cultures. The difficulties of our social creeds and practices have arisen in great measure from our refusal to recognise this fact. In other words it has been the sense and practice of the vested ownership of culture goods which has been responsible for the tragedies of history and for the paradoxes of scholarship in this matter. It is not the facts of the existence of race which are wrong, but our attitudes toward those facts. The various creeds of race have been falsely predicated. The political crimes of nations are perpetuated and justified in the name of race; whereas in many instances the cultural virtues of race are falsely appropriated by nationalities. So that in the resultant confusion, if we argue for raciality as a desirable thing, we seem to argue for the present practice of nations and to sanction the pride and prejudice of past history. Whereas, if we condemn these things, we seem close to a rejection of race as something useful in human life and desirable to perpetuate.

But do away with the idea of proprietorship and vested interest,—and face the natural fact of the limitless interchangeableness of culture goods, and the more significant historical facts of their more or less constant exchange, and we have, I think, a solution reconciling nationalism with internationalism, racialism with universalism. But it is not an easy solution,—for it means the abandonment of the use of the idea of race as a political instrument, perhaps the second most potent ideal sanction in the creed of the Western nations—the "Will of God" and the "good of humanity" being the first. But we are in a new era of social and cultural relationships once we root up this fiction and abandon the vicious practice of vested proprietary interests in various forms of culture, attempting thus in the face of the natural reciprocity and our own huge indebtedness, one to the other, to trade unequally in proprietary and aggressive ways. There are and always will be specialised group superiorities; it is the attempt to capitalise these by a politics of civilisation into theoretical and practical group supremacies which has brought the old historical difficulties.

Freed from this great spiritual curse, the cult of race is free to blossom almost indefinitely to the enrichment and stimulation of human culture. On the grand scale, as between East and West,—European, Asiatic, African; and on the small scale as well, within the borders of our political units, as the self-expression and spiritual solidarity of minorities. I have often thought that the greatest obstacle that has prevented the world from realizing unity has been a false conception of what unity itself meant in this case. It is a notion, especially characteristic of the West, that to be one effectively, we must all be alike and that to be at peace, we must all have the same interests. On the contrary, apart from the practical impossibility of such uniformity, and its stagnant undesirability, we have, in the very attempt to impose it, the greatest disruptive force active in the modern world today.

That way, with its implications of "superior" and "inferior," "dominant" and "backward," "legitimate" and "mongrel," is the path of reactionism and defeat. If this all too-prevalent psychology is to survive, then it is a modern crime to encourage minorities and preserve races, either in the physical or the cultural sense; for one is only multiplying the factors of strife and discord. But the modern world is doing just these things, hoping meanwhile for internationalism, peace and world cooperation. It is easier, and more consistent to change our false psychology than to stem the rising tide of resurgent minorities, which have every right and reason for self-expression which the older established majorities ever had; and in addition the moral claims of compensation. The new nations of Europe, Zionism, Chinese and Indian Nationalism, the awakened American Negro and the awakening Africa have progressed too much to be pushed back or snuffed out. The revision of thought which we are speaking about now as an ideal possibility, tomorrow will be a practical necessity, unless history is tragically to repeat itself in terms of other huge struggles for dominance and supremacy. The best chance for a new world lies in a radical revision of this root-idea of culture, which never was soundly in accordance with the facts, but which has become so inveterate that it will require a mental revolution to change it.

For a moment let us look at some of its anomalies, Missionarism, so dear to our Western hearts, is one of them, and one of the gravest. The very irony of self-asserted superiority and supremacy of an adopted Oriental religion turned against the Oriental world as an instrument of political and cultural aggression ought to chasten the spirit of a rational Christianity. Or, to take another instance, the Aryan myth has no validity if political expediency demands a rationalization of the domination of an Asiatic branch of Aryans by a European branch of Aryans. America, for example, appropriates as characteristically "American" the cultural products of their Negroes, while denying them civic and cultural equality. A North Teutonic tribe, with a genius for organisation, appropriates a Palatinate culture-history and what was largely a South German culture, and sets out to dominate the world under its aegis. These are typical anomalies. And they are not cited in a spirit of accusation. They could be matched for almost every nation or race or creed, and are cited, to prove by the force of their mutual self-contradiction, their common underlying fallacy. Shall the new nations, the insurgent minorities, the awakening races adopt the same psychology, advance in the name of their race or nation the same claims, avow the same antiquated sanctions? Inevitably,—unless there is rapid and general repudiation of the basic idea, and a gradual but sincere abandonment of the old politic of cultural aggression and proprietary culture interests. We began by talking about the cult of race—but this is not beside the point. For the cult of race is dangerous and reactionary if the implications of the old creeds of race are not disposed of or revised. There can be two sorts of modern self-determination,—one with the old politic of revenge and aggressive self-assertion, another with a new politic of creative individuality and cultural reciprocity.

With this new ideology lies the only hope for combining the development of a greater solidarity of civilisation successfully with a period of greater intensification and fresh creativeness in our individual cultures. Divorced from the political factors, this is possible. It is not an accident that Switzerland is the foster home of internationalism. By good historical fortune it has arrived at culturally neutral nationhood, and so is a prototype of the reconstructed nationality of the future. We may just as naturally have several nations sharing a single culture, as, on the other hand, have several cultures within a single nation. But we must revert to the natural units of culture, large or small, rather than try to outrival one another, like Aesop's ox-emulating frogs, in these artificially inflated, politically motivated cultures. Let us notice that the same motive is responsible for two sorts of cultural violence, not always associated in the common mind,—external aggression for building up artificial combinations for the sake of power and size, arbitrary internal repressions for the sake of dominance and uniformity.

To summarize, the progress of the modern world demands what

may be styled "free-trade in culture," and a complete recognition of the principle of cultural reciprocity. Culture-goods, once evolved, are no longer the exclusive property of the race or people that originated them. They belong to all who can use them; and belong most to those who can use them best. But for all the limitless exchange and transplanting of culture, it cannot be artificially manufactured; it grows. And so far as I can understand history, it is always a folk-product, with the form and flavor of a particular people and place, that is to say, for all its subsequent universality, culture has root and grows in that social soil which, for want of a better term, we call "race."

18. Who and What is "Negro"?

One of the most difficult features of Locke's complex
explication of race and culture is his insistence that
they were not always identical. "The fallacy of the
'new' as of the 'older' thinking is that there is a type
Negro who, either qualitatively or quantitatively, is
the type symbol of the entire group. To break arbitrary
stereotypes it is necessary perhaps to bring forward
counter-stereotypes, but none are adequate substitutes
for the whole truth." The counterstereotypes Locke
refers to are the simplistic pictures of blacks as
emotive and spiritual that are the dominant images
of blacks in his *The New Negro* (1925). Locke was
promoting black proletarian folk art at the writing
of this article, but not because it represented the
"real Negro." What makes a work of art or literature
Negro, that is, socially African or Afro-American,
are primarily its main theme, idiom, style, and form,
which are not biological products, unchanging social
phenomena, or the necessary property of a race.

Locke explores how artistic works are characterized
as peculiarly Negro African because of their theme,
author, or idiom. Negro art, as a social medium for
Locke, is continually engaged in a search for what is
truly Negro. The search is itself one of the defining
characteristics of Afro-centric art.

This is the last yearly retrospective review of black
literature Locke wrote for *Opportunity*. He argued in
"Jingo, Counter-Jingo and Us: Retrospective Review

"Who and What is 'Negro'?" *Opportunity* 20 (1942), 36–41, 83–
87. Reprinted by permission of The National Urban League.

of the Literature of the Negro: 1937," *Opportunity* 16 (January-February 1938), 7–11, 27, 39–42, that focusing on black contributions to civilization was not a form of ethnic chauvinism or harmful to the unity of workers. In "Jingo, Counter-Jingo and Us" he was arguing against Bernard Stolberg's "Minority Jingo," a review of Benjamin Brawley's *Negro Builders and Heroes* in the *Nation*, October 23, 1937. Locke had also argued against Richard Wright's characterization of the Negro as a function of folk art in "Freedom Through Art: A Review of Negro Art, 1870–1938," *The Crisis* 45 (July 1938), 227–229. Locke's argument in "The Contribution of Race to Culture" for the legitimacy of differentiation and unity without uniformity, provides a basis for entering into an explication of a particular group.

Who and What is "Negro"?

PART I

A Janus-faced question, "who and what is Negro"—sits like a perennial sphinx at the door of every critic who considers the literature
or the art of the Negro. One may appease it, as many do, with literary honey-cakes and poppy-seed, but hackneyed clichés and non-
committal concepts only postpone the challenge. Sooner or later the
critic must face the basic issues involved in his use of risky and perhaps untenable terms like "Negro art" and "Negro literature," and
answer the much-evaded question unequivocally,—who and what is
Negro?

This year our sphinx, so to speak, sits in the very vestibule with
almost no passing space; for several of the most important books of
1941 pose this issue unavoidably. It is useless to throw the question
back at the sociologist or the anthropologist, for they scarcely know
themselves, having twin sphinxes in their own bailiwicks. Indeed it
is a pertinent question in its own right whether the racial concept
has any legitimate business in our account of art. Granted even that
folks are interested in "Negro art" and "Negro literature," and that
some creative artists consciously accept such a platform of artistic
expression, it is warrantable to ask whether they should and whether
it should be so. After all, mayn't we be just the victims of an ancient
curse of prejudice in these matters and so, unwittingly blind partisans
of culture politics and its traditional factionalisms?

Let us take first the question "Who is Negro," provocatively
posed by the challenging foreword of Richard Wright's *Twelve Million Black Voices*. "This text," he says,

while purporting to render a broad picture of the processes of Negro life in
the United States, intentionally does not include in its considerations those
areas of Negro life which comprise the so-called "Talented Tenth," or the
isolated islands of mulatto leadership which are still to be found in many
parts of the South, or the growing middle-class professional and business
men of the North who have, in the past thirty years or more, formed a certain liaison corps between the whites and the blacks. Their exclusion from
these pages does not imply any invidious judgment, nor does it stem from
any desire to underestimate their progress and contributions; they are omit-
ted in an effort to simplify a depiction of a complex movement of debased

feudal folk toward a twentieth-century urbanization. This text assumes that those few Negroes who have lifted themselves, through personal strength, talent or luck, above the lives of their fellow-blacks—like single fishes that leap and flash for a split second above the surface of the sea—are but fleeting exceptions to that vast tragic school that swims below in the depths, against the current, silently and heavily, struggling against the waves of vicissitudes that spell a common fate. It is not, however, to celebrate or exalt the plight of the humble folk who swim in the depths that I select the conditions of their lives as examples of normality, but rather to seize upon that which is qualitatively and abiding in Negro experience, to place within full and constant view the collective humanity whose triumphs and defeats are shared by the majority, whose gains in security mark an advance in the level of consciousness attained by the broad masses in their costly and tortuous upstream journey.

Here is a clear and bravely worded challenge. Who is the real Negro? Well, not only the mass Negro as over against both the culturally "representative" elite or Talented Tenth and the "exceptional" or "untypical" few of the bourgeoisie, but that "mass Negro" who in spite of the phrase about what is "qualitative and abiding in Negro experience," is common denominator proletarian rather than racially distinctive. For all its local and racial color, then, this approach practically scraps the racial factor as inconsequential and liquidates that element culturally as well as sociologically.

As I shall say later, this is an important book, a valuable social analysis, dramatically exposed and simplified, more than that,—a sound working hypothesis for the proletarian artist who has a right to his artistic *Weltanschauung*. But a school of thought or art or social theory that lays claim to totalitarian rectitude must, I think, be challenged. The fallacy of the "new" as of the "older" thinking is that there is a type Negro who, either qualitatively or quantitatively, is the type symbol of the entire group. To break arbitrary stereotypes it is necessary perhaps to bring forward counter-stereotypes, but none are adequate substitutes for the whole truth. There is, in brief, no "*The Negro.*" More and more, even as we stress the right of the mass Negro to his important place in the picture, artistically and sociologically, we must become aware of the class structure of the Negro population, and expect to see, hear and understand the intellectual elite, the black bourgeoisie as well as the black masses. To this common stratification is added in the Negro's case internal splits resulting from differential response to particular racial stresses and strains, divergent loyalties which, in my judgment, constitute racial distinctiveness, not by some magic of inheritance but through some very obvious environmental conditionings. For just as we have, for comparative example, the orthodox and the assimilate, the Zionist and anti-Zionist Jew, so in Negro life we have on practically all of these levels, the conformist and the non-conformist strains,—the conformist elite and the racialist elite, the lily-white and the race-patriotic bourgeois, the folk and the ghetto peasant and the emerging Negro proletarian. Each is a significant segment of Negro life, and as they severally come to articulate expression, it will be increasingly apparent that each is a representative facet of Negro life and experience. For a given decade one or the other may seem more significant or "representative," chiefly as it may succeed to the historical spotlight or assume a protagonist role in group expression or group movement. However, as our historical perspective lengthens and our social insight deepens, we should no longer be victims of the still all-too-prevalent formula psychology. Common denominator regional and national traits are there to be taken into account, as are also, more and more as overtones, the factors of group and racial distinctiveness. In cultural and creative expression, the flavor of idiom seems to count especially, which to me seems a valid reason for not scraping the racialist emphasis, provided of course, it does not proceed to the isolationist extreme of ghetto compartmentalization. But more important even than this emphasis is the necessity of an objective but corrective insistence on the variety of Negro types and their social and cultural milieu.

Turning to the other basic question,—what is Negro, we may ask ourselves what makes a work of art Negro, if indeed any such nomenclature is proper,—its authorship, its theme or its idiom? Different schools of criticism are obviously divided on these criteria. Each has had its inning, and probably no one regrets the comparative obsolescence of the artificial separatist criterion of Negro authorship. Only in the hectic early striving for credit and recognition could it be forgotten that the logical goal of such a viewpoint is an artistic Ghetto of "Negro art" and "Negro literature," isolated from the common cultural heritage and the vital and necessary fraternalisms of school and generation tendencies. The editors of the brilliantly panoramic anthology, *The Negro Caravan*, pose the issue this way:

> In spite of such unifying bonds as a common rejection of the popular stereo-types and a common racial cause, writings by Negroes do not seem to the editors to fall into a unique cultural pattern. Negro writers have adopted the literary traditions that seemed useful for their purposes. They have therefore been influenced by Puritan didacticism, sentimental humanitarianism, local color, regionalism, realism, naturalism, and experimentalism. . . . The editors do not believe that the expression "Negro literature" is an accurate one, and in spite of its convenient brevity, they have avoided using it. "Negro literature" has no application if it means structural peculiarity, or a Negro school of writing. The Negro writes in the forms evolved in English and American literature. A "Negro novel," "a Negro play" are ambiguous terms. If they mean a novel or play by Negroes, then such works as *Porgy* and *The Green Pastures* are left out. If they mean works about Negro life, they include more works by white authors than by Negro, and these works have been most influential upon the American mind. The editors consider Negro writers to be American writers, and literature by American Negroes to be a segment of American literature. . . . The chief cause for objection to the term is that Negro literature is too easily placed by certain critics, white and Negro, in an alcove apart. The next step is a double standard of judgment, which is dangerous for the future of Negro writers.

Again, these are brave and necessary words. But there is a trace in them of corrective counter-emphasis, and the objective truth lies probably somewhere between, as indeed the dual significance of the anthology itself evidences. Simultaneously, a segment of American literature and a special chapter of racial expression and reaction, most of the materials in this same anthology have a double character as well as a double significance. The logical predicament is in not seeing the complete compatibility between nationally and racially distinctive elements, arising from our over-simplified and chauvinistic conception of culture. Neither national nor racial cultural elements are so distinctive as to be mutually exclusive. It is the general composite character of culture which is disregarded by such over-simplifications. By that logic, a typical American character could never have been expected as a modification of English artistic and institutional culture, but there it is, after some genera-tions of divergence, characteristically Anglo-Saxon and American at the same time. Strictly speaking, we should consistently cite this composite character in our culture with hyphenate descriptions, but more practically, we stress the dominant flavor of the blend. It is only in this same limited sense that anything is legitimately styled "Negro"; actually it is Afro- or Negro-American, a hybrid product of Negro reaction to American cultural forms and patterns. And when, as with many of our Negro cultural products, it is shared in the common cultural life,—our jazz music, as a conspicuous example,—it becomes progressively even more composite and hybridized, sometimes for the better, sometimes not. For we must abandon the idea of cultural purism as a criterion under the circumstances just as we have abandoned the idea of a pure race under the more scientific and objective scrutiny of the facts of history.

Thus the interpenetration of national and racial characteristics, once properly understood, resolves the traditional dilemma of the racialists and on the cultural level puts an essential parity on racial, national and regional idioms. As the point of view matures, perhaps we shall regard all three as different dimensions of cultural variation, interchangeably blended in specific art forms and combinations. Such reciprocity actually exists, and would have been recognized but for our politically minded notions of culture, which flatter majority strains in our culture and minimize minority culture elements. As a matter of fact, the racial evolves by special emphasis from the general cultural heritage and in turn flows back into the common culture. With neither claiming more than its proper due, no such invidious and peculiar character accrues to the racial, and, on such a basis, it should not be necessary to play down the racial contribution in order to prove the essential cultural solidarity of Negro creative effort with American art and letters. The position leads, if soundly developed, not to cultural separatism but to cultural pluralism. To be "Negro" in the cultural sense, then, is not to be radically different, but only to be distinctively composite and idiomatic, though basically American, as is to be expected, in the first instance.

According to such criteria, the critic has, like the chemist, the analytical job of breaking down compounds into their constituent culture elements. So far as characterization goes, this involves the task of assessing the accent of representativeness among the varying regional, racial and national elements. Theme and idiom would bulk more significantly than source of authorship, and important expressions of Negro material and idiom by white authors would belong as legitimately in a Negro as in a general anthology.

Turning to the novels of the year, the most publicized of them all, Mrs. Wheaton's *Mr. George's Joint*, Jefferson Prize Award winner, turns out by my analysis as Negro in theme only but unrepresentative in idiom, despite its laboriously studied local color and dialect. It is comforting to learn that since the decision, the editor of the *Virginia Quarterly Review* has disavowed further responsibility for the award series. Far too often, as in this case, meticulous photographic reporting passes in these days of realism for vital interpretation. At best a second-rate regional novel of small-town Texan life, there is nothing deeply interpretative of Negro life in the book; there is more insight in single short stories of Faulkner or Caldwell, who know how to find the human significance of the sordid and otherwise trivial.

Julian Rayford's *Cottonmouth*, however, for all its slight sketchiness, has much of the genuine feel and tempo of the deep South, and an emotional insight into Negro-white relationships. The regional Southern novel has not had a particularly good yield: only Idwal Jones' *Black Bayou* and the late William Percy's *Lanterns on the Levee* approach any close companionship with the previous high levels in this genre. In initiating a new approach, Arthur Kuhl's *Royal Road* is significant, but it is scarcely a full realization of its potentialities at that. A melodrama with dimensions of moral symbolism, it fails to convince either in the realistic vein or in its symbolic overtone. And so the tragedy of Jesse Stewart, born of Mary and Joseph in Bethlehem, Pa., scarcely warrants the atonement motive insinuated into a sad story of persecution, false witness and miscarriage of judicial procedure. The social forces responsible are not sufficiently delineated; so that Jesse's electrocution seems more a bizarre accident than a racial tragedy.

William Attaway's *Blood on the Forge*, however, fully evokes its milieu and also most of its characters. The story of the three Morse brothers, temperamentally so different, tragically caught in the slum-ghetto of a Pennsylvania steel-mill town, fighting rather blindly the tides of labor feuds just as they had previously struggled with the tragic precariousness of their Kentucky sharecropper farm is a contribution to the still small stock of Negro social analysis fiction.

The stock of slave-trade fiction, with its romantic appeal is, on the contrary, overfull. As these lurid historical canvasses multiply, one marvels at the general state of the reading public that apparently so avidly consumes them. *The Sun Is My Undoing* promises to become another *Gone With the Wind* sensation. Interspersed with its romance and adventure is some rather unorthodox truth about the slave trade's social complications, its intrigue, concubinage and miscegenation, but the endless rehearsing of these particular chapters of history seems worse than gratuitous. *The Unquiet Field* is a much more sober and integrated account of the same materials, but it will in all likelihood be much less popular than its glamorous competitor.

With the postponement of Langston Hughes's *Shakespeare in Harlem*, the poetry output dwindles to almost negligible proportions. Several books of verse in the category of children's verse will be considered later; and even Arna Bontemps' *Golden Slippers* anthology is gauged for youthful readers, with emphasis on the lighter lyric vein. He has nevertheless had the taste to include principally the better poets, so that the book becomes an acceptable anthology of the lighter genre apart from age limitations. Surely the poetic lull must have some other explanation than a creative drought; probably the disinclination of publishers to venture verse publication for "fledgling" poets, but just possibly also the distraction and disillusionment prevailing in the ranks of Negro youth.

One of the major contributions of the year thus becomes the very comprehensive and much needed anthology of Negro authors in all the literary forms which Sterling Brown, Arthur Davis and Ulysses Lee have collated in *The Negro Caravan*. Here is definitive editing of the highest order, combined with authoritative historical and critical annotation. For years to come it will be the indispensable handbook for the study of the Negro's contribution to the literature of the Negro. In the critical introductions to the various literary types, brief mention is wisely added to give some notion of the important correlation of Negro creative effort with that of white authors treating Negro themes; which somewhat offsets the inconsistency of the anthology's non-racialist critical platform and its actual restriction to Negro authorship.

Steig's *Send Me Down* is a very authentic and penetrating analysis of Negro jazz and jazz-makers, proving that in competent hands even the picturesque side of Negro life can be instructively presented. In blatant contrast is the elaborate but superficial *Harlem* of Saroyan and Albert Hirschfeld. The flippancy, both literary and artistic, is condescending, and though the types have changed in the decade that has elapsed, Miguel Covarrubias's *Negro Drawings* still remain the unchallenged superior version of Harlem types and atmospheres. Hirschfeld has caught only surface values, with little psychological or social penetration; clever as caricatures, his drawings only occasionally [are] apt as type portraiture.

Victor Lawson's maiden critical effort is a very competent analysis of Dunbar as man and poet; the one from a not too insistent or enlightening psycho-analytic approach and the other from a rather illuminating analysis of the strains of sentimental romanticism from which his literary pedigree derives. The study quite outdistances the only other extant critical study and biography of this poet, and should supersede it with students of Dunbar or his period of race poetry.

In the field of drama, the joint version of *Native Son* by Richard Wright and Paul Green is the highpoint of the dramatic crop. Oddly enough the climaxes of the drama toward the close die down to dramatic monologues and tableau, while earlier scenes are electric with the best of both drama and melodrama. This only accentuates in some ways the faults of the novel itself, which is more skillfully contrived in its earlier chapters. But no dimuendo of values in the sequence can stifle the power and veracity of the material, which after all is one of the most incisive versions of contemporary Negro life and its social implications. The success of the drama with audiences of all types has already demonstrated the importance of such frank veracity and such uncompromising vitality.

Shirley Graham's full length drama of the West Virginia coal mines, *Dust to Earth*, was elaborately presented by the Yale University Theatre group. Its social background reporting is unfortunately overlaid by a melodramatic plot interest which does not gain force by the defeatist sacrifice of the hero, a denouement which decidedly takes the edge off a play that could have been a pioneering essay in Negro labor tragedy. Our dramatists have on the whole not yet shaken off the timidity which once so banefully beset our novelists. In *On Strivers Row*, Abram Hill has written a good groundbreaking excursion into social comedy. It still remains to be seen what success this type of play will have with Negro audiences, who have yet to become conditioned to dramatic self-criticism. It is to be hoped that the Harlem Peoples Theater will have eventual success in so obvious a need of the Negro drama.

PART II

Neither history nor sociology nor even anthropology have as yet any definitive answer to our eternal question. But they are steadily though not directly approaching that goal. Progress toward such an objective, it seems, cannot follow the bee-line, but must go, like the sailboat, on a tactical course, now overshooting the mark and tacking back on a counter zig-zag in the other direction. Out of successive emphases and from the polemical clash of differing interpretations, we are finally getting where the objective truth about the Negro can be pieced together and put into a clear and meaningful perspective.

In what is one of the richest seasons of sociological yield, we have in the factual literature of 1941 several cases in point,—as an important historical example, the corrective counter-statements of Buckmaster's unconventional history of the anti-slavery movement, *Let My People Go*; or in the sociological field, the unorthodox approaches and conclusions of the current American Youth Commission studies of Negro youth; or again, in the case of anthropology, the provocative counter-statements of Herskovits' *The Myth of the Negro Past*. The older commonplaces about the Negro are being challenged on every hand, and the last phase,—let us hope, of the generation-long polemics of race theory is coming to a head. As I have already stated, there is often over-emphasis and over-simplification in these new provocative counter-statements; and they, too, in many cases lack the full objectivity and final equilibrium of the ultimate truth. However, they are far more objective and realistic than the points of view and theories which they challenge and threaten to displace or modify, and unlike them, are not grounded either in majority bias or minority apologetics. Two very vital requisites for scientific objectivity and final truth are rapidly establishing themselves,—race scholarship is shedding its protective sentimentalities and apologetic bias, while white scholarship, on the other hand, both by more sympathetic penetration and through wise interracial collaboration, is getting almost for the first time an "inside" view of Negro life. Such collaboration, in fact, is becoming the order of the day, as will be even more apparent when the full series of the Carnegie-Myrdal monographs becomes published. The American Youth Commission series is another notable example of this warrantable and fruitful type of collaborative study.

As such scholarship matures, scientific integration removes more and more the isolation and the "peculiar" uniqueness of the Negro's situation and its problems. Common denominator forces and factors are increasingly used to explain and interpret Negro life. The *en bloc* conceptions of the Negro are breaking down gradually into proper and realistic recognition of the diversifications as circumstances and environment vary from place to place, or from generation to generation. Both sociologists and anthropologists are beginning to recognize the complementary effect of the Negro on whites as well as the effects of the white on the Negro; class stratification among Negroes is at last being taken into serious account, and general economic and social factors are coming to the fore as transcending in influence the traditionally "racial." A book like *Color and Human Nature*, as last year's *Children of Bondage*, introduces the welcome novelty of the case study approach and psycho-analytic interpretation, as well as the diversification of individuality alongside those of class stratification and type of community environment. *Thus Be Their Destiny* specifically stresses community structure and the part it plays in racial and interracial reactions. *Color, Class and Personality* not only takes into account all these vital variables, but poses the basic problems of Negro youth over the common denominator of the cognate issues in the life of American youth generally. Community studies of the Negro, like that on the *New Haven Negroes*, wisely styled a "social history," take on increasingly what the Chicago school calls an "ecological" approach, that is, revealing the influence on the Negro of the immediate environment and its socioeconomic forces. Indeed some of them treat the Negro condition as one of the significant indices of these common community factors. Even Professor Herskovits' study, in spite of its emphasis, (indeed, I would say, its overemphasis) on the hypothesis of African culture

survivals, uses the Negro as a base for the study of general sociological and cultural phenomena, and thus makes the analysis yield
something beyond the mere explanation of the Negro's own situation in terms of insight into the general nature of social forces and
cultural process. The positive side of *The Myth of The Negro Past*
thus becomes its analysis of the interplay of the forces of cultural survival and assimilation and its evidence about the general character of
acculturation. A book like *When Peoples Meet*, sub-titled "A Study
in Race and Culture Contacts," generalizes even further, and places
the so-called race question in a universal context of culture contacts
and conflicts, emphasizing the common features and forces involved
in majority and minority relations and their interaction on a world
scale. In a period of world crisis, precipitated by a global war, it is
particularly significant and promising when the study of race and
interracial problems broadens out into an integrated analysis, on the
one hand, of basic problems of human group relations and on the
other, of wide-scale comparative study of universal forces in group
interaction.

Henrietta Buckmasters' well documented story of the "Underground Railroad" and the Abolition movement, in addition to being
the most outspoken evaluation of the part played by the Negro himself in the struggle for freedom, rightly stresses the sustained and
widespread collaboration of the white and Negro anti-slavery forces.
Historically authoritative, the narrative is lifted from the level of
dead history to its proper plane of a great national crusade. Even
more than in the previous studies of slave revolts and insurrections,
the figure of the militant Negro is strikingly documented and vindicated in his all too underestimated role of co-author of his own
freedom; the Negro abolitionists, Purvis, Forten, Redmond, Lenox,
Wells Brown, Delaney, Douglass and Harriet Tubman are properly
paired with their white sponsors and collaborators,—Garrison, Tap-
pan, Coffin, Parker, Burney and John Brown. Carrying the same
heroic story, with less documentation and somewhat less accurate
perspective, Anna Curtis' *Stories of the Underground Railroad* performs a similar service for the less sophisticated reader.

In a more traditional historical vein, A. A. Taylor continues his
reconstruction period studies with a factual but not too interpretive
narrative of *The Negro in Tennessee*; important principally for its

documentation of the Negro factors in the politics of a border state. Of decidedly different scope and interpretative power is the social history already mentioned of *New Haven Negroes* by Robert A. Warner. Here, with the aid of obviously competent Negro research assistance, the life story of a Northern Negro community has been illuminatingly told from colonial times to the present day. This is a type of story sorely needed despite the somewhat discouraging revelation in this instance of a group tragedy of economic displacement downward to marginal and less skilled labor, typical, we fear, of the older Northern centers of the Negro population and especially of New England. More and more Negro studies will need, as in this case, to be put on an intensive regional or local basis, both for historical and sociological accuracy and for the correct evaluation of interracial reactions.

Two pioneer chronicles of the history of Wilberforce and Howard Universities open up the lagging field of institutional history. Each garners the materials needed for the definitive histories that must eventually be written of these institutions, which in that case, must discuss them more penetratingly in terms of their contemporary social conditions and educational policies. The Howard narrative, product of a lifetime's avocational interest on the part of Professor Walter Dyson, though cast in the reminiscent "alumni mould," more nearly approaches a generally useful and interesting public chronicle of one of our most important educational centers. In a documentary way, it has performed a very necessary service.

But history has long since outgrown the traditional job of factual chronicling; the modern brand stands or falls by interpretation. In a less traditional, in fact in a provocatively unorthodox vein, Richard Wright has attempted in *Twelve Million Black Voices* a folk history of the Negro. His identification of the mass Negro with the whole historical Negro cause has already been discussed; with the qualified reservation that however over-generalized, a neglected segment of our problem and an important economic analysis of our disadvantaged minority status is not to be ignored. But although such a gift horse is not to be looked at too much askance, from the point of view of a complete and objective historical story the work has to be challenged and taken with the reservations necessary to polemical and *partis pris* interpretations. Frankly stated as a thesis at the outset, the reader knows, however, precisely what assent or discount to apply; certainly Mr. Wright cannot be accused of sailing or riding under false colors.

In the field of biography a wide gamut is covered by a minimum of publications; at least they do not overlap in type. One of the most significant is the timely re-publication by the Pathway Press of one of the few classics of Negro autobiography,—Frederick Douglass's *Life and Times.* Here, of course, we not only have this heroic past and its still pertinent example, but the field of statesmanship and public movements. At the other pole of achievement, we have an intimate and first-hand account of Marian Anderson's mid-career by her friend and accompanist, Kosti Vehanen. This authentic record of her phenomenal and rather sudden international success after years of painstaking preparation becomes a rare item of Negro biography in the field of formal music, and preserves the record in undisputed inside documentation. It also gives us inspiring glimpses of the imperturbable personality around which the exciting drama seems to revolve without considerable change or effect; to the extent that the symbolic element rather than the human eventually dominates the book, particularly with that historically symbolic climax with which the narrative ends,—the Easter Sunday Lincoln Memorial concert.

Quite more earthly and human in its appeal is the chatty, almost garrulous narrative of W. C. Handy, the *Father of the Blues.* Here is the inning of the Negro folk element and its Cinderella story of early persecution and disdain and eventual fame and glory. The riches of that bonanza of jazz and ragtime were not vouchsafed to Mr. Handy, but at least from an authoritative source the Negro credit for the original contribution that Tin Pan Alley and the commercial music trust have all too glibly claimed is set down beyond all dispute and gainsaying. To have accomplished this culminating task of a lifetime of loyal music pioneering is probably one of Mr. Handy's deepest satisfactions as it will also be one of his most appreciated racial services. In quite another field, that of research science, Dr. Maloney contributes the autobiography of a pioneering pharmacologist. Aside from its personal significance, this book will undoubtedly have inspirational value in documenting the possibilities of Negro success in a field that, as a matter of fact, has had considerable achievement, like that of Delaney, Turner, Carver, Hinton, Imes, Julian, and Just, but far too little biographical chronicling.

In the historical chapters of the various state guides sponsored by the Federal and now the State Writers' Projects, from time to time the honorable precedent set at the outset of including the Negro has taken firm root and flourished. With variable interpretative power, but almost without exception, such chapters or passing mention have been a creditable feature of this mounting list of publications that now includes almost every state in the union. Two specialized studies of Negro life, both of folk-lore and folkways, have also appeared this year,—Mason Crum's *Gullah* and the Georgia Project's *Drums and Shadows*. They are both acceptable contributions to the documentation of our folk-lore, though in each case, I think they are too naively primitivist in their interpretation of the materials. They do the invaluable service, whatever reservations will ultimately be placed on the commentary, of collating this material before it vanishes completely. But they reveal the South and the Negro that are vanishing.

The South that is still very much with us, and that remains one of the basic concerns of national reconstruction is presented by another series of books, three of which are definitive studies of prime sociological importance. *Sharecroppers All*, the joint work of Ira Reid and Arthur Raper, in addition to being a sound economic and sociological diagnosis of the breakdown of the Southern rural economy, provides a basis of constructive remedy not merely for the economic nub of the "race problem" but of the much needed economic rehabilitation of the entire South. It finds common factors behind the regional as well as the racial differentials, furnishing scientific confirmation of Booker Washington's instinctive common-sense which expressed itself in the epigrammatic—"You can't hold a man down in the ditch without staying down there with him." The book's bold analysis is matched by its brave prophecy, for on the one hand it frankly says:

The representative of the new South knows that the region is less handicapped by the sharecroppers than by the heritage of the plantation system, less by outside opposition than by inside complacency, less by the presence of the Negro than by the white man's attitude toward him, less by the spectre of class uprisings and Negro domination than by the fear of them

—and then concludes that "the South, by integrating national and community efforts may be able to pay the bills of yesterday's exploitation of land and man, may be able to conserve and use her natural resources and so restore the region to its rightful place in the nation."

With usual statistical thoroughness, but with the implementation of case studies and personality profiles, Dr. Charles S. Johnson adds to his impressive series of studies the latest,—*Growing Up in The Black Belt*. His picture gains an important human dimension thereby, and to the usual analysis of the Southern rural economy is added a picture of a restive, changing though bewildered younger generation. No one reading the analysis can overlook the imminence of momentous psychological change in spite of all the expected provincialisms and inferiority depressions: the almost frightening paradox of a changing Negro in a recalcitrant South that either refuses to change or to recognize change.

The Deep South takes a more academic turn in a painstaking analysis of the structure of what a group of researchers have chosen as the "typical Southern society." As a general thesis the authors emphasize the rigid dominance of the bi-racial "caste system," but in spite of its almost endless documentation have to report from time to time such numerous anomalies and exceptions as almost to invalidate the practical usefulness of this much-mooted "caste theory" for a practical understanding of Southern social code and practise. Both sex and business relations have always had their devious ways of bridging the "great social divide," and the Old South, never any too consistent in its actual practise of race relations, except on the basis of anything pragmatically conducive to dominance and exploitation, should not have been taken so seriously according to the letter of its stock rationalizations. The longer one resides in the South the more conscious one becomes of its inconsistencies and exceptions. Not only more notice should have been taken of these, but also of the forces of insecurity and challenge which the South now faces. Scant attention has been paid, however, to the insecure economic structure of the entire society or to the increasing conflict of economic interests with the traditional social values both among the whites and Negroes. For lack of this, the study is on the whole academic, sterile and retrospective, whereas with emphasis on such economic factors, it could so easily have been enlighteningly diagnostic and practically helpful.

Color and Human Nature, the parallel story of Negro life in an urban industrial center, furnishes, in marked contrast, a vital, dynamic account of what it means to be a Negro in America of today. The basic forces and reactions to which it calls attention are common even to the rural Southern situation which *The Deep South* so dully anatomizes, but in addition, the peculiar stresses of urban competition, of wider class differentiation and of economic and cultural advancement are illuminatingly reported. Nor are the findings too highly generalized, for case reports emphasize both the successful and the unsuccessful accommodations which circumstance and personality introduce into the racial equation. The reader gets the impression that there are important variables of color, class, economic and educational status, and even of sex and personality which defy any mass or even any regional formula, and make of each individual life a rather unpredictable drama of personality development and adjustment in spite of the handicaps of prejudice. Superimposed, one gets, of course, the other side of the picture, a clear knowledge of the group predicament and its resistant, reactionary traditions and limitations. The net result is a balanced sane perspective.

The Myth of the Negro Past, culminating years of painstaking comparative study of the Negro in Africa, North, Central and South America, is inevitably an important book. In line with the progressive wing of anthropological scholarship, it attempts considerable and vindicating revision of traditional conceptions of the Negro. Over against the stereotype of the Negro's childlike, docile character, it documents the little known facts of considerable social and cultural resistance to slave subordination. Against conventional notions of low-grade African stock and of "inferior," negligible culture background, it advances and justifies the facts of biological hardihood, seasoned social discipline and considerable cultural development in the African racial background. It is argued that a knowledge of this cultural background will lessen prejudice and rehabilitate the Negro considerably in American public opinion,—a strangely moralistic corollary, arguing well for the author's humanity but scarcely realistic enough to justify this moralistic departure from scientific objectivity. What is of most value in the book is neither this cultural vindication, salutary as it is for the lay public, black and white, nor this moral reformism, but the broadly gauged analysis of the African background and its widespread linkages with all parts of the American continent through the dispersion of the slave trade. This, as has already been said, is a story of reciprocal cultural interchange and influence, of Negro on white, and white on Negro, and constitutes a pioneer contribution to the ground problems of acculturation as it has affected the African peoples and their Western descendants. In this area, the study is as valuable for the lines of prospective research it forecasts as for those it tentatively summarizes.

But here again, a reformist zeal overemphasizes the thesis of African survivals, transforming it from a profitable working hypothesis into a dogmatic obsession, claiming arbitrary interpretations of customs and folkways which in all common-sense could easily have alternative or even compound explanations. Instead of suggesting the African mores and dispositions as conducive factors along with other more immediate environmental ones, the whole force of the explanation, in many instances, pivots on Africanisms and their sturdy, stubborn survival. The extreme logic of such a position might, as a matter of fact, lead to the very opposite of Dr. Herskovits' liberal conclusions, and damn the Negro as more basically peculiar and unassimilable than he actually is or has proved himself to be. As elsewhere, the truth would seem to be in between either extreme of interpretation, either that of the Negro as the empty-handed, parasitic imitator or that of the incurably atavistic nativist. In fact, because of his forced dispersion and his enforced miscegenation, the Negro must eventually be recognized as a cultural composite of more than ethnic complexity and cultural potentiality.

James Saxon Childers in *Mumbo Jumbo, Esquire* recognizes the same growing complexity in the African. Of Africa today he says: "Any book that limits itself to either the primitive or the modern in Africa is unfair; such a book does not tell the whole story. A reporter must leave the city and go into the jungle, leave the jungle and return to the city; he must travel over paved highways in automobiles and over the desert on camels." Sketchy but highly suggestive, and what is more important, open-minded, this enlightened and enlightening travelogue represents a new symptom of broadened interracial and intercultural understanding. Dr. George Brown's competent *Eco-*

nomic History of Liberia is particularly gratifying, as an American Negro's evaluation of this offshoot of American Negro colonization. The Oxford Press reprint of the Baganda scholar's study of his own people's customary law is equally symptomatic; as is also Professor Schapera's comprehensive study of *Married Life in An African Tribe*, a study of constructive modifications of Kgatla tribal customs after the initial forced changes and disruption of colonial South African contact. Such studies are no longer exotica; they are at the heart of our contemporary problems of world crisis and world reconstruction. Though sentimentally interested as Negroes, we should more and more become interested in these issues as world citizens. The international significance and import of Africa today may very well add another dimension to the experience of being Negro, and lead even to the renovation and enrichment of the all too confused and limited current concept of who and what is Negro.

NOTES

POETRY AND BELLES LETTRES

The Negro Caravan—Sterling Brown, Arthur P. Davis, and Ulysses Lee. New York: Dryden Press.
Golden Slippers—Edited by Arna Bontemps. New York: Harper & Bros.
Harlem—Al Hirschfeld and William Saroyan. New York: Hyperion Press.
Send Me Down—Henry Steig. New York: Alfred A. Knopf.
Dunbar Critically Examined—Victor Lawson. Washington, D.C.: Associated Publishers.

FICTION

Mr. George's Joint—Elizabeth Lee Wheaton. New York: E. P. Dutton & Co.
Cottonmouth—Julian L. Rayford. New York: Charles Scribner's Sons.
Royal Road—Arthur Kuhl. New York: Sheed & Ward.
Blood on the Forge—William Attaway. New York: Doubleday, Doran & Co.
The Sun Is My Undoing—Marguerite Steen. New York: Viking Press.
The Unquiet Field—Beatrice Kean Seymour. New York: Macmillan.

DRAMA

Native Son—Paul Green and Richard Wright. New York: Harper & Bros.
Dust to Earth—Shirley Graham. New Haven, Conn.: Yale University Theatre, Jan., 1941.
On Strivers Row—Abram Hill. New York: Harlem Peoples Theatre, March, 1941.

HISTORY AND BIOGRAPHY

Let My People Go—Henrietta Buckmaster. New York: Harper & Bros.
Stories of the Underground Railroad—Anna L. Curtis. New York: Island Workshop Co-op. Press, Inc.
The Negro in Tennessee, 1865–1880—A. A. Taylor. Washington, D.C.: Associated Publishers.
New Haven Negroes—Robert Austin Warner. New Haven, Conn.: Yale University Press.
A History of Wilberforce University—F. A. McGinnis, Wilberforce, Ohio: Wilberforce Press.
Howard University: A History, 1867–1940—Walter Dyson. Washington, D.C.: Howard University Press.
Twelve Million Black Voices—Richard Wright. Photo-direction by Edwin Rosskam. New York: Viking Press.
Life and Times of Frederick Douglass. New York: Pathway Press.
Father of the Blues: An Autobiography—W. C. Handy. New York: Macmillan.
Marian Anderson—Kosti Vehanen. New York: Whittlesey House.
Amber Gold—Arnold H. Maloney. New York: Wendell Malliet & Co.

EDUCATION AND SOCIOLOGY

Gullah—Mason Crum. Durham, N.C.: Duke University Press.
Drums and Shadows—Georgia Writers' Project. Athens, Ga.: University of Georgia Press.
Sharecroppers All—Arthur Raper and Ira De A. Reid. Chapel Hill, N.C.: University of North Carolina Press.
Growing Up in the Black Belt—Charles S. Johnson. Washington, D.C.: American Council on Education.
Deep South—Allison Davis, Burleigh G. Gardner and Mary R. Gardner. Chicago: University of Chicago Press.
Thus Be Their Destiny—J. Howell Atwood, Donald W. Wyatt, Vincent J.

Davis and Ira D. Walker. Washington, D.C.: American Council on Education.

Color and Human Nature—W. Lloyd Warner, Buford N. Junker, and Walter A. Adams. Washington, D.C.: American Council on Education.

The Negro Federal Government Worker—J. W. Hayes. Washington, D.C.: Howard University Press.

When Peoples Meet—Alain Locke and Bernhard J. Stern. New York: Progressive Education Assn.

The Myth of the Negro Past—Melville J. Herskovits. New York: Harper & Bros.

AFRICANA

Mumbo Jumbo, Esquire—James Saxon Childers. New York: D. Appleton-Century.

Focus on Africa—Richard U. Light. Washington, D.C.: American Geographic Society.

Native African Medicine—George Way Harley, M.D. Cambridge, Mass.: Harvard University Press.

The Customs of the Baganda—Sir Apolo Kagwa. G. Kalibala. New York: Oxford University Press.

Married Life in an African Tribe—I. Schapera. New York: Sheridan House.

The Colour Bar in East Africa—Norman Leys. London: Hogarth Press.

The Economic History of Liberia—George W. Brown. Washington, D.C.: Associated Publishers.

19. Frontiers of Culture

A draft of this article was presented at the thirty-fifth
annual conclave of Phi Beta Sigma Fraternity on
December 28, 1949, at Rankin Memorial Chapel,
Howard University. Locke's conception of culture is
a set of idioms, styles, forms, and temperaments that
are open to adoption but are likely to be developed
and sustained by a given group. An integrationist, and
not an assimilationist, Locke provides in this short
article a critique of the New Negro movement and an
offering for the future. That offering relies on a
"democratic" rather than "aristocratic" notion of
culture. In brief form, Locke presents his view on
the relationship of social race, culture, identity, and
democracy.

"Frontiers of Culture," *The Crescent* 33 (Spring 1950), 37–39. Reprinted courtesy of the Phi Beta Sigma Fraternity.

Frontiers of Culture

I appreciate deeply the very kind introduction and tribute; I also appreciate the opportunity of appearing on this well-planned and inspiring cultural session of the Thirty-fifth Anniversary Conclave of the *Fraternity*. The excellent musical program has provided pure and inspiring pleasure; my own remarks cannot hope to be so unalloyed.

My assigned topic, *The Frontiers of Culture*, was doubtless supposed to tie in appropriately and harmoniously. I hope it may but I warn you that I shall have to set my own key and I am not so sure how harmonious that will be. Certainly it will not be in the traditional close harmony of "barber-shop" tonality so characteristic of old-fashioned fraternal reunions. Neither in time nor place are we assembled tonight "by the fire, by the fire; let it glow, let it glow" with its associated atmosphere of smug self-praise and sentimental satisfaction. The cup of fellowship comes on later; so there is no excuse for mawkishness at this hour. It was suggested that I discuss some of the vistas of modern art in relation to culture. I shall try in doing so to speak my own mind soberly and truthfully; yet certainly with no unusual sense of authority or finality.

WHAT IS CULTURE?

First a word or so about culture itself. It was once a favorite theme-song word with me. Now I wince at its mention and frankly would like to keep silent on the subject—so great have the misconceptions and misuses been. I recall how focal the world culture was for many movements I have been interested and involved in. In fact, I may have had something to do with its appearance in this *Fraternity's* motto: "Culture for Service, Service for Humanity" (I refuse to recall how responsible). We may have thought we knew what it all meant. God knows there was little enough culture either locally or nationally in those distant days; there is still far too little now, as I shall try later to explain. Do not be unduly alarmed: I haven't a tub or a lantern backstage, though as I warned you, I cannot be too pleasant at the expense of the truth as I see it.

Fortunately, one can live without culture, which accounts for the survival of so much both in the past and the present. But I do believe that, though not vital, culture is nevertheless an essential. In fact, after its achievement, it always had and always will rank first; though I am commonsense enough to admit readily the basic importance of bread, with or without butter. I, too, confess that at one time of my life I may have been guilty of thinking of culture as cake contrasted with bread. Now I know better. Real, essential culture is baked into our daily bread or else it isn't truly culture. In short, I am willing to stand firmly on the side of the democratic rather than the aristocratic notion of culture and have so stood for many years, without having gotten full credit, however. I realize the inevitability of such misunderstanding; what price Harvard and Oxford and their traditional snobbisms! Culture is so precious that it is worth even this price, if we can have it only at the high cost of nurturing and conserving it on the upper levels of caste and privilege. But one should not have to pay that exorbitant price for it.

Accordingly, when the "culture clause" was incorporated in the motto of this *Fraternity*, there was the ambition to propagate the culture democratically, to help it permeate ordinary living, to root it in the soil of the group life, to profess it as a folk rather than a class inheritance. It was a daring notion—this of trying to carry culture to the people and have it leaven the lump with the yeast and richness of humane and gracious living. Behind this aim there was necessarily the hope and expectation that a title of leadership could be induced to dedicate itself to the services of the masses and that their richer insight and vision would thus be multiplied a thousand-fold throughout the land.

THE NEW NEGRO NOW

In the context of the life of the Negro there was also the ambitious prospect of developing in areas of lessened competition and handicap, superiorities meriting and capable of winning effective and lasting recognition both for the group and the individual exponents of culture. You will pardon passing mention of the movement that a decade or so after the founding of this *Fraternity* became known, a little too well known, as "The New Negro." Far be it from me to disclaim or disparage a brain child. But in my view, if a "New Negro" is not born and reborn every half generation or so, something is radically wrong, not only with the society in which we live but with us also. According to this calendar, we should have had at least two "New Negroes" since 1925. Be that as it may, the one of 1925 that I am both proud and ashamed of having had something to do with, failed to accomplish all that it could and should have realized. This does not mean that it accomplished nothing. It does mean, however, that because of a false conception of culture it fell short of its potentialities. This is why I bring this matter up this evening. Having signed that "New Negro's" birth certificate, I assume some right to participate in the post-mortem findings. In sum and substance, that generation of cultural effort and self-expression died of a fatal misconception of the true nature of culture.

Both the creative talent of that day and its audience were infected with sound and abortive attitudes: they made culture a market-place commodity and out of this shallow and sordid misunderstanding did it to death prematurely. Two childish maladies of the spirit—exhibitionism and racial chauvinism—analogues one may say of St. Vitus dance and whooping cough, became epidemic and the basic health of the movement was thereby sapped. Permit me to say that both these attitudes, fatal to any soundness in culture, were disavowed by most of the responsible leaders but to no avail. Once the movement took on public momentum and offered that irresistible American lure of a vogue of success, a ready means of quick recognition, an easy, cheap road to vicarious compensation, this dangerous infection was on. True, it was a typically American misapprehension, a characteristic American popular abuse but it brought about lamentably a Negro-American tragedy of the first magnitude. Permit me to say, further, that it need not have been. From the beginning racial chauvinism was supposed to be ruled out; five of the collaborators of *The New Negro* were whites whose readily accepted passport was competent understanding of the cultural objectives of the movement and creative participation in them. The substance of Negro life was emphasized, not its complexion. Similarly, it was not promulgated as a movement for cliques and coteries or for the parasitic elite but a movement for folk culture and folk representation, eventually even for folk participation. Ultimately, it was hoped, it would be for, by and of the people. It was democratically open to all who might be interested on the basis of collaboration and mutual understanding. Some of the most effective and welcomed spokesmen were not Negro. Negro self-expression, moreover, was expected to include the saving salt of self-criticism. It was never intended that so vital a movement should be plagued with profiteering parasites almost to the point of losing decent public presentability. And above all, it was realized that no considerable creative advance could carry the dead weight of those hangers-on whose participation was merely in terms of keeping up with the cultural Joneses.

I say these things, however, in a constructive mood, since my emphasis from now on is not to be on the somewhat wasted past but on the vital present and the promiseful future. One important characteristic of the frontiers of culture is that they are always moving (not necessarily forward but at least always moving). I welcome an opportunity to apply the principle of the criticism I have just made as constructively as I can to that present and to the future. It is no new principle, as I hope I have made clear; but it does have a new chance of test and application.

GHETTO CULTURE

Let us take for granted, if it hasn't been conclusively proven, that culture has no color, that although Negro life and experience should have and are having increased and increasingly effective expression, there is no monopoly, no special proprietary rights, no peculiar credit and no particular needs or benefits about culture.

(In my definition of culture I would include science as well as the arts.) On that basis, then, all we should be sanely concerned about is freer participation and fuller collaboration in the varied activities of the cultural life and that with regard both to the consumer and the producer roles of cultural creation. Democracy in culture means equally wide-scale appreciation and production of the things of the spirit.

Doubtless you will grant these cardinal principles in principle; with even, I dare say, a certain amount of ready acceptance. But follow the corollaries and wince, as well we all may, at their consistent consequences. I shall point out only a few of them. The most obvious, as well as the most important, is that there is no room for any consciously maintained racialism in matters cultural. The generation to which I belong had to do more than its normal share of defensive, promotive propaganda for the Negro but it is my greatest pride that I have never written or edited a book on a chauvinistically racialist basis. Seldom has farsighted Negro scholarship or artistry proceeded on such a basis and today racialism cannot and should not be tolerated. We can afford to be culturally patriotic but never culturally jingoistic.

Moreover, situations are changing fast; movement after movement in its progressive vanguard takes on not even the working principle of the interracial but the aegis of full integration. Let us ask boldly and bravely, what then are the justifications of separate Negro churches, of separate Negro fraternities, schools, colleges? One of the wisest and best statements that I have read recently is that from a colleague and former student—Professor E. Franklin Frazier—who in speaking of Howard, his alma mater, said in effect that its best future goal might well be to "lose its racial identity and become simply a great university." The logic of increasing integration demands, of course, active cooperation and action on our part; we must of necessity do our share in the liquidation of segregation and all forms of separatism. (I was not aware until after this was written of the very recent action on the part of the Conclave to declare *Phi Beta Sigma* open to all without regard to race. Congratulations!)

All this is not going to be easy, for it means restaking considerable vested interests and devaluating considerable double-standard currency. But this is as right as it is inevitable. Competition will be harder and swifter but healthier and fairer for all that. Fraternity will be more rational and be based on commonalities of interest. Attitudes must comparably become more objective, less partisan. Counter-bias must be canceled out and psychologically neutralized.

NEW FILMS

Now in a final page or so I come to what I presume the program chairman had in mind when he gave me the assignment: *Frontiers of Culture*. This is the new frontier and *integration* is its best single caption. Its conquest means collaboration and fraternization, at a considerable present cost and effort but at eventual gain and enlightenment. Had I more time at my disposal I could document more specifically from personal experiences both its costs and its long-term rewards. Suffice it to point out some present-day instances and vindications of cultural integration. The National Board of Review of Motion Pictures recently announced its 1948 citations. Of nine selections on an international basis, three were films of Negro life and situation, *The Quiet One, Intruder in the Dust* and *Home of the Brave*. The first came out of an essentially Negro situation, what was once a corrective school for Negro juvenile delinquents, which fortunately had recently been broadened out to an interracial clientele. This made all the more human and significant the star role of the Negro lad who was the protagonist. *Intruder in the Dust* emerges through Hollywood from Oxford, Mississippi, where at the wise insistence of the author, William Faulkner, and the brave good sense of the director, it was filmed by a mixed cast, with local crowd and bit-part recruits. Here is a truly new horizon and a portentous conquest of a new psychological cultural frontier. And *Home of the Brave*, I hope you have noticed, was not a pro-Negro undertaking at all, despite its hero, but basically an anti-prejudice polemic. Time being short, I make a particular point of these symbolic examples of the new trends I am discussing and trying to vindicate though they are self-vindicating to any open-minded observer. Note that these are films and, therefore, in the most democratic mass medium we have, short of radio. When film and radio begin to change, we can have some realistic hope of a changed American public mind.

When the mass media begin to show signs of social enlightenment and cultural integrity, I repeat, there is a new light on the horizon. First, because they go so far with their message and their reformative influence. But close second to that, they are so accessible to all. Even in the dark zones of segregated living, if enlightened leadership will only take upon itself to praise, support and circulate them. The cultural move of prime importance today is to turn these great and almost limitless resources to the mass media of radio, films and television to the ends of truer, more objective, mutual understanding and let that become the leaven of a people's culture. The breadth of participation which they make possible happily carries along also that high quality of art and insight which befits true culture. I am, of course, not ignoring the force or role of the more traditional arts, where, as a matter of fact, the new values and attitudes must first experimentally express themselves. *Intruder in the Dust*, for example, was an ultra-literary novel before it became a Hollywood film. However, if work of fresh insight and great artistry is to remain within such limited confines, the hope of a high democratic culture would be indefinitely below the horizon of our time.

CULTURAL DEMOCRACY

But I cannot end on too optimistic a note, even though I believe firmly that a people's culture of high grade will eventually come about somehow, sometime, somewhere. Under conditions that permit it, it does not necessarily follow that a culture with breadth and depth will automatically or inevitably realize itself. Where Town Hall and Senator Claghorn, Jack Armstrong and Quiz Kids, Hillbilly and the Philharmonic simultaneously crowd the ether and are to be had just for the turn of the switch and the dial, it doesn't follow that the average selectivity will be right. But fortunately that issue is a matter of education and the general public taste rather than a mere question of racial condition or conditioning. There is, however, that special enemy, ghetto-mindedness, which may well give us more than momentary concern. So we still have two arch enemies of mass culture to fight and conquer—Phillistinism and prejudice—class bias and group bias.

I know this discussion has not been altogether pleasant going but prose must be conceded its utilitarian uses and obligations. As serious-minded Americans we must all be thinking gravely and rigorously about the present state of the national culture and mindful of the special and yet unrealized demands of culture in a democratic setting. Perhaps it is truism but it is worth repeating that a few present liberal trends with the radical changes of popular attitude potentially involved are projecting helpful incentives toward a more democratic American culture. So far is the emancipation of the public mind from prejudice and group stereotypes, this may be properly regarded as, in large part, a new Negro contribution to the broadening of the nation's culture. But for us as Negroes, it is even more important to realize how necessary it is to share understandingly and participate creatively in these promising enlargements of the common mind and spirit. To be democratic is as important as it is to be treated democratically; democracy is a two-way process and accomplishment.

IV. Identity and Education

20. Negro Education Bids for Par

Locke was in the midst of controversy at Howard University when this article was published. He was promoting the teaching of a course on race relations, the teaching of African studies, and pay equity between black and white faculty. All were rejected by the white administration, and in June, 1925, Locke was fired from Howard and would not return until 1928.

There were student strikes at nearly every traditionally black college in the 1920s. The strikers protested the Calvinist rules regulating student campus life; the racially separate pay scales for faculty; the employment of conservative, usually white, faculty; and the exclusion from college life of public debate and research programs about racism and segregation. In this article, Locke argues that under a system of segregation the role of black colleges involves the right to provide an education that is in the Negro's interest such that that interest is consonant with the Negro's liberation. The article provides us with important insight into Locke's understanding of what cultural groups should do to promote their interest under conditions of duress. It also provides insight into the way Locke treats various educational programs that seem ostensibly unreconcilable or were offered as *the* program for black education.

"Negro Education Bids for Par," *Survey Graphic* 54 (1925), 567–570.

Negro Education Bids for Par

The stock of Negro education has a heavy traditional discount, and is chronically "under the market." Whatever the local variation, one can usually count upon a sag in both standard and facilities for the education of the Negro, section for section, program for program, below the top current level, so that to reach relative parity with surrounding systems of education, Negro education must somehow "beat the market." This extra spurt to overcome its generation-long handicaps is the immediate practical problem in Negro education. Its gravity, even as affecting general educational standards, can be gauged if we stop to consider that, counting the regional concentration of the Negro population in Southern and border states legally committed to separate education, plus the large numbers in many large cities even of the North and middle West that maintain separate or partly separate teaching of colored children, separate race education prevails over more than two-thirds the total potential school population of Negro children.

Since we cannot say that this dual system is on the wane, what ought, theoretically, to be an anomaly in our democracy exists as a definite and inescapably practical educational problem. Further, by reason of its being in ninety per cent of the instances a discriminatory separation, and only in ten per cent a voluntary group arrangement or a special effort to compensate the handicaps of a socially disadvantaged group, the situation presents a problem of general public responsibility, and a clear issue of public justice and fair play. Fortunately the last few years have seen a marked change of public attitude on the matter, not merely renewed effort to remove some of the most outstanding disparities, but more promising still, a shift of the appeal from motives of charity to motives of justice and the "square deal." Particularly the last year has been a boom year for Negro educational interests, and there is some warrant for hope that with the momentum of special campaigns for improving the facilities of both private and public schools for Negroes, our educational stock may somehow in the near future approximate par.

Fifteen, ten, even as late as five years ago, in Southern states, the ratio of division of state expenditures, per capita, between white and Negro pupils ranged as high as twenty to one, and averaged fifteen to one, as the Jones report startlingly revealed; and that might be taken as a general index of the situation as it then was, except for large cities and a few favored privately reenforced centers. Though few such glaring discrepancies now prevail, the disparity is still very considerable: a recent appeal in the Tuskegee-Hampton endowment campaign estimates that "the Negroes constituting about one-tenth of the total population, receive less than 2 per cent of the billion dollars annually spent here for education; and of $875,000,000 spent annually on public schools, only a little more than one per cent is expended for Negroes." Certainly, even if allowance is made for the lumped expenditures of areas where no separate account is taken, there is enough in these figures to warrant our picturing the Negro school child as still wearing educational shoddy instead of wool, with the adolescent Negro youth inadequately provided for by threadbare educational "hand-me-downs" or spirit-rasping missionary clothes.

Indeed the missionary type of school, necessary and helpful as it has been, has nevertheless done much to conceal and palliate the fundamental lack in the common school system. Here where the greatest disparity has existed is just where basic parity must first of all be established. Philanthropy and private endeavor do a real dis-service even when they aid the education of the Negro if they assume the moral burden of the deficiencies of public state education. Fortunately the more enlightened philanthropic effort of today, as exemplified in the policy of the Jeannes and Slater funds and the Rosenwald grants, extends only cooperative aid in the improvement of public school facilities, and is thus based on the only sound principle.

A standardized public school education must become the standard in the education of the average Negro child. Otherwise, Negro education costs double and yields half. As an indirect, but heavily mulcted taxpayer, the Negro, under the present system in the South, either pays for some one else's education and himself goes without, or with the aid of the philanthropist pays twice, once through the public system, and once again through the special agency of the private school. After a trying period of vexing publicity in criticism of these conditions, a really constructive and public-spirited reaction has gradually gathered momentum in the South. A new social vision is really involved in this new feeling of local and public responsibility for the education of the Negro. State appropriations, private fund grants, and voluntary contributions of black and white citizens have been cooperatively enlisted in this movement, but the true gauge of its value has been not so much the considerable sums that have been added to the meager resources of the public schools for Negroes in the South, but the recommitment of the state to its fundamental duty, and the reawakening to the principle of local responsibility in matters of education.

An outstanding instance of this is the progressive North Carolina state program, which by special appropriations invested five millions in permanent school equipment for Negro schools in the four-year period 1921–1925, and practically doubled its maintenance expenditures for the same period. Another outstanding instance is reported from Atlanta, where through the interracial committee and the wise direction of the colored vote on the Atlanta school bond referendum, $1,250,000 of the $4,000,000 bond issue was by agreement devoted to the facilities of the Negro schools. The same sort of pressure and leadership wrote into the Kentucky state bond issue for education the provision of a fixed percentage for the uses of Negro education. Recent news of agreements under the auspices of an interracial commission for additional high school facilities for Negroes in Texas, the extensive sharing of the Negro communities in private educational benefactions such as the Duke gifts in North Carolina and the Du Pont improvements of rural schools in Delaware all point, in spite of a continuance of much unfair and reactionary practice, to a new era in public policy. In the existing situation, efforts of this sort are to be regarded as the greatest hope and the safest guarantee of progress in the education of the Negro. To foster it in its most constructive spirit, however, we must not consider such progress any more than the plain duty and common obligation of every community. The improvement of Negro education is overwhelmingly a public task and responsibility; never for any reason of temporary advantage or special appeal must it be allowed to assume in the public mind the aspect of a special responsibility, a private enterprise, or a philanthropic burden. Many a well-intentioned friend of the Negro and of educational progress still thinks of Negro education largely in terms of something special and private rather than something basically standard and public, but by the right insistence the public conception in this regard must be brought to par.

It has been an undesirable and not necessarily permanent condition, then, that has brought the education of the Negro so overwhelmingly into the control of private institutions of all sorts—good, bad and indifferent. Many of these are non-standardized missionary enterprises, conceived in sentiment rather than scientific pedagogy, supported by long-distance philanthropy, and in numerous instances not strategically located or wisely planned as to the division of educational labor with other schools. It is no particular marvel that the South has for so long considered Negro education an alien concern, and, allowing for the aberrations of prejudice, an unwelcome intrusion.

No friend of progressive education can afford today to take a sentimental attitude toward the motley crop of "colleges," "seminaries," and nondescript "collegiate-industrial" schools still in operation despite the weeding-out process of the last decade attendant upon the exposures of the Jones report and other survey agencies. Standardization is the paramount demand of Negro education. This must come about partly by ruthless curtailment of philanthropic support for unworthy institutions, partly by voluntary consolidation of competing schools, and partly through the absorption of students by the increased facilities of the land-grant colleges and state normal schools. All these forces are at present working, but not with the force of thorough conviction behind them. Undoubtedly the next important forward step in Negro education must be the long-delayed but urgently needed concentration of the type once proposed by one of the great educational foundations. It was suggested that the five rival collegiate institutions in Atlanta combine to form one standard and resourceful college and university center thereby pooling their plants, faculties, students and resources. Backed by heavy endowment grants, a few such liberal professional training centers must be provided at strategically placed points like Atlanta, Nashville, one for the great Southwest, one for Texas and one for the Mississippi Delta region, to bring a progressive and standardizing influence into every important region of the Negro population. It has been the history of American education that its schools have been standardized from the top down, and largely through the influence of the private colleges and universities—and there seems no reason for expecting Negro schools to be the exception. As the public education of the Negro expands the private schools concerned with his education must concentrate, which is their one great opportunity to lift themselves to modern standards of efficiency.

Within the group of private schools founded to aid the Negro, those that have been the outgrowth of the Hampton-Tuskegee program have had an influence and a public acceptance far beyond their relative number. Because of their spectacular success and unique appeal to practical Americanism, they have indeed in the public mind become the outstanding elements of Negro education. The reaction of this appeal and popularity upon other types of Negro school, especially the program of the Negro college, has led to a feud of almost Kentuckian duration and intensity in Negro educational circles. Support of the school with a liberal or academic curriculum of the collegiate or professional sort unfortunately came to mean antagonism to the school with the industrial-vocational or "practical" curriculum, and *vice versa*. The question resolved itself often into the question of "what kind of education the Negro most needed," or was "best fitted for," or was most "worthy of public support," instead of the position backed equally by the best educational idealism and common-sense, that the Negro, like any other constituency, needed all types of education that were not actually obsolete in American educational practice.

Only now, when the antagonisms of this issue are beginning to disappear, does a dispassionate analysis become possible. Certainly, whatever the justifications or grievances on either side, the cause of Negro education as a house divided against itself has been in anything but a favorable position before the public. One of the most hopeful recent developments has been the waning of this feud, and the growing realization that the Tuskegee-Hampton program and that of the traditional Negro college are supplementary rather than antagonistic. One factor in this new understanding has been the relinquishment by the younger generation of college youth of the traditional fetishes of so-called classical education that during the missionary period of Negro college management were nevertheless important compensations for an ambition struggling up against colossal odds. The general American college world in fact has had to pass through the same conversion of values, but the "genteel tradition" has its special sentimental hold in the mind of the educated Negro of the older generation. But with a more practical and modernized conception of education, on one hand, growing up in the younger generation of liberally educated Negroes, the program of the "industrial wing" of Negro education, on the other hand, has itself grown. This year Hampton Institute graduated its second and Tuskegee its first crop of degree graduates from standard collegiate courses in education, science and economics.

Thus the year that has so been signalized by the successful seven million dollar joint campaign for Hampton-Tuskegee endowment, and that promises to net resources of nine millions for those valuable institutions, has fortunately seen such a resolution of old antagonisms that in the near future a united front may reasonably be expected in the ranks of Negro education. With close cooperation and understanding established between its two equally important wings, we can optimistically look forward to a new era in Negro education, especially when the powerful forces of public opinion and of philanthropic benefaction come to realize the significance and promise of this understanding and cooperation and lend support generously to both types of educational effort. We shall then see the education of the Negro not as a conflict between two programs or types, but as a mutually supplementary program of collegiate-professional education on the one hand, and of the collegiate-economic, technical and agricultural training on the other, with the field of teacher and social-service training divided between them, that for the great urban centers and their needs on the one hand and that for the important rural situation on the other.

It was not the fault of the Hampton-Tuskegee idea that the so-called higher education of the Negro could not for a generation compete with it in dramatizing its own values. The conception of education back of that idea was original; indeed in its day it was in advance of American educational reform. Before the general vogue and acceptance of technical and vocational types of education and the widespread use of the "project method," its practical demonstration and application of their value was a contribution to American education at large. In addition to its appeal to the American sense of the "practical," the Hampton-Tuskegee program exerted, as it still does, a strong sentimental appeal through its race and community service, and through making all institutions and agencies that come under its influence missioners of the masses, galvanizers of "the man farthest down," and exponents of a naturally popular doctrine of economic independence and self-help. But for every adherent this program has won through what its critics have called its "concessions" to the popular American way of thinking, including the characteristic conciliatory optimism of its philosophy of race contacts, it has, I think, won ten by its concrete appeal and demonstration of results. These it was spectacularly able to offer through the personality and career of Booker Washington, who became, along with a host of other successful products of the system, convincing exhibits of its value. If the type of education that felt itself threatened and depreciated by the vogue of the "industrial program" had been able to stress its social results as dramatically—as is quite possible, considering the indispensable service of the professions—it would have shared liberally in public favor and support.

The essential difference in the relative public success of the two types of education was not in their intrinsic worth but in the quite different caliber of their propaganda and leadership. At the particular time of the strong competition of the Washington program, the higher education of the Negro was in far weaker administrative hands than those of the hardy and zealous missionary pioneers who a generation before had founded it. Having made a success of its initial appearance, Negro collegiate education in the last twenty-five years or more has made the mistake of allowing its social appeals to lapse, of making only an individualistic appeal to its adherents, and of trying to justify itself either by depreciating the rival program or merely by abstract self-appraisal of its own values. Its leadership has been vitally at fault.

Oddly enough, the administrative leadership of the "higher education" wing of Negro education has always been less native and racial than that of the "industrial-vocational." Contrary to general knowledge or expectation, therefore, it has been the so-called liberal education of the Negro that has suffered the heavier effects of the missionary blight. As a consequence what has been liberal in name and intention has not always been liberalizing in effect. When we consider that the great service of Booker Washington to the mass education of the Negro consisted in transforming charity-education into work-education, and in revitalizing missionary motives with the positive tonic of the ideals of self-help and practical community betterment, we can realize that missionarism, as a tradition either of attitude or of management in Negro collegiate education, is doubly out of place. Indeed missionarism and self-leadership are incompatible. And if we assess the success of the "vocational program" as due largely to the public demonstration of its ability to develop its own leaders and effect a marked racial awakening, we can readily see that the non-success of the Negro college of the traditional sort to hold public attention and favor and elicit general support is in part due to the coddling and emasculating missionarism which still traditionally controls it. The Negro college represents too largely yet a reactionary, old-fashioned program, distantly though idealistically administered, second-hand in aim and effect. In short, it has not yet produced its own leadership to give it a vital and distinctive program and to justify it according to its true relation to racial development and advance. It has not failed as a medium of supplying in increasingly adequate numbers well-educated men, but it has failed in recognized social leadership and reform. This branch of our education needs then more than a theoretical defense, or renewed public support: it needs a practical reform of the first magnitude to recover its social values and purposes, and thus bring itself to par again.

This is not to say that Howard, Fisk, Morehouse, Atlanta, Wilberforce, Virginia Union, Johnson Smith and Lincoln—to name the outstanding Negro institutions of college and university grade—are not increasingly important centers of a modernized collegiate education and standardized professional training. Since the war they have all increased considerably in student numbers, faculty strength and in equipment, and most of them have attained standard scholastic rating. But in strange, almost paradoxical contrast to their material expansion and advance, there has persisted a reactionary conservatism of spirit and atmosphere. The mind of Negro youth senses and describes it as "missionary paternalism." It is significant in this connection that at a forum conference of over one hundred Negro college students representing eighteen different institutions, held recently at Nyack, N.Y., it was voted as the consensus of opinion that "because of the paternalistic attitude so prevalent in Negro colleges and so offensive and uninspiring to their students, Negro colleges should be headed by Negroes selected strictly on the basis of efficiency, though the faculties should contain both white and colored teachers." What it amounts to, in last analysis, is really that along with the maintenance of the obsolete system of theological control in the Negro college there has persisted an autocratic and conservative tradition of management. Indeed it is a tradition so rooted in them that it persists in cases where there is direct race control; but the situation is naturally accentuated in psychological effect where, as in the great majority of instances still, there is white executive control. Certainly the regime that inspired a former generation with race zeal and courage only irritates and antagonizes the present clientage of the Negro colleges. A case in point is the recent protest of the alumni body of Lincoln University, Pennsylvania, against the election of Rev. Dr. Gaston to the presidency of that institution on the ground of his "having exhibited a reactionary attitude in his administration of the board controlling the Presbyterian schools for Negroes in the South, and of his not being in favor of a standard progressive program of college education for the Negro." The fact is, having outgrown the idealisms of the missionary impulse which once galvanized them, Negro colleges have not been free to develop a modern emancipated spirituality of their own. Indeed to do this requires more self-direction and autonomy than the present tradition and practice of control and management permits.

The widespread student and alumni unrest of the last eighteen months in one Negro college after another—Tallahassee, Lincoln University in Missouri, Fisk, and Howard, with the situation at Fisk resulting in the ousting by a student strike and alumni agitation of a conservative president in spite of his recent completion of a successful million-dollar endowment campaign—is significant evidence of this rising demand for liberal reform, educational self-direction and autonomy. For while these breaks occur nominally over questions of alumni control and student discipline, they all come to a head in a feeling of racial repression and the need for more positive and favorable conditions for the expression and cultivation of the developing race spirit. So obviously there is a set to Negro collegiate education that does not conform to the psychology of the young Negro. Partly as a negative reaction to conservative management, partly as a response to developing race consciousness, Negro student bodies are developing the temper of mind and mood that has produced the nationalist universities and the workers' colleges.

This development is as reasonable as it is inevitable. Negro education, to the extent that it is separate, ought to be free to develop its own racial interests and special aims for both positive and compensatory reasons. Otherwise it becomes a flagrant anomaly and self-contradiction. But without autonomy and race control there is little or no opportunity for developing any such compensating interest: in short, racial separation presents under these circumstances a negative and irritating challenge or disparagement instead of a welcomed and inspiring opportunity. As organized today for the most part, this type of education constantly reminds Negro youth, in the midst of a sensitive personal and racial adolescence, of the unpleasant side of the race problem, instead of utilizing it as a positive factor in this education. The very noticeable negative reactions on this issue ought to be taken as unmistakable symptoms of an urgent need for a profound change of policy to restore the lapsing morale of important centers of Negro education. The highest aim and real justification of the Negro college should be the development of a racially inspired and devoted professional class with group service as their integrating ideal. Certainly the least that can be expected and demanded of separately organized Negro college education is that in the formative period of life the prevailing contacts should be with the positive rather than the negative aspects of race, and that race feelings of a constructive sort should be the stimulating and compensating element in the system education. But this element, in solution in the positively saturated group feelings of Negro youth at these centers, is inhibited from expression and precipitation by atmospheric conditions that range all the way from spirit-dampening condescension at its worst to spirit-repelling moralism at its best. The mind of the average Negro youth under these conditions turns rebelliously individualistic, and the finest social products of his education are lost.

This loss in the social coefficient of the education of the most promising section of Negro youth, under the very conditions where it should be most carefully conserved and nurtured, is one of the tragic wastes of the race situation. If there is anything specially traditional and particularly needed in Negro education it is the motive and ideal of group service. And though the loss of it in the more capably trained Negro of the present generation is partly due to the influence of the prevalent materialistic individualism of middle-class American life, a still larger loss is due to an inevitable and protective reaction against the present atmosphere of his education.

The lapsing social values of higher education for the Negro can, I think, be recovered only under race leadership, for they must be tactfully coaxed back in an atmosphere of unembarrassed racial councils, charged with almost a family degree of intimacy and confidence. To provide such a positive-toned community ought to be one of the first aims and justifications of the Negro college. Under such conditions, the Negro problem itself can be taken up into the very substance of education, and made, from the informational, the disciplinary and the inspirational aspects, a matter of vital consideration. Occasionally in the atmosphere of very liberal inter-racial exchange this is possible, but under average conditions of the present, decidedly not. Like its analogue, the nationalist university or the class-conscious group, the Negro college of the present day requires and demands, if not group exclusiveness, at least group management and the conditions of self-determination—in brief, spiritual autonomy. Just so long as so obvious and reasonable an advantage is not available will the Negro college remain below the level of its fullest educational potentialities.

This brings the pressing current problem of the Negro college in close alignment with the contemporary movement for the liberal reform of the American college, but for a very special and perhaps more urgent reason. Whatever the needs for more adequate financial backing and support of the Negro college, the need for liberalizing its management and ideals is greater. The less free a people are socially, the greater their need for an emancipating atmosphere in their education. Academic freedom is nowhere any too secure, but to see it so exceptionally curtailed as to be almost non-existent in Negro education is to realize what revolutionizing reform must come about before these schools can hope to attain their full spiritual growth and influence, and function actively in general race development. Under present circumstances and management, few if any of the Negro colleges are in a position to realize these newer demands or even experiment toward catering to these special needs of an increasing body of Negro youth, who cannot be spiritually content with the present regime, however standardized and effective may be the education which it offers. Of course, some of this insistence is only the liberal urge of the youth movement and the common needs of the younger generation, which know no color line and seep over into Negro college life. But when we remember that the present generation of young Negroes is in process of moulting the psychology of dependence and subserviency, and if we stop also to consider that the Negro college student earns his education in far larger proportion than the general college population, the urgency of his requirement for a liberal program and sensitively responsive control becomes apparent. It is something more than a youth problem; there is a racial significance and insistence to these demands.

If they are ignored, reactionary management may drive from the Negro college the constituency which is psychologically most virile and may once again goad reform into revolution. Offered scope and constructive expression in a legitimate field, this spirit of Negro youth is capable under the right native leadership of transforming a half-dozen segregated centers of Negro professional education into radiant centers of Negro culture. As it is, without race control and self-expression the Negro college is more than an anomaly: it is a potential seedbed of unrest. It is the thwarted force that is dangerous. All who fear the truly vitalized Negro college, labelling it a radical menace, will, if they succeed in repressing it, have actually chosen the radicalism of the half-educated charlatan who makes a precarious vocation of revolution and agitation instead of the liberalism of the fully educated and responsible professional man who makes an avocation of social service and reform. The only alternative about the forces of race assertiveness today in America is whether they shall be allowed constructive channels of expression. Certainly education and the Negro college ought, of all agencies, to be able to use them constructively. Indeed without some special motive force, the

Negro college cannot hope in the very near future to overcome its particular handicaps.

The safest guarantee of parity in the higher education of the race, finally, is the open and balanced competition of Negro institutions for race patronage with other institutions of higher learning accessible to Negro students. The ratio of the total enrollment of Negro college students in mixed as compared with separate institutions, allowing for a strictly collegiate grade of instruction in the latter, is nearly one to three, and the ratio of degree graduates, according to the careful yearly statistics of the education number of *The Crisis*, is roughly one to two; that is, for every two degree graduates from standard Negro institutions for the last few years, there has been one from the private and state universities of the country at large. These facts reenforce two important principles. First, the inter-racial contact that is lost at the bottom of the educational ladder is somewhat compensated for at the top. It is of the most vital importance to race relations and the progress of democracy in America that contact be maintained between the representative leaders of the white and black masses. The greatest danger of separate school systems would be the removal of these surfaces of contact, and the detriment would be mutual enough to be national. In the second place, the Negro college has yet to justify itself in the full estimation of the college-going Negro constituency. Even when it does, it will take care only of a fraction of Negro college students, but that its clientele should diminish or that its product should lack a justifying distinctiveness and racial effectiveness would be the only indictment of separate education for which the Negro might in any way hold himself accountable. Developed in modern ways to its full possibilities, however, the Negro college ought to become the prime agency in recruiting from the talented tenth the social leadership which is an urgent need, both racial and national, in the difficult race situation of America.

21. Negro Needs as Adult Education Opportunities

The various sponsors of the conference were among the primary agents promoting adult education in the black community as an extension of black collegiate activity. As with most educational endeavors dependent on federal and private foundation funding, the resources for blacks were limited. The program was intended, from the standpoint of the funding agents, as very often an exercise in improving the patriotic commitment, manners, morals, and rudimentary skills of reading and writing among disenchanted minorities. Morse A. Cartwright, then director of the American Association for Adult Education, was the keynote speaker along with Locke. Cartwright gave the usual description of adult education as a good for the general improvement of the citizenry. Locke uses the opportunity to argue against the contrived segregation of adult education programs; he argues for the value of adult education in terms of the satisfaction of "Negro Needs" and as a need the Negro had identical to other groups. In addition, Locke considers the limitations and benefits of race-specific educational policies and the future of such policies.

"Negro Needs as Adult Education Opportunities," *Findings of the First Annual Conference on Adult Education and the Negro*, held at Hampton Institute, Virginia, October 20–22, 1938, under the auspices of the American Association for Adult Education, the Extension Department of Hampton Institute, and the Associates in Negro Folk Education. Mimeograph available at Hampton University, Hampton, Virginia.

Negro Needs As Adult Education Opportunities

My title, "Negro Needs as Adult Education Opportunities," poses a delicate question, and poses it purposely. Construed one way, with the emphasis on Negro needs, it raises the vexing issue of the Negro's special situation and whether or not his needs are peculiar. There is no more controversial question than this very one, whether because of his handicaps and disabilities the Negro stands in need of a special variety or program of education, just as there is no more reactionary and dangerous position than the offhand assumption that he does. Construed another way, however, with the emphasis on adult education and the challenge which the Negro's situation makes to it, no more fundamental and progressive question can be raised in this entire field of our common interest and effort. Need I say which of these two emphases I have chosen for our mutual consideration tonight?

This conference, specializing on the topic "Adult Education and the Negro," focused even though it is upon a particular constituency and those who serve its needs cannot afford, nevertheless, to commit itself to or insult itself with the outmoded doctrine of separate and peculiar types of education for Negroes. If ever that doctrine had vogue—and we must admit with regret that it did—it is now educationally dead, though it may not yet be everywhere altogether and effectively buried. We have in spite of that come to the place where we clearly recognize its tragic misconceptions, misconceptions that have not only diverted much Negro education into shallow, backwater channels but which have seriously impeded the movement for general mass education in the South. If Booker Washington's inspiring formula of practical education had been applied wholesale in the South an educational reconstruction that has yet to be accomplished would have been successfully inaugurated. Education of the mind, heart, and hand, education for social adjustment and practical living, such as the adult education movement envisages, would have become a generally accepted formula for the mass education of both black and white and a basis laid down for a truly democratic and democratizing type of public education—as indeed it must yet be laid down. But instead, a narrow notion that what was educational meat for one racial group must be educational poison or anathema to another intervened to frustrate the general application of an educational discovery that was common denominator human, even though it did come out of the special exigencies of the Negro's handicapped situation and universally sound, even though a pathological, social situation did warp its practical applications.

Let us not in our generation, and in our special field of adult education repeat this tragic mistake. Nor forget that we are prone to make it, as was only too clearly shown by the limited and one-sided procedures of the "Americanization" program, where also in our narrow zeal to Americanize and make over the foreigner through conformity we forgot to liberalize the typical American attitude toward and about the foreigner through education for social tolerance and cultural understanding. Let us, then, take the Negro case merely as a special instance of a general problem requiring special attention and effort, perhaps, because of its acute degree but in its significance and bearing upon educational problems and methods considered generally diagnostic and universally applicable. The condition of the Negro and its educational implications will fit and parallel any similarly circumstanced group and, in addition, like many another acute situation, will point the lesson of new and generally applicable techniques.

So let us inquire briefly what the objective situation of the Negro adult constituency is in its basic elements. At bottom, it seems to me to be that of any semi-literate, working-class group deprived of social opportunity and cultural contacts. For all such groups, after the initial and obvious mistake of playing down to their disadvantaged condition, the educationally successful approach has invariably found the educational task to be first and foremost a job of inspiration, of establishing galvanic contacts to counteract the lethargy and discouragement incident to their depressed condition. This lesson has been verified from the earliest days of educational work with culturally disadvantaged groups, from Toynbee Hall and Ruskin College down to Hull House and Reedsville, from the Cheapside Cockney and the Ghetto Jew to the emancipated Southern Negro to the Sovietized Russian peasant. It is just human under these conditions to require manna rather than dry bread. The starved intellectual palate requires to be tempted, else it will not respond at all. It is thus nothing exceptional that our few experimental attempts with adult education for Negro groups the appeal of the cultural subjects has been found relatively greater than that of the practical. Why should this thrice learned lesson have to be specially vindicated in the Negro's case? Yet from all I can gather, far too many workers in this field accept the traditional and often officially imposed doctrine of confining an adult education program for Negroes to the practical elementals, ignoring this very prevalent and understandable reaction. The lure and fascination of what is "beyond them" (beyond them, it will be noticed, is in quotation marks) is more than pardonable, it is educationally encouraging and effective. For this, we need not go to the lessons of the adult education movement in Denmark or of worker's education in England and Wales; the early educational history of the Negro himself illustrates the same story. In the Reconstruction period, when Negro education began, as it has been aptly said, with adult education, he learned to read from the Bible more than from the primer and leapt under the spur of zeal and enthusiasm from illiteracy to very mature educational materials and results. Of course, sometimes with awkward and incongruous results, but nevertheless with a momentum that got ahead by leaps and jumps rather than by inches. The movement for adult education among any disadvantaged group must have a dynamic and enthusiasm-compelling drive. Beyond the mere literacy level, enlarging horizons and broadening human values must dominate it or the movement will stall. It can never be successful in terms of the surface scratching of remedial programs designed primarily to remove handicaps. Too much of the present programs are of this character and have behind them only the pressure of some official program rather than the pull of a people's movement. Fortunately from several quarters private programs of mass education are beginning, several of them of radical social character, and they thrive on just some such dynamic as I have described. The programs under public auspices, with which we are primarily concerned in this conference, can successfully compete with them in only one way and that is by also developing an inner momentum of zeal and enthusiasm by the appeal to emotionally strong interests. In this respect, the cultural values with their humanizing appeal are practical in the best and most effective sense; it is their job to vitalize the program. A left-handed or obviously remedial program or one evidently behind that in operation for other more favored groups may be accepted as crumbs or half an educational loaf but never with enthusiasm or inspiration.

Some of us, condemned to work under just such conditions as these, may feel that I am pointing this out in ironical and futile criticism. But on the contrary, it is to advise that whatever the official program may be, these inspirational materials and cultural values should be brought into it by our own initiative and ingenuity in the interests both of greater efficiency and of larger group service. They will not only register, they will help carry through any program to which they are harnessed. For they have, under most circumstances, the power to counteract the depressing stigma of a segregated system of instruction and to lift the psychological level of a sub-standard educational program.

What can be said of the cultural appeal in general can be said with even greater force of the racial appeal, provided it, too, takes the cultural approach. No one will question the fact of a special need for compensatory attitudes, as psychologically fundamental for groups and for individuals subject to the outer restrictions of prejudice and the inner handicaps of inferiority. No one will claim that enhanced group pride and morale and self-respect can alone effect a general social transformation, but they are powerful initial factors and must often precede the practical economic and political effort by which group progress is made real and secure. Certainly such compensatory pride and self-respect are among the best contributions which education can make to the social situation. As has been well said: "Cultural activities and their special appeals and incentives enhance the self-respect of the people and enable them to assert themselves in healthy fashion in their social and economic group life, urging them on toward the transformation of their social and economic conditions to constantly rising levels of security and opportunity."

It is obvious that the Negro section of the population stands deeply in need of such compensating and inspiring materials. More than that, in addition to serving the adult group directly, educational effort in this direction serves a double duty. Through the influence of the parent generation upon the youth, we can particularly check the artificial discouragements of the limited past of their elders and keep from adding unnecessarily to the actual, situational disabilities of the young. Indeed, there is little use in the teaching of race pride to the younger generation unless it be reinforced—and intelligently reinforced, in the attitudes of the elder generation. This is a special obligation and opportunity of the adult educational movement among us: in my judgment, the most serious special duty in our program of folk education. To carry it through effectively should be one of the prime objectives of our adult education work for Negroes.

There is, however, an important limiting proviso for such racially motivated phases of education, to which one must call special attention. To be educationally sound and effective, it must be kept from the extremes of racial chauvinism. We must play rather than blow or toot the racial horn. That means that at bottom the racial element must be factually based and soberly balanced instead of childishly emotional or violently partisan. We must in this avoid the errors of our adversaries and not compound bias with counter-bias. No better safeguard to this can be found than by addressing the majority and the minority, the racial and the general audience at the same time with the same facts and the same language, and of not shouting even though the majority ear seem indifferent or deaf. Moreover, on these matters, the majority needs adult education in the worst way, as has been aptly put by the saying that the Negro problem is a problem of the white mind. Though this task may seem an extra and unwarrantable burden, it is after all our job to undertake it. I hope it is pardonable in this connection to refer to the basic policy of our Associates in Negro Folk Education which addresses the same materials (to quote) "not merely to the growing Negro audience that desires and needs to understand itself more fully, but also to that wider general audience which is beginning to face the Negro and the race question more fairly and with intelligent open-mindedness." If, then, we point up the racial phases of our adult education efforts to such a policy and program, we escape spiritually at least from the dilemmas of segregation. It is both sound pedagogy and good strategy to do so. This is a practical instance of maintaining the principle I mentioned at the outset of keeping a racial situation out of shallow and dangerous backwaters and safely in the mainstream of educational effort and progress. Indeed, to the extent we are successful, we are performing a much-needed service in general social education at the same time that we universalize what otherwise would be merely provincial values. The same materials, if properly presented, will inspire and compensate minority minds and educate and liberalize majority minds. I am fully aware that this will not in itself solve a national race problem, but here again, it is the most effective contribution education can make toward it.

And now to a third and final point. Here, also, an obvious Negro need reveals a particular adult education opportunity. If we look over the wide range of the adult education program and note the areas of most vital Negro needs—noticing incidentally that they are, sadly enough, the very areas of greatest educational discrimination—we find them to be: (1) the field of health and hygiene, (2) vocational training with the modern frontage of vocational guidance and job placement, (3) agricultural extension with emphasis on the important new aspects of cooperative management, marketing, and buying, (4) training in the community aspects of social and economic problems, and (5) practical cultural education through amateur production in the craft and the applied arts. Merely to mention them is depressing in view of the obvious and critical need on the one hand, and the pitiful disparity of effort, especially in publicly supported education in the South, on the other hand. The situation would be hopeless but for two comparatively recent trends.

First is the growing realization that the social reconstruction program for the entire nation and particularly for the South must not only include the man farthest down but must begin with him. Further, that for realistic and basic rather than sentimental or philanthropic reasons, these situations cannot be effectively handled with color differentials and that to do so imperils the success of the whole program. The other favorable factor is that the declared policy and better trends of the Federal emergency programs are pointed in this progressive direction. The emergency programs have also done some very important pioneering in just these fields, although regularized Federal participation and subsidies alone, it seems to me, can put these beginnings in a position to make accumulative our remedial attack on these critical chronic needs. The brightest hope of the situation is the likelihood now that the educational prescription and treatment will be made out according to condition and not according to race. How much further along, for example, the program addressed to the tenant farmer and his improvement would be if this common bond of condition had been intelligently faced even a half generation ago! The Tuskegee program of practical farmer education would have swept through the South with full local and state support and with a single eye to the economic improvement of the standard of production and of living. Perhaps it was too much to expect, but all that stood in the way were entrenched traditions of stubborn custom upon which a courageous and intelligent and realistic attack should have been made.

With the pressure of the present crisis, an effective though unorthodox movement with its own propaganda technique that might well be envied and studied by adult educators has actually faced this situation and in terms of the sharecroppers' movement has transformed these same stubborn traditions for thousands of Southern farmers, black and white. A crisis has added its pressure, but after all the movement has had to proceed on the basis of changing mass attitudes through informal education. No official or even semi-official system can propagandize so suddenly or so successfully, but the demonstration of the possibilities is there for us educators to learn, if we will. Social change can be speeded up and directed by direct attack on the mass mind and inveterate, backward group ways of thinking: the man farthest down can be reached, and that not in terms of mere A, B, C's or surface trivialities. At the same time, we see by the same example that an intelligent linking up of basic interests can bring the Negro from an excluded and subordinated part of the picture into the very foreground and center of a progressive program. Adult education is essentially "an unconventional educational program" because of its connection with vital issues and the immediate needs of its constituency. It forfeits its essential character when it ceases to be frontier pioneering. As a mere extension of traditional methods and values it ceases to be worthy of its name, which is my reason for a final warning that adult education for Negroes, or for that matter any group, cannot possibly be second-hand, traditional, or conservatively directed. To the extent that we can influence it, we must see that it becomes increasingly progressive and experimental. If it is to serve minority group interests, this becomes more than desirable; it becomes imperative.

Thus we must conclude first that the adult education movement among Negroes cannot maintain itself reasonably or effectively as a separate or special program, even though it is condemned over a large area to separate organization and effort; second, that even with its body in the fetters of a segregated set-up, it must maintain a grasp on universal values and address itself beyond the narrow racial constituency to a general social and cultural service, and finally it must align itself with more progressive programs of educational reform and social reconstruction. In so doing, there is opportunity to meet Negro needs as they are and yet not curtail the progressive character of the educational effort. With our formal education under a very heavy lag and handicap, this chance of a short cut to the frontier of educational pioneering is a real opening of promise and value. By seizing hold on it there is the possibility of converting Negro needs into fresh educational inspiration and opportunities. That challenge and situation lies on our doorstep; let us assume it.

22. The Need for a New Organon in Education

This article is Locke's most extensive critique of what in 1950 was, and continues to be, a controversial major objective of educational policies intent on reshaping dogmatic and fallacious cognitive thinking processes—the promotion of logic and critical thinking as the fundamental "integrating elements for knowledge." Locke argues for his approach of "critical relativism" to replace the sterile, formalistic, and contentless critical thinking that was being taught as a set of reasoning methodologies and logical techniques.

Locke's view of the relation of values to education was formed over a long career of publication and participation in shaping educational policies. Of particular note as indicators of Locke's consistent involvement with educational issues are his "Moral Training in Elementary Schools," *The Teacher* 8 (1904), 95–101; "More than Blasting Brick and Mortar," *Survey Graphic* 36 (January 1947), 87–89; "Minorities and the Social Mind," *Progressive Education* 12 (March 1935), 141–146; *World View on Race and Democracy: A Study Guide in Human Group Relations* (Washington D.C.: American Library Association, 1943); "Stretching our Social Mind," speech Before the Hampton Institute Commencement, August 18, 1944 (Box S-T, Alain

"The Need for a New Organon in Education," *Goals for American Education*, Ninth Symposium of Conference on Science, Philosophy and Religion (New York: Conference on Science, Philosophy and Religion, 1950), pp. 201–212.

Locke Collection, Howard University); "The Negro in the Three Americas," *Journal of Negro Education* 13, no. 1 (Winter 1944), 7–18.

The modernity of the issues Locke addresses and his novel timeless approach, based on his mature value theory, are in some ways the pragmatic capstones of his work. If Locke's herculean efforts on behalf of African art, Afro-American art, literature, and drama have influenced intellectual history, the way those influences were intended to function in his eyes as modes of education has not received due attention. Given his promotion of African studies and of courses on race relations and the nature of social differentiation, ardent building of adult education projects, contributions to the *Journal of Adult Education*, service as editor and secretary of the Associates in Negro Folk Education and service as president of the American Association for Adult Education, it is fitting that his value theory and views of identity find an extensive expression in the field of education.

The Need for a New Organon in Education

For nearly two decades, scholars and educators have been intensively engaged, though too often on divided fronts, in what now appears a quest for a common objective—the discovery of integrating elements for knowledge and the search for focalizing approaches in education. Though not altogether fruitless on either side, these explorations have been unduly confusing and not overwhelmingly successful because of the lack of coordination between the philosophical and the educational activity and effort. The prospects of ultimate solution and success at present are immeasurably improved, however, through the comparatively recent realization of the common cause character of their problem and interests on the part of philosophers and educators. Both groups, accordingly, find themselves in a more strategic and hopeful position. There is agreed coordination, it seems to me, on three points; and pending tactical cooperation. The points of agreement are: first, that contemporary learning suffers from a serious and immobilizing lack of any vital and effective integration, both as a body of knowledge and as a taught curriculum (excepting, of course, the pragmatic vocational clusters in the various professional fields); second, that this "ineffectiveness" is not so much an internal fault as it is an external dislocation in the relationship of knowledge to the problems of the social culture; and third, that unless some revitalizing integration is soon attained, not only the social impotence of our knowledge must be conceded in spite of its technological effectiveness, but a breakdown of the culture itself may be anticipated.

These pragmatic pressures of a culture crisis, when added to the normal concerns for the systematization of knowledge and to our special contemporary need for "unified knowledge" after decades of an unprecedented expansion of the scientifically known, result cumulatively in a problem of great weight and urgency. To the natural desire on the part of educators not to evade their traditional social responsibility is added an anxiety not to forfeit their customary intellectual leadership. Although felt only vaguely in the earlier stages—that period of educational reform when "orientation courses" were proposed as the problem's "solution"—these concerns have now deepened to reach the present widespread preoccupation with the problem in terms of "general education" and the "core-curriculum." I have no desire to deprecate any of these promising and in many cases galvanizing reorganizations of the college curriculum, or to prejudge their coordinating potentialities, especially since so many are yet in the experimental stage. Particularly not to be thus minimized should be those programs which, in contradistinction to the "Great Books" plan, aim at broadening directly the student's present day perspectives of social vision and at connecting student thinking realistically with major practical interests of contemporary life, be they personal or social, local or global. Common to all such educational directives is the laudable attempt to link academic learning with the practical issues of living, and thus develop critical acumen and trained aptitudes for responsible intelligent action.

My ground of general criticism (and generalized criticism has its admitted limitations and risks) rests not on the contention that such general education plans lack merit and usefulness, but that, to use Matthew Arnold's phrase, "one thing more is also necessary." Accordingly, these suggestions of a much needed supplementation are brought forward in the conviction that mere curriculum extension or revision is insufficient, and that a more fundamental methodological change both in ways of teaching and in ways of thinking is necessary, if we are to achieve the objectives of reorientation and integration so obviously required and so ardently sought.

Any educational reconstruction adapted to a culture crisis as acute and deepseated as ours should be expected to be radical enough to call for more than mere realignment of subject-matter content or just new emphases in focus and perspective. Comparable culture transitions in the past have been characterized by a new methodology as well as a "new learning"; each age or stage of scholarship seems to have developed a new way, as well as a new scope, of thinking. In illustration, one need only cite the priority of the inductive logic which the scientific Renaissance instated, and its eventual methodological revolution of the laboratory method itself. However, to be even more specific, one might mention such later methodological departures as the genetic-functional approach which initiated evolutionary theory and scientific naturalism, the historico-comparative and statistical methodologies which combined to produce our modern social science, or quantum mechanics and mathematical relativity which evoked our contemporary atomic science. A new phase of scholarship and learning, so far as historical precedent shows, presupposes a new organon.

It seems somehow curious, then, that in this whole educational consideration of the present culture shift, whereas proposals of curriculum revision have been legion, suggestions of new methodology have been so few. And of these few, only the proposals of the semanticists and the "logical positivists" have been at all thoroughgoing and systematic. On one point, certainly, one can tangentially agree with the logical positivists to the extent that their project of "unified knowledge" calls for a more precise and more relevant logic than the verbalist and formalistic one, which, even when it is renounced as a formal logic, still dominates us so tyrannically through its deep embodiment in our language terms and the modes of thinking they have conditioned. But from there on, those of us interested primarily in a pedagogically useful organon, will, I take it, not pin our hopes on a "new logic" which, instead of yielding a clarifying and critical instrument, remains up to the present more recondite and abstract than the old logic it plans to supersede.

One can also find oneself in passing agreement with one of the prime objectives of the "Chicago Plan"—its insistence on the need for sharpening the instruments of critical thinking as an educational prolegomenon. But here again, as with its companion school of thought, the approach is too aridly formalistic.[1] As practical integrations of knowledge neither new "encyclopedic unity," nor the disciplinary unity of formal training in the abstract virtues of clear thinking, seems immediately promising. So, if for no other reason than its practical orientation toward the contemporary world and its problems, the curriculum reorganizations proposed by the "general education" plans seem to offer the wisest preference in the present field of choice. Even without a corrective methodology aimed expressly at implementing integration, they have considerable educational promise.

But it is by no means an excluded possibility to envisage a methodological approach superimposed on the new type curriculum, which would be calculated to assure the development of new ways of thinking *about* its newly reorganized content. It is such supplementation that this paper suggests. For without some specific correctives for traditional ways of thinking, it would by no means be certain that the wider horizons and broader content correlations of the general education program would really broaden the student's thinking, actually integrate it sufficiently to ensure a process understanding of the facts reviewed, and develop in him the capacity for evaluative criticism. We are making the assumption, of course, that global thinking, and what has been called "process understanding," and the capacity for evaluative criticism are compositely the prime objectives of the several general education schemes.

As a matter of fact, none of these objectives is assured except as the student's way of thinking is made the focus of pedagogic attention and ability for interpretation and capacity for critical evaluation explicitly placed above information and analytic skills. Can we be sure that content coordination and broadening the curriculum in time and space perspective will, of themselves, produce these results? Let us suppose, for example, that we have extended the study of history or of man and his cultures from the conventional Western hemispheric scope to a global range and setting, have we automatically exorcised parochial thinking and corrected traditional culture bias? As I see it, not necessarily. It surely is a patent fallacy to assume that a change in the *scope* of thinking will change the *way* of thinking. To convert parochial thinking into global thinking, involves meeting head on their issues of conflict, realistically accounting for their differences by tracing the history of their development, and out of a process-logic of this development, bravely to take a normative stand. If on the other hand, we keep scholarship's traditional neutrality as to values in the name of impartial objectivity, if we proceed with the old academic balancings of *pros* and *cons,* no matter how wide the scope of the curriculum, we are likely to have as an end-product a student, more widely informed, but with the same old mind-sets, perhaps more substantially entrenched in the conceit of knowing more. In that event, we have augmented rather than resolved the problems which, as intellectual defaults and dilemmas, constitute so large a part of the current "culture crisis."

If modernized contemporary education is to deal with attitudes, it must perforce grapple realistically with values and value judgments; if it is to build constructive mind-sets, or even fashion efficient critical ones, it must somehow restore the normative element in education. On more elementary educational levels, under the pressure of critical social issues and their behavior problems, a considerable vanguard of progressive teaching, particularly in the areas of "social" and "intercultural" education, has already crossed this educational Rubicon. Only in retrospect will it be realized what a departure this initiates from the standard educational traditions of descriptive objectivity, and *laissez-faire* neutrality with its "hands off" policy on controversial issues. The new programs openly involve a normative responsibility for attitude formation and even for remedial attitude reconstruction. In the latter, we go beyond the reconditioning of the pupil's thinking to situational recasting, in some cases, of his behavior patterns. Yet because this new "doctrine" has for its base objective findings in anthropology, social psychology, mental hygiene, and scientific child study, there is an authoritative consensus back of these newer educational procedures that few would care to challenge. Certainly no one would think of putting them in the same category, let us say, with religious teaching or political indoctrination.

But it is not easy to discover analogous procedures on the level of higher education, where independent thinking and self-forming opinion are conceded objectives. No matter how urgent the educational need for developing critical discrimination or inducing constructive attitudes, I take it we would not seriously consider reinstating, even in a modified modern guise, the old doctrinal didacticism which, at such pains and effort, education shed several generations ago. So our problem resolves itself into the very difficult and crucial one of finding a way to treat materials on this level with critical and normative regard for values, but without becoming didactic or dogmatic.

These difficult specifications set up criteria for a basic new methodology, as suited to meeting these new demands for our contemporary problems and interests as the empirical method, with laboratory science as its embodiment, was suited to the characteristic problems and interests of the first scientific age. Ironically, it was just the latter's fixation on fact to the exclusion of value, which led—by its neutral objectivity and consequent incapacity to consider values and their goals—to the present-day bankruptcy of the objective scientific method in certain important areas of contemporary concern.

It is for just these areas and their problems that intellectually and educationally a new organon is a pressing need. Adequate thinking on social issues needs above all to be critically evaluative rather than stop short at descriptive neutrality. So far as possible we must learn to handle values as objectively as we are able to handle facts, but in the social science fields we stand in further need of some way of correlating significantly and realistically their factual *and* their value aspects.

Objectively critical and normative judgments have been the despair of the social sciences (and for that matter, too, of the humanities in problems of comparative criticism), ever since scholarship subscribed to its modern scientific basis. However urgent our normative social interests or educational needs may become, we cannot secede from that alliance. So the only practical alternative is to discover a way of projecting into the study of social fact a normative dimension objective enough to be scientifically commensurable.

Though difficult, such a development is methodologically feasible. It could stem from a broadly comparative and critical study of values so devised as to make clear the vital correlations between such values and their historical and cultural backgrounds. By so regarding civilizations and cultures as objective institutionalizations of their associated values, beliefs, and ideologies, a realistic basis can be developed not only for a scientific comparison of cultures but for an objective critique of the values and ideologies themselves. Study and training in such analyses and interpretations should develop in students a capacity for thinking objectively but critically about situations and problems involving social and cultural values.

Considerable ground has already been broken for such an approach in recent studies undertaking realistic historical analyses of the ideological framework of various periods of civilization and systematic value comparisons between varying types of culture. The well-known work of Arnold J. Toynbee, F. S. C. Northrop,[2] Charles Morris, Margaret Mead, Geoffrey Gorer and others in this field, attempts this extension of the study of culture and history into the history and development of ideas and ideologies and the formation of various value orientations in social cultures. They are pioneering, in their several ways, in the techniques of objective and comparative social value analysis. "Area studies," also, from another angle of emphasis on the study of all aspects of a given society or culture as organically correlated, have similar, if not so clearly developed potentialities. These new approaches, emphasizing "civilization-type," "overall culture pattern," "paths of life" and "culture orientations," as determined by historical value emphases and predilections, all seem to reflect a common trend toward bridging the gap between the "factual" and the value aspects of the social sciences by using values objectively as key concepts for historical interpretation.

The methodological basis of such studies must be carefully distinguished from the earlier nonrealistic philosophies of history with their superimposed dialectics. These newer attempts, on the contrary, with no preconceived dialectics of history, try to make history reveal its own process logic, by following on a comparative historical basis the operational connection between an age and its beliefs, a culture and its system of values, a society and its ideological rationale. Here in this sort of integrated study of history may lie the implementation of a new scholarship that will not only afford us an objective panoramic outlook on history, but will also develop critical criteria for analyzing, comparing, and evaluating the varieties of human culture, and for explaining their cultural differences. The advantages from the point of view of a more objective understanding of society, culture, and history are rather immediately apparent; the normative implications, of equal if not greater importance, will be presently considered.

In this connection it is interesting to note, that with very few exceptions, the general education curricula center around the history of civilization. This seems a general recognition of the prime importance today of a fuller and more comprehending knowledge of man. This generally conceded goal of an "integrated" education is, of course, the old humanist ideal and objective of the best possible human and self-understanding. But it recurs in our age in a radically new context, and as something only realizable in an essentially scientific way. Instead of being based as before on the universal, common character of man, abstractly and rationalistically conceived, it rests on the concrete study of man in all his infinite variety. If it is to yield any effective integration, that must be derived from an objective appraisal and understanding of the particularities of difference, both cultural and ideological. These it must trace to the differentiating factors of time, place, and circumstance, largely on the framework laid down by recent cultural anthropology. The modern version of the "proper study of mankind is man" is, therefore a comprehensive, comparative study of mankind with realistic regard for difference, instead of a rationalistic study with a zeal for commonalities and conformity. We face, accordingly, a type of scientific humanism, with an essentially critical and relativistic basis. Its normative potential can issue only from the more objective understanding of difference and the laying down of a scientific rather than a sentimental kind of tolerance and understanding. If we are not to renounce the scientific approach, the hopes for integrated understanding must be grounded not on any doctrinaire normativism of agreement but upon this relativistic normativism of the realistic understanding of difference. And the question there has always been—how integrating can that be?

Although proposing a scientific type of core-curriculum, Professor Deutsch[3] in his paper for the current Conference, faces this same question, and from a somewhat similar methodological approach envisages a sound and constructive normativism derived, however, from relativistic premises. Answering his own query, "What could such a type of training accomplish," he remarks:

Perhaps in the most general terms it could aid students to achieve a larger measure of understanding of processes and of the nature of change and growth. It might aid them to achieve a better understanding of the nature of values and a greater openness to the values of other peoples and other cultures without weakening their understanding and attachment to their own. It might help students to acquire a rational appreciation of reason, and at the same time not only of the function but of the nature of tradition and intuition and perhaps, to some degree, of mysticism and religion; it might help them to keep their minds open to the insights and values which have been attained and which may be attained again through any and all of these approaches without forcing them at the same time to despair of the powers of reason.

A more rigorous and systematic program of value analysis and comparison would not leave such admittedly desirable results to chance or indirection. These broadening intellectual emancipations should be considered direct normative objectives of the process of education. The historical-comparative approach could then warrantably be maintained as the only proper (in the sense of the only scientific) way of understanding values, including particularly those of one's own culture and way of life. It would be regarded as educationally mandatory to view values relativistically in time perspective, so as to comprehend value change and development, and likewise, to see them in comparative perspective, so as to understand and appreciate value diversity. Thus there could be derived from critical relativism a corrective discipline aimed at the undermining of dogma-forming attitudes in thinking and the elimination of the partisan hundred percentist mentality at its very psychological roots. Instead of correcting here and there in palliative fashion specifically objectionable manifestations and superficial symptoms of an intellectually reinforced irrationality, we should then be attacking it at its generic source. For all absolutistic thinking, however idealist, has totalitarian potential; the characteristic end-product of the abstract intellectual tradition is dogma.[4]

We have come to a partial realization of this in our modern study of public opinion and in propaganda analysis. We have grappled with the problem at a deeper level in semantics, by searching out the mechanisms of dogmatic thinking and exposing the fallacies of symbol identification and the like. But until we have based the training of the student mind on a thoroughly grounded educational corrective for dogmatic thinking and its traditional rationalizations, we will not have effectively established scientific critical thinking in general, and objective thinking about values in particular.

The normative consequences of such a critical relativism can be realized only when it is carried through to a consistent and coordinated methodology. It then reveals not only how extensive are its normative implications, even though based on essentially nonnormative scientific procedures, but how radically reformative its effect can be. One can survey these in general outline by making an inventory with their limiting and in many cases, corrective criteria. Carried through as a consistent methodological approach, *Critical Relativism* would

1. implement an objective interpretation of values by referring them realistically to their social and cultural backgrounds,

2. interpret values concretely as functional adaptations to these backgrounds, and thus make clear their historical and functional relativity. An objective criterion of functional sufficiency and insufficiency would thereby be set up as a pragmatic test of value adequacy or inadequacy,

3. claim or impute no validity for values beyond this relativistic framework, and so counteract value dogmatism based on regarding them as universals good and true for all times and all places,

4. confine its consideration of ideology to the prime function and real status of being the adjunct rationalization of values and value interests,

5. trace value development and change as a dynamic process instead of in terms of unrealistic analytic categories, and so eliminating the traditional illusions produced by generalized value terms—*viz.*, static values and fixed value concepts and "ideals,"

6. reinforce current semantic criticism of academic value controversy by stressing this realistic value dynamics as a substitute for traditional value analytics, with its unrealistic symbols and overgeneralized concepts.

It should be made clear that this approach does not necessarily involve substantive agreement on specific value interpretations, but merely methodological agreement to keep value analysis and discussion on a plane of realism and the maximum attainable degree of scientific objectivity. It could even be a conceded educational device to maintain neutrality and permit constructive educational consideration of value issues so controversial as to be irreconcilable otherwise, especially with public educational institutions.

Critical thinking, however, could make no greater headway in a single line of uncompromising advance than, with such a strategic methodology as tactic, to invade the innermost citadel of dogmatic thinking, the realm of values. Nor could it provide a more vital integrating element in a modernly oriented general education than by carrying the scientific approach into content areas hitherto closed to objective scientific treatment. Conversely, it would be a real supplementation to scientific method itself, which has its admitted limitations, to be stretched by the necessity of handling value materials to the inclusion of new techniques of critical appraisal and formative attitude-conditioning. The gains would thus be mutual, to value analysis on the one hand, and to scientific method, on the other.[5]

Such methodological procedure could not be expected to settle many of these controversial value issues, especially their theoretical aspects, in concrete answers or demonstrable conclusions. But there would at least be an end to the inconclusive neutrality which education has been forced to exercise on many vital matters. It should be an educational boon to be able to handle them realistically and systematically off the plane of dogmatic solutions.

But while it is possible, and even strategic, to sidestep opposition with specific dogma not directly refutable by scientific proof, it is also nearly impossible to generate and implement critical thinking without challenging dogmatic thinking in general. As previously pointed out, it is necessary to attack the psychological roots of dogmatism. No restricted, formalistic discipline seems to me calculated to accomplish this in the present day college curriculum; neither the new scientific logic, nor the newer semantic logic, not to mention a rejuvenated traditional logic. We should remember that in the days when the traditional logic was effective and vitally alive, it was a real organon of learning, developed in application to the content of almost every other subject in the curriculum. Accordingly any reform in methodological approach which can carry its techniques, discipline, and influence into a large area of curriculum content has, it would seem, a favorable chance of being effective in the training and orientation of student thinking. A realistic critique of values, aspects of which run importantly throughout the whole range of the social science and humanistic subjects of the curriculum, has a definite advantage and wide prospect of influence, once adopted and set to work. It can become a new organon of critical thinking as well as a new apparatus of integration in the present educational situation, which is one of extreme, almost emergency need, with respect to both critical thinking and integration. Beside internal integration within the areas of the subjects with important value aspects and problems, there is a further overall curriculum integration in the extension of the scientific method to cover so much more intellectual territory. After all its success in the natural science segment, and for that matter, wherever facts are in question, has already established potential dominance of the scientific method and approach throughout the scope of modern scholarship. The conquest of the field of values would be almost the concluding triumph.

NOTES

1. For further discussion of the "Chicago Plan," see Chapter 2 by Lyman Bryson, Chapter 3 by T. V. Smith, Chapter 9 by Howard Mumford Jones, Chapter 11 by John U. Nef, Chapter 13 by Mordecai M. Kaplan, Chapter

15 by George N. Shuster, Chapter 16 by Earl J. McGrath, Chapter 17 by Ordway Tead, and George B. de Huszar's comment in Appendix 3.

2. With limiting reservations in the cases of Toynbee and Northrop because of the remnants in their thinking of the abstract dialectical principles of interpretation.

3. See Chapter 4 by Karl W. Deutsch.

4. For further discussion of the problems of ethical absolutism and relativism, see Chapter 10 by Donald C. Stone (including comments by Quincy Wright and Clem C. Linnenberg, Jr.) and Chapter 14 by Theodore Brameld (including comments by B. Othanel Smith, John D. Wild, and Louis J. A. Mercier).

5. See Chapter 6 by John Courtney Murray, S.J., for a criticism of the limits of scientific method with the proposal that there are other rational techniques available for dealing with questions of value and metaphysics.

An Interpretation

Rendering the Subtext: Subterranean Deconstructive Project

LEONARD HARRIS

The formulation of a unitary science based on what seemed to undergird all human endeavors—values—was the thrust of value theory in the early 1900s. Such a theory would be capable of accounting for or explaining nearly all forms of human endeavor. As Ralph B. Perry put it, the "realms of value coincide largely with man's major institutions."[1] A general theory of value would tell us what a "value" meant, what its nature was and how valuation occurred. If the general theory was metaphysical in character, then it would tell us the way values cohere or were constituted like the nature of the universe. If anthropological in character, the general theory would tell us the way values cohere or constitute a foundational feature of our personhood. If "value" was construed broadly, then a general theory would tell us not only what was entailed in having a value (pleasure, relation, interest, affection, satisfaction, quality of being) and how it originates but what sorts of phenomena we should consider to be of worth in matters of personal virtues, psychology, sociology, politics, and economics. If constructed narrowly, then a general theory would tell us what was entailed in having a particular value and how it originates, and what we should consider of worth in matters of a particular area, for example, ethics or labor. Locke conceived value theory broadly.

Locke spoke in the code of value theory, particularly value relativism and cultural pluralism, as his master code of deconstruction. His views consistently rejected the hierarchical constitution of metaphysics, the possibility of a meta-metalanguage or presupposition-less valuation, and what William James termed the "block universe" picture of reality. But that code was itself not the magic of the magi-cian, not the conjuring of the conjurer, not the voodoo of the hoodoo man. The magic was the subterranean message conveyed in a subter-ranean world for which the deconstructive code was itself a master form that also served, in Baker's terms, deformatively. That is, it served to convey meanings and messages that served the purpose of positively evaluating features of black culture that were treated derogatorily in the dominant media. It served, in addition, to in-ject a universal that constrained the master code of value relativism and cultural pluralism—the common features of our humanity. That we each transvalue and thereby differentiate uniquely is simultane-ously recognition for Locke of value equivalences. A logical proof, for example, can be beautiful; importance can be attached to the sounds of spirituals equally as the cadence of a political speech. We are all the same in our condition of being transvaluers. Within that common being we are all individuated. Our individuation is consti-tuted through an already given social world, and within that social world we form and reform cultural loyalties of personhood, poli-tics, and religion. Individual and social identities do not correspond to essences or natures but are integral to systems of self-regard and transvaluation. These views were expressed in a subterranean world.

The doing of philosophy occurred for Locke in a subterranean world in at least two senses: first, his views on the nature of values were central to his views of race relations, literary criticism, and education, but his views on the nature of values received less atten-tion than his views on race, literature, and education; and secondly, on his account no one's belief system is totally available to them or others, so that the world of cognition is to some degree always hid-den. Discourse about general conceptions divorced from normative commitments, as if general conceptions were justified in a value-free fashion or were themselves free of normative implications, was not a human power because all forms of thought were necessarily en-twined to some degree with prereflective preferences. Locke's phi-losophy consequently informed his articles on cultural issues, but compared to his voluminous works on cultural issues his works ex-plicitly addressing philosophical issues rarely surfaced as a discourse unto itself. When it did, Locke exposed the illicit way that value ultimates were constituted and used to legitimize cultural chauvinism. Discourse about general conceptions was thus also discourse about the relevance of general conceptions to our prereflective beliefs and daily cultural life. Locke's discourses about daily cultural life were, conversely, discourses used as examples to reflect or portray a general conception consciously as a feature of his value relativism. Locke's deconstructive project not only entailed a rejection of metaphysics but an effort (a) to go beyond the illusion that a given group held inherently preferable beliefs or values that in some way cohered with the nature of things, (b) to denude the romanticism of cultural pluralists who believed in the likelihood of a world without regulative value guides or imperatives, and (c) to expose the way pluralism was misguidedly used as a rouge for the perpetuation of the segregated status quo.

The Diltheyian problematic that language tends to elicit metaphysical standpoints, intentionally or unintentionally, is in Locke's writings analogous to the problematic that even radical value relativism is compelled to set itself up as an epistemologically privileged position warranting itself as an absolute. Identifying the common features underlying our cultural realities and constructing imperatives that would limit the imposition of debilitating authoritarian guidelines should be the primary constructive project of human endeavors.

The common denominators of our humanity are invariant across historical reference systems. The differences between cultures are a reflection or manifestation of our nature—*our common nature to differentiate and valuate uniquely*—rather than different cultural or racial essences. The processes of unique valuations, revaluations, and transvaluations is not tangential to our being but natural to it. Locke's relativism holds that the existence of cultural differences is not a manifestation of different and inalterable natures but a manifestation of our nature to differentiate. The context within which common properties occur is definitive of a thing's nature. For Locke, monism is thus an erroneous philosophic approach, because it defines essences in terms of the sameness of properties across reference systems. Analogous to conceptions of the nature of things, cultural properties are not essences but the historical reference system (inclusive of the material condition germane to that system) within which they exist in tandem with the "common denominators" of humanness (which includes irreducible powers of differentiating and valuating), and are definitive of our being.

The subterranean integration of Locke's philosophy can be seen in his disagreement with Lothrop Stoddard and his support of proletarian art. He argued, for example, against Stoddard's view that whites had an "indefensible right to their racial heritage" that warranted segregation.[2] Locke argued, white orthodoxy "fumes about keeping society closed at the top and insists on keeping it viciously open at the bottom. It claims to eliminate social contracts between the races, but actually promotes race mixing."[3] Locke held that people naturally differentiate themselves and that so doing is warranted under certain conditions but that there is nothing natural about structured systems of segregation. Instead, "making possible free and unbiased contracts between the races on the selective basis of common interest and mutual consent" is a condition for an open society.[4] The culture of a people develops, for Locke, not in isolation but in tandem and contact with others. Contrary to Stoddard's biracialism, a culture does not have a right to exist in isolation or at the expense of another. Analogously, privileging one reasoning method by awarding it the status of objectivity and thereby treating it as pure, as an isolated good to be untainted by the intrusion of other reasoning modalities, is dysfunctional because this overlooks other modalities of thinking potentially of use. Privileging a given cultural domain limits cultural contacts and the exchange of modalities of living that are potentially of benefit. Locke did not rest his hopes for a peaceful world on a method of inquiry as such, including his method of critical relativism, but on the possible positive outcome of the human spirit, recognition of cultural equivalences, real social struggles, and the use of tolerance, reciprocity, and parity.

Locke identified with the proletarian struggle during the 1930s. The "class proletarian creed" of the black arts movement of the 1930s was perceived by Locke as being committed to expressing black art just as the then-outdated "racialism" of the New Negro movement was committed to expressing black art of the 1920s.[5] Proletarian art, as expressing and promoting the interest of the working class, received Locke's applause not because the proletariat is the historically necessary agent of universal human liberation but, I suspect, because at a point in history its expressions and interests were promoting universal human liberation. The interest of premier concern to Locke was regard for uniquely African and African-American cultural genres as legitimate modes of valuation. In addition, Locke's support of Richard Wright's *Native Son*—seen in the 1940s and 1950s as a radical novel that exploded the myths that white socialists were bereft of racist attitudes and that no serious class conflicts occurred within the black community—was an expression of his support for proletarian art committed to sounds echoing from the depths of the black world. Locke's promotion of the "New Negro" as the harbinger of self-respecting black artistic expression and his later support for the "class proletarian creed" are not as antithetical as they may appear—each presupposes an elite group with an interest in promoting warranted modes of valuing originating from the African world. Cultural pluralism provided a framework within which that interest was legitimated in tandem with the warranted cultural moorings of other peoples.

Under the general rubric of cultural pluralism, Locke worked out the constructive and pragmatic side of his subterranean deconstructive project. That side entailed establishing the legitimacy of the way African people differentiate themselves and exploring the conditions for cross-cultural communication and cultural conflict resolution. Locke's cultural pluralism emphasized, on Horace Kallen's interpretation, the possibility of the "free intercommunication of diversities —denoting the cultivation of those diversities for the purpose of free and fruitful intercommunication between equals." On Kallen's account, cultural pluralism meant for Locke a situation of "voluntary cooperative relationship where each, in living on, also helps, and is helped by, the others in living."[6] Locke did not conceive of culture as a static phenomenon, nor did he argue that any cultural grouping in existence has a right to be protected from forces affecting its change. His cultural pluralism presumed the continued existence of cultural change and conflict but not the continuation or production of grievous forms of domination and exploitation. He consistently explicated cultural continuities and considered them a requirement for personhood. He believed that humans tend to differentiate in ways that produce and reproduce modes of antagonistic thinking and acting. The possibility of peaceful coexistence between diverse cultural communities existed for Locke, but not as a uniform cultural reality devoid of continual revaluation, transposition, and transvaluation or of always-fluid social identities.

I have drawn similarities or analogies between Locke's views and James's pragmatism, Meinong's and Urban's value theories, Habermas' conception of communicative competency, and Derrida's deconstructive philosophy in order to suggest the strengths of Locke's critical relativism, value relativism, and cultural pluralism. The similarities, analogies, and convergences are also intended to reveal his subterranean deconstructive project. Moreover, they indicate that Locke's philosophy emerges from the master code enlivening his deconstructive value theoretic project. That is, historically embedded in early twentieth century value theory trends, Locke's philosophy arises as a school of thought.

Locke conceived of value theory broadly, at least in the sense that values undergird all human endeavors, that to some degree they can be correlated to various human institutions and reasoning modalities, and that we share a common nature to differentiate and valuate. In some cases of broadly conceived value theories, the root metaphor of a conception of value was used as the root metaphor for depicting the nature of reality. Meinong's *Psychologisch-ethische Untersuchungen zur Werththeorie* (1894) was followed by *Über Annahmen* (1910); and Ehrenfels' "Werttheorie und Ethik," *Vierteljahrsschrift für wissenschaftliche Philosophie* (1893–94), was followed by *System der Werttheorie*, (1897–1898). Ralph B. Perry's *General Theory of Value* (1926) was followed by Euro-American histories of philosophy, patriotic valorizations of America, a classical study of William James, and eventually *Realms of Value* (1954); Wilbur Urban's *Valuation: Its Nature and Laws* (1909) was followed by *The Intelligible World, etc.*, (1929) and *Fundamentals of Ethics* (1930); and William James's *The Principles of Psychology* (2 vols., 1890) was followed by a number of articles and books that took the root metaphor of experience and its characteristics as the root metaphor of reality. My point is not that an individual value theorist necessarily presented his conception of value and valuation and then worked out the ways central features of that conception should be mapped onto understanding political institutions or reality in general. Nor is the point that all value theorists were aware of what other theorists were doing or held the same views throughout their careers. Rather, value theory as a field was predicated on a conception about what a general theory of value involved. The world of value theory that Locke chose to enter was not the world of reductionist general theories of value in the way that emotivism is reductionist. That is, emotivism reduces, or explains, modes of social behavior by reference to feelings. Nor was his world the same as that of the neo-Kantians, logical positivists, or the then-budding phenomenologists Brentano, Husserl, and Scheler. Rather, Meinong, Urban, James, Perry, and Ehrenfels, at the point that Locke entered their worlds between 1907 and 1918, correlated modes of behavior to conceptions of value or experience. They were metaphysical pluralists, value relativists, and fallibilists, and believed that their views rested on facts about human cognition. In addition, they believed that their general theory of value or experience could be used to account for a wide variety of cognitive endeavors and realities. Noting these similarities in their agendas is not intended to suggest that their philosophies were identical but to suggest certain basic guiding beliefs were common to their projects.

The master code of the broadly construed value theory, it can be argued, was burdened with inescapable problematics, particularly, because it tended to both describe how we make value judgments and, simultaneously, to prescribe. In addition, it treated subjective conditions as causes of social situations. However, it is also arguable that given that prescriptions and descriptions are produced by historically situated valuing agents, Locke's naturalization of epistemology surmounts the prescription–description problematic. Locke grounds prescriptive considerations in the conditions shaping, and the conditions definitive of, human conduct.[7] These were described in social-psychology terms and were always open to revision. Provincialism, partisanship, proprietorship, patriotism, pride, exaltation, tension, acceptance, or repose, for example, are changeable features of human thought. They may be expressed in terms of racial, national, ethnic, or class loyalties, but the causal variables shaping interests and identities and the correlation of subjective conditions with social entities are best described, for Locke, by objective research guided by critical relativism.

It is arguable that Locke was too optimistic about the prospects of cultural pluralism, the possibility of cultural reciprocity, the role of literature, art, and music in reshaping race relations during the Harlem Renaissance, and the likelihood of social recognition of the way identities shape and re-shape perceptions. The Science, Philosophy, and Religion Conferences (SPR) were a classic example of the failures of the cultural pluralism movement. Locke regularly attended the meetings of SPR and was a member of its Board. The SPR first met in 1940 at the Jewish Theological Seminary in New York, and met annually between 1941 and 1958 at Columbia University. Albert Einstein, Aldous Huxley, Bertrand Russell, F. S. C. Northrop, Margaret Mead, Talcott Parsons, Mortimer J. Adler, Paul Weiss, Ruth Benedict, Charles S. Johnson, and E. Franklin Frazier were a few luminaries that participated in various meetings and published articles in the annual book of SPR proceedings. The SPR conferences returned to the seminary in 1959, and by 1962, its purpose and foci were much more ethnocentric than its initial thrust. Although this forum, and numerous others such as the National Negro Congress, did not weather the storm of sectarian interests, it is arguable that numerous benefits did result from their pluralistic efforts. Moreover, Locke's optimism was no more misguided than Marx's expectations of a socialist revolution in nineteenth-century England; no less fantastic than Dewey's hopes and efforts to promote and use pragmatism in pre-revolutionary China; and no more visionary than W. E. B. Du Bois' promotion of Pan-Africanism through the barely independent state of Ghana in the 1960s. Socialist revolutions have occurred, most often in the First World (rather than continental Europe); pragmatism has had its uses in China, but not by virtue of Dewey's efforts; and Pan-Africanism is a constituting ideology and direction of Africa and the diaspora, but not because the Ghanaian model is regularly emulated. Communicative competency between agents requires radical reorientation of already given linguistic forms of predication, explication, and symbols. It simply takes longer for realities to be seen and possibilities actualized than philosophers usually recognize.

Locke emerges from the master code by setting a new agenda. Issues current among value theorists were rarely his central consideration; for example, whether or not there are discoverable scientific laws of proper explanation and interpretation, codifiable methods of logical reasoning, possible ways for one subject to enter into, apprehend, and represent the reality of another subject, or a meta-normative definition of values. Instead, the issues that fuel Locke's concerns include how to represent an entity that is both real and simultaneously a reification. A group, for example, that sees itself, and is seen as, a people, who have common cultural norms and similar material and political interests, is a real social entity always in formation and re-formation. Yet, peoplehood, be it racial, ethnic, or national, is a reification. Moreover, such reifications cloak both class and cultural differences and similarities. Social identities for Locke are foundational components of our ontologies, not immutable Hegelian givens with transcendentally shaped teleologies, nor historical fetters of the uncivilized in contrast to an enlightened a-textual self purified of privincialisms. The nature of personhood and human conduct are central issues in tandem with such issues as what should be the meta-criteria of representation, perceiving, and symbolizing across relative modes of valuation; what modes of reasoning require continual critical reflection; how to picture personal and group identities; explications of theoretical tendencies that unintentionally confer credibility to authoritarianism and uniformity. Locke's philosophy, as a body of texts, emanates from the world of philosophy he joined, it articulates itself, and sounds the emancipatory vibrations of the maroons.

No biography of Locke nor comprehensive collection of his works now exists. Moreover, relatively few articles have been publishing focusing attention on specific concepts and the use of terms in Locke's works. This anthology functions as an introduction to an emerging appreciation of Locke's philosophy, recognition of a subterranean deconstructive project, acknowledgment of an enigmatic moment that gave rise to a creative praxis, and a praise song for a philosophy that lived in the Harlem Renaissance and lives beyond.[8]

NOTES

1. Ralph B. Perry, *Realms of Value* (Cambridge, Mass.: Harvard University Press, 1954), p. vii.

2. Lothrop Stoddard, "The Impasses at the Color-Line," *Forum* 77 (October 1927), 503.

3. Alain Locke, "The High Cost of Prejudice," *Forum* 77 (December 1927), 505.

288 / *An Interpretation*

4. *Ibid.*, pp. 504–505.
5. See, for example, *Official Proceedings of the National Negro Congress* (Washington, D.C.: National Negro Congress, 1937), pp. 15–17.
6. Horace Kallen, "Alain Locke and Cultural Pluralism," *Journal of Philosophy* 57 (February 1957), 124. See also Eugene Clay Holmes, *The New Negro Thirty Years Afterward* (Washington, D.C.: Howard University Press, 1955), pp. 3–7; Ernest D. Mason, "Alain Locke's Social Philosophy," *World Order* (Winter 1978–1979), 25–34; Ernest D. Mason, "Alain Locke on Race and Race Relations," *Phylon* 40 (1979), 1–17; Mark Helbling, "Alain L. Locke: Ambivalence and Hope," *Phylon* 40 (1979), 291–300.
7. See Locke, "Values and Imperatives," p. 315. Also see Charner M. Perry, "The Arbitrary as Basis for Rational Morality," *International Journal of Ethics* 18 (January 1933), 127–144, and W. Watts Cunninham's response, *International Journal of Ethics* 18 (January 1933), 147–148. Locke agrees with Cunninham's view that "choices are not ultimately arbitrary because preferences are necessarily relative, rather, we should ground choice in a principle of value and of determining this principle with reference to the conditions of human conduct" (Cunninham, p. 147).
8. I have focused this anthology on Locke's works in philosophy. The concepts that Locke emphasized as definitive of the constitution of human experience and conduct are due special consideration, for example, the notions of affectivity, cognate, form quality, and imperatives; the analysis of valuation, transvaluation, and revaluation as processes endogenous to our being; the notion of "difference" (parasitic structures) and what it means to differentiate; incommensurability, particularly as it manifests itself in cultural distinctions and modes of ascribing meaning to phenomenon; the relationship of the "common denominators" definitive of our being and their interplay with our particularities; and the conception of personhood as most often tied to a group identity and its role in shaping and reshaping senses of self-worth.

Locke's works in philosophy often utilize terms in unique ways. These terms are due close attention to determine, where possible, their precise meaning. Mason's "Alain Locke's Philosophy of Value" (in Russell J. Linnemann [ed.], *Alain Locke: Reflections on a Modern Renaissance Man* [Baton Rouge: Louisiana State University Press, 1982], pp. 1–16) clarifies the meaning of Locke's value relativism from his occasional use of "subjectivism"; Mason's "Deconstruction in the Philosophy of Alain Locke" (*Transactions of the Charles S. Peirce Society* 24 [Winter, 1988], 84) traces Locke's argument against metaphysical absolutism in comparison to Derrida's, and the contours of his value relativism as deconstructive. Locke's critique of pragmatism's Western biases in favor of the reasoning methods of experimental science, conceptual anticipation of Rorty's critique of foundationalism, and view of "imperatives" as modal commitments (lacking in Rorty's pragmatism) are explored by this editor in "Legitimation Crisis in American Philosophy" (*Social Science Information* 26 [1987], 57–73); the significance of identity, particularly racial identity, self-worth, and nativistic approaches are addressed by this editor in "Identity: Alain Locke's Atavism" (*Transactions of the Charles S. Peirce Society* 24 [Winter 1988], 65–83). Locke's political ideas and their possible application to contemporary issues are discussed in Johnny Washington's *Alain Locke and Philosophy: A Quest for Cultural Pluralism* (Westport, Conn.: Greenwood Press, 1986). The above works provide major analyses or uses of Locke's conceptions within the arena of modern philosophy and in so doing offer important guideposts for further clarification, exploration, and analysis of Locke's unique use of terms.

Issues of interest in relation to culture involve the reasonableness of Locke's suggestions on the way culture should be studied, the usefulness of his suggestions on the preconditions for the possibility of peace between cultures, and the efficacy of symbol systems as phenomena shaping our attitudes.

Several issues involving the arts are due additional consideration: whether folk art accurately portrays social reality; the way a work of art pictures or depicts; the advocacy role of literature, and Locke's critique of literature by authors who rejected that role; and whether the universals considered as such by Locke are really universals. The above issues do not exhaust the possibilities, but they capture some of the more contemporary areas of interest for which Locke's works are rich in suggestive theoretical avenues.

Chronology,
Bibliography,
and Index

Chronology: Alain Leroy Locke, 1885–1954

The Chronology is divided into sections that roughly parallel important transition periods in Locke's professional life.

1885

Born Arthur Locke, September 13, 1885, the only child of Pliny Ishmael Locke and Mary Hawkins Locke. Paternal grandfather, Ishmael Locke, free Negro, teacher in Salem, N.J., supported by Society of Friends to attend Cambridge University, established schools in Liberia for four years; maternal grandmother, Sarah Shorter Hawkins, established schools in Liberia; maternal grandfather, Charles Shorter (free Negro and soldier in the War of 1812); paternal uncle, Phaeton Locke. Pliny I. Locke taught freedmen in North Carolina during Reconstruction, worked as accountant in the Freedmen's Bureau and the Freedmen's Bank, was private secretary to General O. O. Howard, matriculated in the Howard University Law Department, completing law school in 1874; returned to Philadelphia in 1874 and became a clerk in the U.S. Post Office, died in 1891. Mary H. Locke, educated at the Institute for Coloured Youth, Philadelphia, supported herself and family as a teacher in Camden and Camden County, was a disciple of the humanist Felix Adler, Ethical Cultural Society, and died in 1922.

1902

Graduated from Central High School in Philadelphia; suffered rheumatic fever, which damaged his heart.

1904

Graduated first in class from Philadelphia School of Pedagogy, B.A. degree; first known publication, "Moral Training in Elementary Schools," *The Teacher*, 1904.

1904–1907

Studied under Josiah Royce, George Herbert Palmer, Ralph Barton Perry, Hugo Munsterberg; graduated from Harvard College *magna cum laude*, B.A. degree; received Bowdoin Prize for an essay in English; elected to Phi Beta Kappa; selected as Rhodes Scholar from Pennsylvania, first black to receive award.

1907–1909

Although Rhodes Scholars held right of admission to an Oxford college, five Oxford colleges refused to admit Locke on grounds of race; admitted to Hertford College, Oxford University, in 1907 and studied philosophy, Greek, and *Literae Humaniores* until 1910; critical of the aristocratic pretensions of Oxford in "Oxford Contrasts," published 1909; one of the founders of the African Union Society.

1910–1911

Attended the University of Berlin, focused his studies on the works of Franz Brentano, Alexius Meinong, Christian Freiherr von Ehrenfels.

1912–1914

September 13, 1912, appointed to the faculty of the Teachers College at Howard University as Assistant Professor of the Teaching of English and Instructor in Philosophy and Education under Lewis B. Moore; taught logic, ethics, education, literature, and English in the Teachers College; Moore retired in 1912 and Locke added to his duties the teaching of ethics and logic at Howard University.

1915

Petitioned Howard University's Board of Trustees to teach a course based on the scientific study of race and race relations; petition rejected; Howard Chapter of the NAACP and the Social Science Club sponsored a two-year extension course of lectures by Locke entitled "Race Contacts and Inter-Racial Relations: A Study in the Theory and Practice of Race."

1916

Joined with Montgomery Gregory and others to form Special Army Training Corps; was appointed an Austin Teaching Fellow at Harvard; Ralph Barton Perry selected as dissertation advisor; helped produce the play *Rachel* by Angelina Grimké.

1917–1918

Submitted doctoral dissertation to Perry, September 17, 1917, entitled "The Problem of Classification in Theory of Value"; graduated from Harvard, Ph.D. in Philosophy, 1918; applauded W. E. B. Du Bois' ideas on the Talented Tenth in "The Role of the Talented Tenth," *Howard University Record* 18 (December 1918).

1919–1923

The Red Summer of 1919 begins, over one hundred blacks lynched; involved with efforts by black faculty to secure salaries commensurate with white faculty; helped establish the Howard University Players in 1921 with Montgomery Gregory and Marie Moore-Forrest; began publishing in 1923 many articles and book reviews for *Opportunity: Journal of Negro Life* (Urban League Journal, ed. Charles S. Johnson), most of which entailed the notion of identity as flourishing through a community and best manifested through folk art; began relations with future important philanthropic and organization sources such as Paul Kellogg, editor of *Survey Graphic*; Ms. Rufus Osgood Mason, philanthropist; the Harmon Foundation; Rosenwald Foundation; Progressive Education Association; Forum of the Air; and American Library Association.

1924

Delegate to Carnegie Corporation–sponsored Adult Education Conference, 1924; took leave of absence from Howard to work in collaboration with the French Oriental Archaeological Society of Cairo; represented Howard and the Negro Society for Historical Research, visited Egypt and the Sudan; was present at Luxor, Egypt, for reopening of the tomb of Tutankhamen; tendered his concept of race and its relationship to culture in "The Concept of Race as Applied to Social Culture."

1925–1926

Edited in March an issue for *Survey Graphic* entitled "Harlem, Mecca of the New Negro," which included contributions by Charles S. Johnson, James Weldon Johnson, W. E. B. Du Bois, Arthur Schomburg, Kelly Miller, and Walter White; was fired in June, 1925, from Howard University, ostensibly on grounds of university reorganization but actually as a part of administrative efforts to remove faculty in favor of black and white equity; published *The New Negro* in December; emerged as a leading literary critic, aesthete, author of introductions to catalogues of African art, conduit for philanthropic sources for art exhibits and for patron funds for literary artists such as Langston Hughes, Zora Neale Hurston, Aaron Douglas, Richmond Barthé, Countee Cullen; continued promoting adult education and published under the American Association for Adult Education "Adult Education for Negroes," in *Handbook of Adult Education in the United States* (1926).

1927

Spent summer researching in Geneva the League of Nations' mandate system and the problem of forced African labor under the auspices of the Foreign Policy Association; co-edited with Montgomery Gregory *Plays of Negro Life: A Source-Book of Native American Drama*; Exchange Professor, Fisk University.

1928

Returned to Howard under auspices of first black president of Howard University, Mordecai W. Johnson; revised proposal for systematic study of race; lobbied for African Studies Program at Howard (not institutionalized until 1954); defended folk art as a people's expression against charges that art should be used for propaganda in "Art or Propaganda?" (1928).

1929–1934

Argued increasingly in *Opportunity* and elsewhere that universal art or the universality and warrant of cultural messages are not at odds with particularity or racial art; received funds from the American Association for Adult Education, Rosenwald Fund, Carnegie Corporation, to evaluate adult education centers in Atlanta and Harlem; assisted in their organization with Ira Reid and E. F. Frazier; held that "race" is essentially a cultural manifestation and that with an end to vested interest in cultural identities universal culture could begin as an allowing of diversity without prejudice in "The Contribution of Race to Culture" (1930); published *The Negro in America* in 1933 for the American Library Association to enhance adult education and group relations.

1935

Harlem race riots; interest in writing philosophy revived; Alfred Dunham joined Howard; Locke published "Values and Imperatives," in *American Philosophy, Today and Tomorrow* ed. Horace M. Kallen and Sidney Hook; argued that pragmatism's fallibilism should entail a rejection of the western valorization of the scientific method; constructed value relativism as epistemological basis; helped establish the Associates in Negro Folk Education under auspices of American Association for Adult Education, Rosenwald Fund, Carnegie Corporation.

1936

Worked on Bronze Booklets under auspices of Associates in Negro Folk Education (nine booklets were eventually published, the first by Ira Reid, "Adult Education Among Negroes"; Locke's were "Negro Art: Past and Present" and "The Negro and His Music"; served as an organizer of the Division of the Social Sciences, which came to function as a focal point for race-specific research.

1937

At the annual meeting of the National Negro Congress, supported a position alluded to in literary critiques since 1931—that the proletarian creed in art that perceived art as a tool for liberation and was supportive of Negro modes of self-expression was the next phase after the racialism associated with the New Negro movement.

1938–1939

Beginning of World War II ended conditions supportive of artistic activity; spent less time promoting art, drama, and literature and more time with adult education; defended black historiography that directed at building Negro pride through chronicling Negro success stories as not being a hindrance to working-class unity in "Jingo, Counter Jingo and Us" (1938); published "The Negro: New or Newer," in 1939; contended that the phrase "New Negro" had become a slogan applauding race idolatry and not the banner of a genuine cultural movement.

1940–1942

Defended Richard Wright's portrait of Bigger Thomas in *Native Son* in "Of Native Sons: Real or Otherwise" (1941); edited with Bernard J. Stern *When Peoples Meet: A Study in Race and Culture* (1942), which was predicated on the ethnicity paradigm of race and the view that cultural pluralism could contribute to world peace through its normative criteria for ameliorating difference (subvention by the Progressive Education Association); edited in 1942 *Color: Unfinished Business of Democracy*; pointed out the racism and hypocrisy of the democracies; pointed out the wrong-heading search for the authentic Negro in "Who and What is Negro?" (1942).

1943

Inter-American exchange Professor to Haiti; wrote *Le rôle du Negro dans la culture des Amerique* (1943) and "Race, Culture et Democratie" (1944).

1944–1945

Participant in the founding and conferences of the Conference on Science, Philosophy and Religion headed by R. M. MacIver; published philosophy articles through its auspices; chaired 1945 conference; served on editorial board of *American Scholar*; philosophy editor for *Key Reporter* of Phi Beta Kappa; elected president of American Association for Adult Education in 1945.

1946–1947

Visiting Professor, University of Wisconsin (1945–1946) and the New School for Social Research (1947).

1948–52

Taught at City College of New York and Howard University (1948–1953); attended the Salzburg Seminar in American Studies (1950); active in American Association for Adult Education; published "The Need for a New Organon in Education" in *Goals for American Education*, rejecting formal logic as a sufficient cornerstone of critical thinking particularly when it is isolated from normative and moral considerations.

1953

Phi Beta Kappa chapter established at Howard; retired from Howard in June and was awarded Honorary Degree of Doctor of Humane Letters; moved to New York in July; published retrospective review of literature "From *Native Son* to *Invisible Man*," integrating historical developments with an understanding of literature since the New Negro movement; worked on *The Negro in American Culture*.

1954

Reviewed Ralph Barton Perry's *The Realms of Value*; experienced recurring heart trouble; died June 9, Mount Sinai Hospital, New York; funeral held at Benta's Chapel, Brooklyn, New York, June 11, Dr. Channing Tobias officiating, cremation at Fresh Pond Crematory, Little Village, Long Island; Margaret Just Butcher, daughter of Ernest E. Just, completed and published *The Negro in American Culture* but faced controversies over its faithfulness to Locke's approach to culture.

SOURCES

Barry, Faith, *Langston Hughes, Before and Beyond Harlem* (Westport, Conn.: Lawrence Hill, 1983).

Crane, Clare Bloodgood, "Alain Locke and the Negro Renaissance" (Ph.D. dissertation, University of California, San Diego, 1971).

Hemenway, Robert E., *Zora Neale Hurston: A Literary Biography* (Urbana: University of Illinois Press, 1977).

Holmes, Eugene, C., "Alain L. Locke and the Adult Education Movement," *Journal of Negro Education* (Winter 1965), 5–10.

Johnson, Abby Arthur, and R. M. Johnson, *Propaganda and Aesthetics: The Literary Politics of Afro-American Magazines in the Twentieth Century* (Amherst: University of Massachusetts Press, 1979), pp. 69–70.

Lewis, David Levering, *When Harlem Was in Vogue* (New York: Alfred A. Knopf, 1981).

Long, Richard A., "Alain Locke: Cultural and Social Mentor," *Black World* 20 (November 1970), 87–90.

Stewart, Jeffrey C., *The Critical Temper of Alain Locke: A Selection of His Essays on Art and Culture* (New York: Garland Publishing, 1983).

Willis, Wilda Logan, *A Guide to the Alain L. Locke Papers* (Washington, D.C.: Moorland-Spingarn Research Center, Howard University, 1985).

Biographical sketch by Michael R. Winston in Rayford W. Logan and Michael R. Winston (eds.), *The Dictionary of American Negro Biography* (New York: Norton, 1983), pp. 398–404.

Bibliography

CHRONOLOGICAL BIBLIOGRAPHY*

1904–1918

"Moral Training in Elementary Schools." *The Teacher*, 8 (1904), 95–101.
"Cosmopolitanism." *The Oxford Cosmopolitan*, 1: 1 (1908), 15–16.
"Oxford Contrasts." *Independent* 67 (July 1909), 139–142.
"The Negro and a Race Tradition." *A.M.F. Quarterly Review* (April 1911), n.p.
"The American Temperament." *North American Review* 194 (August 1911), 262–270.
"Emile Verhaeren." *The Poetry Review of America*. Ed. William S. Braithwaite (January 1917), 41–43.
"*The Problem of Classification in the Theory of Value.*" Ph.D. dissertation, Harvard University, 1918.
"The Role of the Talented Tenth." *Howard University Record* 12:7 (December 1918), 15–18.

1919

"Howard University in the War—A Record of Patriotic Service—'The Des Moines Training Camp.'" *The Howard University Record*, 13 (1919), 159–178.

1922

"Steps Toward the Negro Theatre." *The Crisis* 25 (December 1922), 66–68.

1923

"The Ethics of Culture." *Howard University Record* 17 (January 1923), 178–185.

   *Includes annual retrospective book reviews; other reviews in next two sections.

"Professional Ideas in Teaching." *Bulletin*, National Association of Teachers in Colored Schools (April 1923), n.p.

"Portrait." *Current History Magazine of the New York Times* 18 (June 1923), 413.

"The Problem of Race Classification." *Opportunity* 1 (September 1923), 261–264.

"The Colonial Literature of France." *Opportunity* 1 (November 1923), 331–335.

"Roland Hayes: An Appreciation." *Opportunity* 1 (December 1923), 356–358.

1924

"Black Watch on the Rhine." *Opportunity* 2 (January 1924), 6–9.

"Apropos of Africa." *Opportunity* 2 (February 1924), 37–40.

"New Themes." *Crisis* 27 (February 1924), 178.

"The Younger Literary Movement." Written with Du Bois. *Crisis* 28 (February 1924), 161–163.

"Negro Speaks for Himself." *The Survey* 52 (April 1924), 71–72.

"Max Rheinhardt [sic] Reads the Negro's Dramatic Horoscope." *Opportunity* 2 (May 1924), 145–146.

"A Note on African Art." *Opportunity* 2 (May 1924), 134–138.

"The Concept of Race as Applied to Social Culture." *Howard Review* 1 (June 1924), 290–299.

"French Colonial Policy (Open Letter to Réne Maran)." *Opportunity* 2 (September 1924), 261–263.

"Dean Cook of Howard." *Opportunity* 2 (December 1924), 379.

1925

"Art of the Ancestors." *The Survey* 53 (March 1925), 673.

"Enter the New Negro." *The Survey* 53 (March 1925), 631–634.

"Harlem." *Survey Graphic* 53 (March 1925), 629–630.

"Internationalism: Friend or Foe of Art?" *The World Tomorrow* 8 (March 1925), 75–76.

"Youth Speaks." *The Survey* 53 (March 1925), 659–660.

"Backstage on English Imperialism." *Opportunity* 3 (April 1925), 112–114.

"To Certain of Our Philistines." *Opportunity* 3 (May 1925), 155–156.

"The Command of the Spirit." *The Southern Workman* 54 (July 1925), 295–299.

"The Art of Auguste Mambour." *Opportunity* 3 (August 1925), 240–241, 252.

"Negro Education Bids for Par." *The Survey* 54 (September 1925), 567–570.
"Technical Study of the Spiritual." *Opportunity* 3 (November 1925), 331–332.
"More of the Negro in Art." *Opportunity* 3 (December 1925), pp. 363–365.
"The Legacy of the Ancestral Arts." *The New Negro.* Ed. Alain Locke, 1925.
The New Negro. Ed. Alain Locke. New York: Albert and Charles Boni, Inc., 1925.
"The Negro Spirituals." *The New Negro.* Ed. Alain Locke, 1925.
"Negro Youth Speaks." *The New Negro.* Ed. Alain Locke, 1925.
"The New Negro." *The New Negro.* Ed. Alain Locke, 1925.

1926

"Nana Amoah: An African Statesman." *The Survey* 55 (January 1926), 434–435.
"The Negro and the American Stage." *Theatre Arts Magazine* 10 (February 1926), 112–120.
"American Literary Tradition and the Negro." *The Modern Quarterly* 3 (May–July 1926), 215–222.
"The Drama of Negro Life." *Theatre Arts Monthly* 10 (October 1926), 701–706.
"America's First Pacifist (Benjamin Banneker)." Letter to the *Nation* (December 1926), 560.
"Adult Education for Negroes." *Handbook of Adult Education in the United States.* New York: American Association for Adult Education, 1926, pp. 121–131.
"The Negro Poets of the United States." *Anthology of Magazine Verse for 1926 and Yearbook of American Poetry.* Ed. William S. Braithwaite. Boston: B. J. Brimmer Co., 1926, pp. 143–151.

1927

"The Gift of the Jungle." *The Survey* 57 (January 1927), 463.
"Art Lessons from the Congo: Blondiau Theatre Arts Collection." *The Survey* 57 (February 1927), 587–589.
"A Collection of Congo Art." *Arts* 2 (February 1927), 60–70.
"African Art in America." Letter to the *Nation* (March 16, 1927), 290.
"The Negro Poet and His Tradition." *The Survey* 58 (August 1927), 473–474.
"The High Cost of Prejudice." *The Forum* 78 (December 1927), 500–510.

"The Drama of Negro Life." *Plays of Negro Life*. Ed. Alain Locke and Montgomery Gregory. New York: Harper and Bros., 1927.

Four Negro Poets. Ed. Alain Locke. New York: Simon and Schuster, 1927.

"Hail Philadelphia." *Black Opals*, 1 (1927), 3.

"The Negro in the American Theatre." *Theatre: Essays in the Arts of the Theatre*. Ed. Edith J. Isaac. Boston: Little, Brown and Co., 1927, 290–303.

"Our Little Renaissance." *Ebony and Topaz*. Ed. Charles S. Johnson. New York: National Urban League, 1927, pp. 117–118.

Plays of Negro Life: A Source-Book of Native American Drama. Ed. Alain Locke and Montgomery Gregory. New York: Harper and Bros., 1927.

"The Poetry of Negro Life." Introduction to *Four Negro Poets*. Ed. Alain Locke. New York: Simon and Schuster, 1927.

1928

"Beauty Instead of Ashes." *Nation* (April 1928), 432–434.

"The Message of the Negro Poets." *Carolina Magazine* 58 (May 1928), 5–15.

"Art or Propaganda?" *Harlem* 1 (November 1928), 12–13.

Foreword. *An Autumn Love Cycle*, by Georgia Douglas Johnson. New York: H. Vinal, Limited, 1928.

"Impressions of Haifa." *The Bahá'í World: A Biennial International Record* 3 (1928–1930), 280–282.

"The Negro's Contribution to American Art and Literature." *Annals of the American Academy of Political and Social Science* 140 (1928), 234–247.

Preface. *A Decade of Negro Self Expression: Occasional Paper No. 26*. Charlottesville, Va.: Trustees of the John F. Slater Fund, 1928, pp. 5–8.

1929

"The Boxed Compass of Our Race Relations." *The Survey* 51 (January 1929), 469–472. Rpt. *Southern Workman* 58 (1929), 51–58.

"1928; A Retrospective Review." *Opportunity* 7 (January 1929), 8–11.

"North and South: The Washington Conference on the American Negro." *The Survey* 61 (January 1929), 469–472.

"Beauty and the Province." *The Styles* (June 1929), 3–4.

"Both Sides of the Color Line." *The Survey* 62 (June 1929), 325–336.

"Negro Contributions to America." *The World Tomorrow* 12 (June 1929), 255–257.

"Afro-Americans and West Africans." *Wasu (Preach)*, no. 8 (1929), 18–24. Address delivered to the West African Students' Union.

"Art or Propagandy." *The Crescent* 8, no. 1 (1929), 11. Locke's first name misspelled as "Alvin" and the title misspelled as "propagandy." Essentially the same as "Art or Propaganda," 1928.

"The Negro in American Culture." *Anthology of American Negro Literature*. Ed. V. F. Calverton. New York: Modern Library Series, 1929, pp. 248–266.

1930

"The Contribution of Race to Culture." *The Student World* 23 (October 1930), 349–353.

"Folk Values in a New Medium." Written with Sterling A. Brown. In *Folk-Say: A Regional Miscellany*. Ed. B. A. Botkin. Norman: University of Oklahoma Press, 1930, pp. 340–345.

"A Notable Conference." *Opportunity* 8 (1930), 137–140.

"Unity Through Diversity: A Bahá'í Principle." *The Bahá'í World: A Biennial International Record* 4 (1930–1932), 372–374.

1931

"This Year of Grace: Outstanding Books of the Year in Negro Literature." *Opportunity* 9 (February 1931), 48–51.

"Slavery in the Modern Manner." *The Survey* 65 (March 1931), 590–593.

"The American Negro as Artist." *The American Magazine of Art* 23 (September 1931), 210–220.

"Negro in Art." *Bulletin of the Association of American Colleges* 17 (1931), 359–364. Rpt. in *Christian Education* 15 (1931), 98–103.

1932

"We Turn to Prose: A Retrospective Review of the Literature of the Negro for 1931." *Opportunity* 10 (February 1932), 40–44.

"The Orientation of Hope." *The Bahá'í World: A Biennial International Record* 5 (1932–1934), 527–528.

1933

"Black Truth and Black Beauty: A Retrospective Review of the Literature of the Negro for 1932." *Opportunity* 11 (January 1933), 14–18.

"The Negro in Times Like These." *The Survey* 69 (June 1933), 222–224.

The Negro in America. Chicago: American Library Association, 1933.

"The Negro Takes His Place in American Art." In *Exhibitions of Produc-*

tions by Negro Artists. New York: The Harmon Foundation, 1933, pp. 9–12.

"The Negro's Contribution in Art to American Culture." *Proceedings of the National Conference of Social Work* (New York, 1933), 315–322.

1934

"The Saving Grace of Realism: A Retrospective Review of the Negro Literature of 1933." *Opportunity* 13 (January 1934), 8–11, 30.

"Some Lessons from Negro Adult Education." *Proceedings of the Sixth Annual Conference of the American Association for Adult Education* (May 1934), n.p.

"Reciprocity Instead of Regimentation: Lessons of Negro Adult Education." *Journal of Adult Education* 6 (October 1934), 418–420.

"Toward a Critique of Negro Music." *Opportunity* 12 (November–December 1934), 328–331, 365–367, 385.

"Sterling Brown: The New Negro Folk-Poet." *Negro Anthology*. Ed. Nancy Conard. London: Wishart and Co., 1934, pp. 111–115.

1935

"The Eleventh Hour of Nordicism: A Retrospective Review of the Literature of the Negro for 1934." *Opportunity* 13 (January–February 1935), 8–12, 46–48, 59.

"Minorities and the Social Mind." *Progressive Education* 12 (March 1935), 141–150.

"The Magic of African Negro Art." *Literary Digest* 30 (March 1935), 28.

"African Art: Classic Style." *American Magazine of Art* 28 (May 1935), 270–278.

"The Dilemma of Segregation." *Journal of Negro Education* 4 (July 1935), 406–411.

"Values and Imperatives." *American Philosophy, Today and Tomorrow*. Ed. Sidney Hook and Horace M. Kallen. New York: Lee Furman, 1935, pp. 313–333.

"Types of Adult Education: The Intellectual Interests of Negroes." *Journal of Adult Education* 8:6 (1935–1936), 352.

1936

"Deep River, Deeper Sea: Retrospective Review of the Literature of the
Negro for 1935." *Opportunity* 14 (January–February 1936), 6–10, 42–43,
61.
"Harlem: Dark Weather-vane." *Survey Graphic* 24 (August 1936), 457–462,
493–495.
"Propaganda—or Poetry?" *Race* (Summer 1936), 70–76, 87.
Editorial Foreword. In Reid, Ira De A., *Adult Education Among Negroes.*
Washington, D.C.: Associates in Negro Folk Education, Bronze Booklet
Series, 1936.
"Lessons of Negro Adult Education." *Adult Education in Action.* Ed. Mary
L. Fly. New York: American Association for Adult Education, 1936, pp.
126–131.
The Negro and His Music. Washington, D.C.: Associates in Negro Folk
Education, 1936.
Negro Art: Past and Present. Washington, D.C.: Associates in Negro Folk
Education, 1936.
"The World of Inter-racial Relations." *The Berea Alumnus* 6 (1936), 252–
257.

1937

"God Save Reality! A Retrospective Review of the Literature of the Negro
for 1936." *Opportunity* 15 (January–February 1937), 8–13, 40–44.
"Spiritual Truancy." *New Challenge* 2 (Fall 1937), 81–85.
Editorial Foreword. In Brown, Sterling, *The Negro in American Fiction.*
Washington, D.C.: Associates in Negro Folk Education, Bronze Booklet
Series, 1937.
Editorial Foreword. In Brown, Sterling, *Negro Poetry and Drama.* Wash-
ington, D.C.: Associates in Negro Folk Education, Bronze Booklet Series,
1937.
Editorial Foreword. In Hill, T. Arnold, *The Negro and Economic Recon-
struction.* Washington, D.C.: Associates in Negro Folk Education, Bronze
Booklet Series, 1937.
Letter to Editor. *Art Front* 3, no. 7 (1937), 19–20.

1938

"Jingo Counter-Jingo and Us. A Retrospective Review of the Literature of
the Negro for 1937." *Opportunity* 16 (January–February 1938), 7–11,
39–42.

"With Science as His Shield the Educator Must Bridge Our Great Divides."
Frontiers of Democracy (May 1938–April 1941), 8–10.

"Freedom Through Art: A Review of Negro Art, 1870–1938." *Crisis* 45
(July 1938), 227–229.

"Negro Needs as Adult Educational Opportunities." *Findings of The First
Annual Conference on Adult Education and the Negro,* 1938, pp. 5–10.

Letter. In *Writers Take Sides: Letters About the War in Spain From 418
American Authors.* New York: The League of American Writers, 1938,
p. 40.

1939

"The Negro: 'New' or Newer: A Retrospective Review of the Literature
of the Negro for 1938." *Opportunity* 17 (January–February 1939), 4–10,
36–42.

Foreword to *Contemporary Negro Art.* The Baltimore Museum of Art.
Exhibition of February 3–19, 1939.

"What Every American Knows." Letter to *The Survey* 28 (February 1939),
155.

"Advance on the Art Front." *Opportunity* 17 (May 1939), 132–136.

"Negro Music Goes to Par." *Opportunity* 17 (July 1939), 196–200.

"The Negro's Contribution to American Culture." *Journal of Negro Education* 8 (July 1939), 521–529.

Americans All: Immigrants All. Ed. Alain Locke. Washington, D.C.: Office
of Education *Bulletin,* 1939.

Foreword to *A Comparative Study of Religious Cult Behavior Among
Negroes with Special Reference to Emotional Group Conditioning Factors,* by Raymond Julius Jones. *Howard University Studies in Social Sciences* 2, no. 2 (1939).

"The Negroes of the U.S.A." *The Aryan Path* 10: 1 (1939), 22–25.

1940

"With Science as His Shield the Educator Must Bridge Our 'Great Divides.'"
Frontiers of Democracy 6 (1940), 208–210.

"Dry Fields and Green Pastures: A Retrospective Review of Negro Literature and Art for 1939." *Opportunity* 18 (January–February 1940), 4–10,
28, 41–46, 53.

"Ballard for Democracy." *Opportunity* 18 (August 1940), 228–229.

"American Negro's Exposition's Showing of the Work of the Negro Artist."
In *Catalog for the Exhibition of the Art of the American Negro (1851–
1940).* Chicago: American Negro Exposition, 1940. n.p.

"Lessons in World Crisis." *The Bahá'í World: A Biennial International Record* 9 (1940–1944), 745–747.

"On Literary Stereotypes." In *Fighting Words*. Ed. Donald Ogden Stewart. New York: Harcourt, Brace and Company, 1940, pp. 75–78.

"Negroes (American)." *Britannica Book of the Year* (1940), 485–486.

The Negro in Art: A Pictorial Record of the Negro Artist and of the Negro Theme in Art. Washington, D.C.: Associates in Negro Folk Education, 1940.

"Popularized Literature." *Findings of the Second Annual Conference on Adult Education and the Negro*, 1940, pp. 48–50.

"Spirituals." In *75 Years of Freedom*. Washington: Library of Congress, 1940, pp. 7–15.

1941

"Of Native Sons: Real and Otherwise." *Opportunity* 19 (January–February 1941), 4–9, 48–52.

Foreword to *We Too Look at America*. Catalogue for an exhibition of paintings, sculpture, drawings at the South Side Community Art Center, Chicago, Ill., May 1941, n.p.

"Chicago's New Southside Art Center." *Magazine of Art* 34 (August 1941), 370–374.

"Broadway and the Negro Drama." *Theatre Arts* 25 (October 1941), 745–752.

Foreword to *Life and Times of Frederick Douglass*, by Frederick Douglass. New York: Pathway Press, 1941.

"Negroes (American)." *Britannica Book of the Year* (1941), 486–487.

"Three Corollaries of Cultural Relativism." In *Proceedings of the Second Conference on the Scientific Spirit and the Democratic Faith*. New York, 1941.

1942

"Who and What is 'Negro'?" *Opportunity* 20 (February–March 1942), 36–41, 83–87.

"Democracy Faces a World Order." *Harvard Education Review* 12 (March 1942), 121–128.

"Is there a Basis for Spiritual Unity in the World Today?" *Bulletin of America's Town Meeting of the Air* (June 1942). George Denny, Jr., Moderator. Discussants: Mordecai W. Johnson, Alain Locke, Leon A. Ransom, and Doxie A. Wilkerson.

"The Case of a Minority: Predicament of a Majority." *The Chicago Defender*, (September 1942), 31.

"Color: The Unfinished Business of Democracy." *Survey Graphic* 31 (November 1942), 455–459.

"Autobiographical Sketch." *Twentieth Century Authors*. Ed. Stanley Kunitz and Howard Haycroft. New York: Wilson Company, 1942.

Editorial Foreword. In Williams, Eric, *The Negro in the Caribbean*. Washington, D.C.: Associates in Negro Folk Education, Bronze Booklet Series, 1942.

"Negroes (American)." *Britannica Book of the Year* (1942), 472.

"Pluralism and Intellectual Democracy." *Second Symposium*. New York: Conference on Science, Philosophy and Religion, 1942, pp. 196–212.

When Peoples Meet: A Study of Race and Culture Contacts. Ed. Alain Locke and Bernhard J. Stern. New York: Committee on Workshops, Progressive Education Association, 1942.

1943

"Haiti to the Fore." *People's Voice*, (June 1943), 11.

Le rôle du Negro dans la culture des Ameriques. Port-au-Prince, Haiti: Imprimerie de l'état, 1943.

"Negroes (American)." *Britannica Book of the Year* (1943), 491–492.

1944

"The Negro in American Culture." *New Masses* (January 18, 1944), 4–6.

"Race, Culture et Democratie." *Cahiers d'Haiti*, 8 (March 1944), 6–14.

"Understanding World Cultures." *Educational Leadership* 1 (March 1944), 381–382.

"The Negro Contribution to American Culture." *Journal of Negro Education* 13 (Winter 1944), 7–18.

"The Negro in the Three Americas." *Journal of Negro Education* 13 (Winter 1944), 7–18. Translation of "Le Rôle du Negre dans la Culture des Amerique."

"Whither Race Relations? A Critical Commentary." *Journal of Negro Education* (Summer 1944), 398–406.

"Cultural Relativism and Ideological Peace." *Approaches to World Peace*. Conference on Science, Philosophy and Religion. Ed., Lyman Bryson, L. Finkelstein, R. M. MacIver, New York: Harper & Brothers, 1944, 609–618.

"Moral Imperatives for World Order." In *Proceedings*. Institute of International Relations, 1944, pp. 19–22.

"Negroes (American)." *Britannica Book of the Year* (1944), 490–491.
"The Negro Group." *Group Relations and Group Antagonisms.* Ed. R. M. MacIver. New York: Harper and Bros., 1944, pp. 43–59.

1945

"Understanding Through Art and Culture." *Africa Today and Tomorrow* (April 1945), 23.
"Areas of Extension and Improvement of Adult Education Among Negroes." *Journal of Negro Education* 15 (Summer 1945), 453–459.
"A Contribution to American Culture." *Opportunity* 23 (Fall 1945), 192–193, 238.
"Address of Welcome." Proceedings of the Eighth Annual Conference of the Division of the Social Sciences. *Howard University Studies in the Social Sciences,* 4: 1 (1945), 3–7.
Diversity Within National Unity. Washington, D.C.: National Council for the Social Studies, 1945. Symposium with Alain Locke, Carey McWilliams, George B. Ford, Otto Klineberg, and Howard E. Wilson (Locke presiding).
"The Minority Side of Intercultural Education." *Education for Cultural Unity,* 17 (1945), 60–64.
"The Negro and the War." *Britannica Book of the Year* (1945), 486–487.
"The Teaching of Dogmatic Religion in a Democratic Society." In *The Authoritarian Attempts to Capture Education.* Papers from the 2nd Conference on the Scientific Spirit and Democratic Faith. New York: Kings Crown Press, 1945, pp. 143–145.
"Up Till Now." Introduction to *The Negro Artist Comes of Age; A National Survey of Contemporary American Artists.* Albany, N.Y.: Albany Institute of History and Art 1945, pp. iii–vii.

1946

"The Negro and World War II." *Britannica Book of the Year* (1946), 517–518.
"The Negro Minority in American Literature." *English Journal* 35 (1946), pp. 315–320.

1947

"Coming of Age." *Adult Education Journal* 6 (January 1947), 1–3.
"More Than Blasting Brick and Mortar." *Survey Graphic* 36 (January 1947), 87–89.

"Address of Alain Locke." *The Max C. Otto Jubilee Dinner Addresses,* Great Hall, Memorial Union, University of Wisconsin (May 1947), 15–17.
"Education for Adulthood." *Adult Education Journal* 6 (July 1947), 104–111.
"The Armed Services." *Britannica Book of the Year* (1947), 537–538.
"Pluralism and Ideological Peace." *Freedom and Experience: Essays Presented to Horace M. Kallen* Ed. Milton R. Konvitz and Sidney Hook. Ithaca, New York: New School For Social Research and Cornell University Press, 1947, pp. 63–69.
"Reason and Race: A Review of the Literature of the Negro for 1946." *Phylon* 8 (1947), 17–27.

1948

"A Critical Retrospect of the Literature of the Negro for 1947." *Phylon* 9 (1948), 3–11.
Foreword to *Witness for Freedom*, by Rebecca Barton. New York: Harper and Bros., 1948.

1949

"Dawn Patrol: A Review of Literature of the Negro for 1948." *Phylon* 10 (1949), 5–14, 167–172.
"Are Negroes Winning Their Fight for Civil Rights?" *Harlem Quarterly*, 1, No. 1 (1949–1950), 23.

1950

"Frontiers of Culture." *The Crescent: Official Organ of the Phi Beta Sigma Fraternity* 33: 1 (1950), 37–39.
"The Need for a New Organon in Education." *Goals for American Education.* New York: Conference on Science, Philosophy and Religion, 1950, pp. 201–212.
"Negroes (American)." *Britannica Book of the Year* (1950), 481–482.
"The Negro and the American Stage." *Theatre Arts Anthology.* Ed. Rosamond Gilder. New York: Theatre Art Books, 1950, pp. 81–87.
"Self-Criticism: The Third Dimension in Culture." *Phylon* 11 (1950), 391–394.
"Wisdom *de Profundis*: Literature of the Negro, 1949." *Phylon* 11 (1950), 5–15, 171–175.

1951

"Changing Values in the Western World." *American Scholar* (February 1951), 343–358. Forum with Alain Locke, Arthur Schlesinger Jr., Walter Mehring, Frederick A. Weiss, Matthew Huxley, Hiram Haydn, Alan Gregg, and Simon Michael Bessie.
"The Arts and the Creative Integration of Modern Living." *Progressive Education* 28 (April 1951), 182–183. (A response to and article by Alexander Dorner.)
"Cultural Ascendancy." *Encylopaedia Britannica*, vol. 16 (1951), 194–196.
"Harlem." *Encyclopaedia Britannica*, Vol. 16 (1951), 200–201.
"L'Apport Intellectual et Cultural du Noir American." *Les Etudes Americaines*, Cahier 28, Bimestriel (1951), 3–6.
"Inventory at Mid-Century: A Review of the Literature of the Negro for 1950." *Phylon* 12 (1951), 5–12, 185–190.
"Negro Art." *Encyclopaedia Britannica*, Vol. 16 (1951), 198–199.
"Negro Poetry." *Encyclopaedia Britannica*, Vol. 16 (1951), 200. (With James W. Johnson.)

1952

"The High Price of Integration: A Review of the Literature of the Negro for 1951." *Phylon* 13 (1952), 7–18.
"The Negro in American Literature." *New World Writing* 1 (1952), 18–33.
"Negroes (American)." *Britannica Book of the Year* (1952), 495–497.

1953

"From *Native Son to Invisible Man*: A Review of the Literature of the Negro for 1952." *Phylon* 14 (1953), 34–44.
"Negro in the Arts." *United Asia: International Magazine of Asian Affairs* 3 (June 1953), 177–181.
"Our Changing Race Relations: Some Educational Implications." *Progressive Education* 30 (1953), 75–76, 91–92.
"The Social Responsibility of the Scholar." *Proceedings of the Conference of the Division of the Social Sciences*. Washington, D.C.: Howard University Press, 1953, pp. 143–146.

1954

"Negroes (American)." *Britannica Book of the Year* (1954), 498–499.
"Minority Side of Intercultural Education." *Education for Cultural Unity:*

Seventeenth Yearbook, California Elementary School Principals Association, n.d., 60–64.

TITLED BOOK REVIEWS

"Back of Mob Violence." Rev. of *The Black Patch War*, by John G. Miller. *Survey* 72 (1936), 187.

"Back of the Problem." Rev. of *Shadow of the Plantation*, by Charles S. Johnson. *Survey* 71 (1935), 28.

"Belated Justice." Rev. of *The Negro in Congress*, by Samuel D. Smith. *Survey Midmonthly* 76 (1940), 278–279.

comp. "Best Books on the Negro." *Publisher's Weekly*, 22 July 1933, p. 228.

"Biography for Beginners." Rev. of *Negro Builders and Heroes*, by Benjamin Brawley. *Survey Midmonthly* 73 (1937), 367–368.

"Black Pawns of Labor." Revs. of *The Negro in The Slaughtering and Meat-Packing Industry in Chicago*, by Alma Herbst; and *the Free Negro Family*, by E. Franklin Frazier. *Survey* 68 (1932), 699–700.

"The City Negro." Rev. of *The Negro Family in Chicago*, by E. Franklin Frazier. *Survey* 68 (1932), 90–91.

"Colonial Commonsense." Rev. of *Kenya*, by Norman Leys. *Survey Graphic* 55 (1925), 380–381.

"Color—A Review." Rev. of *Color*, by Countee Cullen. *Opportunity* 4 (1926), 14–15.

"Common Clay and Poetry." Rev. of *Fine Clothes to the Jew*, by Langston Hughes. *Saturday Review of Literature* 9 (April 1927), p. 712.

"Conant's Solution: Pro and Con." Rev. of *Education in a Divided World*, by James Bryant Conant. *The Key Reporter* 14, no. 2 (1949), 4.

"Contribution to Culture." Rev. of *The Negro Author*, by Vernon Loggins. *New York Herald Tribune Books*, 27 March 1932, Sec. 11, p. 17.

"Dark History." Rev. of *Black Laws of Virginia*, by June Purcell Guild. *Survey Midmonthly* 73 (1937), 171.

"Darwinian Negro Study." Rev. of *The Negro's Struggle for Survival*, by S. J. Holmes. *New York Herald Tribune Books*, 24 July 1938, Sec. 9, p. 8.

"Elegy in the Modern Manner." Rev. of *Lament for the Stolen*, by Katharine Garrison Chapin. *Voices: A Journal of Poetry* 97 (1939), 56–58.

"Fire: A Negro Magazine." Rev. of *Fire*, ed. Wallace Thurman. *Survey* 58 (1927), 563.

"Flaming Self Portrait." Rev. of *A Long Way From Home*, by Claude McKay. *Christendom* 2 (1937), 653–654.

"Fresh History." Rev. of *The Negro in the Reconstruction of Virginia*, by A. A. Taylor. *Survey Graphic* 59 (1927), 175.

"The Gift of the Jungle." Rev. of *Tom Tom*, by John W. Vandercook. *Survey Graphic* 57 (1927), 463.

"Haiti Up to Date." Rev. of *Black Democracy*, by H. P. Davis. *Survey* 72 (1936), 256.

"Heads or Tales on the Race Question." Revs. of *Black America* by Scott Nearing; and *What the Negro Thinks*, by R. R. Moton. *Survey Graphic* 72 (1929), 198–199.

"Inside Negro Groups." Rev. of *The Negro's Morale*, by Arnold Rose. *The Progressive* 14 (1950), 31–32.

"Interpreting the Negro." Rev. of *Anthology of American Negro Literature*, ed. V. F. Calverton. *Survey Graphic* 64 (1930), 49–50.

"Major Prophet of Democracy." Rev. of *Race and Democratic Society*, by Franz Boas. *Journal of Negro Education* 15 (1946), 191–192.

"Martyrdom to Glad Music: The Irony of Black Patriotism." Rev. of *From Harlem to the Rhine: The Story of New York's Colored Volunteers*, by Arthur W. Little. *Opportunity* 14 (1936), 381.

"Mixed Bloods in Society," Rev. of *Race Mixture*, by Edward B. Reuter. *Survey Graphic* 66 (1931), 57–58.

"Moral Pivot." Rev. of *From Slavery to Freedom*, by John Hope Franklin. *Saturday Review of Literature*, 8 November 1947, p. 16.

"Negro Angle." Rev. of *The Ways of White Folks*, by Langston Hughes. *Survey Graphic* 23 (1934), 565.

"The Negro as Spender." Rev. of *The Southern Negro as a Consumer*, by Paul K. Edwards. *Survey* 68 (1932), 380.

"Negro Eloquence." Rev. of *Negro Orators and Their Orations*, by Carter G. Woodson. *Nation*, 4 August 1926, p. 110.

"Negro Folk Songs." Rev. of *On the Trail of Negro Folk Songs*, by Dorothy Scarborough. *Saturday Review of Literature*, 28 November 1915, p. 339.

"The Negro Poet and His Tradition." Rev. of *God's Trombones*, by James Weldon Johnson. *Survey* 58 (1927), 473–474.

"Negro Portraiture." Rev. of *Portraits in Color*, by Mary White Ovington. *Nation* 126 (1928), 414.

"The Negro Trek." Revs. of *The Negro Peasant Turns Cityward*, by Louise V. Kennedy; and *The Rural Negro*, by Carter G. Woodson. *New York Herald Tribune Books*, 23 November 1930, Sec. 11, p. 14.

"The Negro Vote." Rev. of *Race, Class and Party*, by Paul Lewinson. *Survey* 68 (1932), 523.

"Negroes and Earth." Rev. of *Black April*, by Julia Peterkin. *Survey* 58 (1927), 172–173.

"Negroes as Americans." Rev. of *Brown America*, by Edwin R. Embree. *Survey Graphic* 67 (1931), 152.

"New Light on an Old Problem." Revs. of *Slavery in Mississippi*, by Charles

S. Sydnor; and *The Anti-Slavery Impulse*, by Gilbert H. Barnes. *Survey Graphic* 23 (1934), 197.

"The New South Takes Stock." Rev. of *The Negro in Richmond Virginia: Report of the Negro Welfare Survey Committee*, by The Richmond Council of Social Agencies. *Survey Midmonthly* 63 (1930), 598.

"An Old Problem in New Perspective." Rev. of *Brown Americans*, 2nd edition, by Edwin Embree. *Survey Midmonthly* 80 (1944), 29–30.

"Out of Africa: Something New." Rev. of *Dahomey, An Ancient Africian Kingdom*, by Melville J. Herskovitz. *Opportunity* 16 (1938), 342–343.

"Outdated Tradition." Rev. of *Tuskegee and The Black Belt*, by Anne K. Walker. *Survey Midmonthly* 80 (1944), 334.

"Philosophy Alive." Rev. of *The Cleavage in Our Culture*, ed. Frederick H. Burkhardt. *The Progressive* 17, no. 2 (1953), 41–43.

"Plight and Dilemmas." Revs. of *The Black Man in White America*, by John C. Van Deusen; and *American Caste and the Negro College*, by Buell G. Gallagher. *Survey Midmonthly* 75 (1939), 91.

"Problem of Race Classification." Rev. of *The Racial History of Man*, by Roland Dixon. *Opportunity* 1 (1923), 261–264.

"Professional Stock-Taking." Rev. of *The Negro Professional Man and the Community*, by Carter G. Woodson. *Survey* 80 (1934), 267–268.

"Reason and Society." Rev. of *New Hopes For a Changing World*, by Bertrand Russell. *The Key Reporter* 18, no. 1 (1952–53), 4.

"Reconstruction Reconstructed." Rev. of *The Negro in the Reconstruction of Virginia*, by A. A. Taylor. *New York Herald Tribune Books*, 17 July 1927, p. 10.

"Santayana." Rev. of *Dominations and Powers*, by George Santayana. *The Key Reporter* 16, no. 4 (1951), 4–5.

"Society's Orginal Sin." Rev. of *God's Stepchildren*, by Sarah Gertrude Millin. *Survey Graphic* 54 (1925), 180–181.

"Sociological Problem No. 1." Rev. of *Race Relations and the Race Problem*, by Edgar T. Thompson. *Survey Midmonthly* 76 (1940), 82–83.

"Southern Triangle." Revs. of *Slavery Times in Kentucky*, by J. W. Coleman; *The Negro in Tennessee*, by A. A. Taylor; and *The Negro in Virginia*, by W. P. A. of Virginia. *Survey Midmonthly* 78 (1941), 343–344.

"Spiritual Truancy." Rev. of *A Long Way From Home*, by Claude McKay, *New Challenge* 2, no. 2 (1937), 81–85.

"The 'Talented Tenth.'" Rev. of *The Negro College Graduate*, by Charles S. Johnson. *Survey Midmonthly* 74 (1938), 252.

"The Technical Study of the Spirituals: A Review." Rev. of *Saint Helena Spirituals*, by N. G. J. Ballanta (Taylor). *Opportunity* 3 (1925), 331–332.

"Values That Matter." Rev. of *Realms of Value*, by Ralph Barton Perry. *Key Reporter* 19, no. 3 (1954), 4.

"The Weary Blues." Rev. of *The Weary Blues*, by Langston Hughes. *Palms* 4 (1926), 25–28.

"Welcome the New South." Rev. of *The Advancing South*, by Edwin Mims. *Opportunity* 4 (1926), 374–375.

"What Is the Negro Doing?" Revs. of *The Negro in American Life*, by Jerome Doud; and *Homes of the Freed*, by Rossa B. Cooley. *New York Herald Tribune Books*, 28 November 1926, p. 7.

"Where the Negro Worker Stands." Rev. of *The Black Worker*, by Sterling D. Spero and Abram L. Harris. *Survey Midmonthly* 65 (1931), 679.

"Why the Communists Failed." Rev. of *The Negro and the Communist Party*, by Wilson Record. *The American Scholar* 21 (1951–52), 116, 118.

UNTITLED BOOK REVIEWS

Rev. of Edwin Mim's *The Advancing South*. *Opportunity* 4 (December 1926), 374–375.

Rev. of *The African Child: An Account of the International Conference on African Children*, by Evelyn Sharp. *Survey Midmonthly* 68 (1932), 333. Unsigned in print but initialed by Locke in Box 157 of the Locke papers.

Rev. of *African Dependencies: A Challenge to Western Democracy*, by Nwanko Chukwuemeka. *Survey* 86 (1950), 470, 472.

Rev. of *The Basis of Criticism in the Arts*, by Stephen Coburn Papper. *Ethics* 57 (1947), 145–147.

Rev. of *Black Metropolis*, by St. Clair Drake and Horace Cayton. *Survey Graphic* 35 (1946), 26.

Rev. of *Color and Democracy*, by W. E. B. DuBois. *Survey Graphic* 34 (1945), 415.

Rev. of *Dark Princess*, by W. E. B. DuBois. *New York Herald Tribune Books*, 20 May 1928, p. 12.

Rev. of *The Dynamics of Culture Change*, by Bronislaw Malinowski. *Survey Midmonthly* 81 (1945), 246.

Rev. of *The Education of Negro Ministers*, by W. A. Daniels. *Survey* 55 (1925), 262.

Rev. of *Encyclopedia of the Negro: Preparatory Syllabus*, by W. E. B. DuBois and Guy B. Johnson. *Survey Midmonthly* 81 (1945), 215.

Rev. of *From Slavery to Freedom*, by John Hope Franklin. *Saturday Review of Literature* 30 (November 8, 1947), 1b.

Rev. of *From Slavery to Freedom*, by John Hope Franklin; and *Masters of the Dew*, by Jacques Roumain. *Survey Graphic* 37 (1948), 374–375.

Rev. of *Goat Alley*, by Ernest Howard Culbertson. *Opportunity* 1 (1923), 30.

Rev. of *The Magic Island*, by W. B. Seabrook. *Opportunity* 7 (1929), 190.

Rev. of *The Mark of Oppression*, by Abram Kardiner and Lionel Ovesey. *Survey* 87 (1951), 446.

Rev. of *The Myth of the Negro Past*, by Melville Herskovits. *Intercultural Education News* 3, no. 4 (1942), 7.

Rev. of *The Negro Ghetto*, by Robert C. Weaver. *Survey* 85 (1949), 60–61.

Rev. of *The Negro in American Life*, by John Becker. *Survey Graphic* 34 (1945), 332.

Rev. of *The Negro in American Life*, by Willis J. King. *Survey Midmonthly* 57 (1927), 530.

Rev. of *The Negro in Our History*, by Carter G. Woodson. *Journal of Negro History* 12 (1927), 99–101.

Rev. of *Negro Migration During the War*, by Emmet J. Scott. *Journal of Negro History* 5 (1920), 490–491.

Rev. of *The Negro Peasant Turns Cityward*, by Louise W. Kennedy. *New York Herald Tribune Books*, 23 November 1930, p. 14.

Rev. of *Paul Laurence Dunbar*, by Benjamin Brawley. *Survey Graphic* 26 (1937), 496.

Rev. of *The Prodigal Century*, by Henry Pratt Fairchild. *The American Scholar* 20 (1950–51), 370, 372, 374.

Rev. of *Public Opinion in War and Peace*, by Abbot Lawrence Lowell. *Opportunity* 1 (1923), 223.

Rev. of Frank L. Schoel's *La Question des Nois aux Etats-Unis*. *Opportunity* 2 (April 1924), 109–110.

Rev. of *Race and Rumors of Race*, by Howard Odum. *Survey Graphic* 33 (1944), 330–331.

Rev. of *Race Relations*, by Charles S. Johnson and Weatherford Willis. *Survey Graphic* 24 (1935), 312.

Rev. of Roland Dixon's *The Racial History of Man*. *Opportunity* 1 (September 1923), 261–262.

Rev. of *The Rural Negro*, by Carter G. Woodson. *New York Herald Tribune Books*, 23 November 1930, p. 14.

Rev. of *Scarlet Sister Mary*, by Julia Peterkin. *Opportunity* 7 (1929), 190–191.

Rev. of *Sex Expression in Literature*, by V. F. Calverton. *Opportunity* 5 (1927), 57–58.

Rev. of *Southern Negroes*, by Bell Irwin Wiley. *New York Herald Tribune Books*, 25 September 1938, p. 19.

Rev. of *There Was Once a Slave*, by Shirley Graham. *Survey Graphic* 36 (1947), 361–362.

Rev. of *A Treasury of the Blues*, by Abbe Miles. *The American Oxonian* 40 (1953), 153–154.

Rev. of *What the Negro Wants*, ed. Rayford Logan. *Survey Midmonthly* 81 (1945), 95.
Rev. of *The World and Africa*, by W. E. B. DuBois. *Survey Graphic* 36 (1947), 452.
Revs. "Notes on the New Books." *The Crisis* 25 (1923), 161–163.

UNPUBLISHED WORKS OF MAJOR PHILOSOPHICAL INTEREST *

"Culture Contact and Culture Conflict." In *Proceedings* of the Workshop in General Education. Chicago: Cooperative Study in General Education, American Council on Education, 1941, pp. 54–62. Box C.
"The Culture Dilemma." Box C.
"Education for Adulthood." Presidential Address, 23d Annual Convention, American Association for Adult Education. May 13, 1947.
"Freud and Scientific Morality." Box F-I.
"The Great Disillusionment." Box F-I.
"International Comparison of Racial Attitudes." Box F-I.
"The Nature of Truth," 1907. Box N.
"A Note on Bosanquet's Doctrine of Judgment as a Basis of a Logic of Values." On Bernard Bosanquet, *Logic*, 1884, and Albert H. Munsell, *Color Notation*, 1907, 1916, pp. 1–12. Box N.
"On Insanity." Box F-I.
"The Preservation of the Democratic Ideal." Box O-R.
"Race Contacts and Inter-Racial Relations: A Study in the Theory and Practice of Race." Syllabus of an Extension Course of Lectures, Washington, D.C.: Howard University, 1916. Box O-R.
"Races and People." Box O-R.
"A Rhodes Scholar Question." Box O-R.
"Stretching Our Social Mind." Speech before the Hampton Institute Commencement. August 18, 1944. Box S-T.

BIBLIOGRAPHIES

Martin, Robert. "A Bibliography of the Writings of Alain Leroy Locke," in *The New Negro Thirty Years Afterward*. Ed. Rayford Logan et al. Washington, D.C.: Howard University Press, 1955, pp. 89–96.
Stewart, Jeffrey C. *Alain Locke: A Research Guide*. New York: Garland Publishing, 1988.

*Available at Moorland-Spingarn Research Center, Howard University.

Tidwell, John Edgar, and Wright, John S. "Alain Locke: A Comprehensive Bibliography of Published Writings." *Callaloo* 4:11, 12, 13 (February–October 1981) 175–192.

BIOGRAPHICAL REFERENCES

Brewer, William, "Alain Locke," *Negro History Bulletin* 18 (November 1954), 26–32.

Bunche, Ralph J., W. E. B. Du Bois, et al., "The Passing of Alain LeRoy Locke," *Phylon* 15 (1954), 243–252.

Crumwell, John W., "Alain LeRoy Locke," *African Times and Orient Review.* (April 1913), 313–314.

Davis, Arthur P., *From the Dark Tower: Afro-American Writers, 1900–1960* (Washington D.C.: Howard University Press, 1974), pp. 51–60, 240–244.

Fennell, Robert E., "From Cain's Other Side: An Informal View of Alain Locke," *Recapit* 1 (February 1959), 1–3.

Harris, Leonard, *Philosophy Born of Struggle: Anthology of Afro-American Philosophy from 1917* (Dubuque, Iowa: Kendall-Hunt, 1983), pp. 308–310.

Hay, Samuel A., "Alain Locke and Black Drama," *Black World* (April 1972), 8–14.

Holmes, Eugene, C., "Alain L. Locke and the Adult Education Movement," *Journal of Negro Education* 34 (Winter 1965), 5–10.

Holmes, Eugene, C., "Alain Locke—Philosopher, Critic, Spokesman," *Journal of Philosophy* 54 (February 1957), 113–118.

Holmes, Eugene, C., "Alain L. Locke: A Sketch," *Phylon* 20 (Spring 1959), 82–89.

Holmes, Eugene, C., "The Legacy of Alain Locke," *Freedomways* 3 (Summer 1963), 293–306.

Kallen, Horace M., "Alain Locke and Cultural Pluralism," *Journal of Philosophy* 57 (February 1957), 119–127.

Logan, Rayford W. (ed.), *The New Negro Thirty Years Afterward* (Washington D.C.: Howard University Press, 1955).

Logan, Rayford, W., and Michael R. Winston (eds.), *The Dictionary of American Negro Biography* (New York: Norton, 1983), pp. 398–404.

Long, Richard A., "Alain Locke: Cultural and Social Mentor," *Black World* 20 (November 1970), 87–90.

Midgette, Lillian Avon, "A Bio-Bibliography of Alain LeRoy Locke" (M.S.L.S. thesis, Atlanta University, 1963).

Stafford, Douglas K., "Alain Locke: The Child, the Man, and the People," *June* (Winter 1961), 25–34.

Stewart, Jeffrey C., "A Biography of Alain Locke: Philosopher of the Harlem Renaissance" (Ph.D. dissertation, Yale University, 1979).

Tidwell, John Edgar, and John Wright, "Alain Locke: A Comprehensive Bibliography Of His Published Writings," *Callaloo* 4 (February–October 1981), 175–192.

Willis, Wilda Logan, *A Guide to the Alain L. Locke Papers* (Washington, D.C.: Moorland-Spingarn Research Center, Howard University, 1985).

COLLECTIONS OF PARTICULAR RELEVANCE

Countee Cullen Papers, Amistad Research Center, Dillard University.

The Beula M. Davis Special Collection, Morgan State University, is a valuable source for memorabilia of the era.

Cullen Jackman Collection, Atlanta University, "Eulogy for Alain Locke," in William Stanley Braithwaite folder.

James Weldon Johnson Collection, Yale University.

Horace M. Kallen Papers, American Jewish Archives, Hebrew Union College. Letters of John Dewey to Horace M. Kallen, March 31, 1915; Kallen to Albert Barnes, January 1, 1919; Kallen to Wendell Bush, January 9, 1919. In this connection, also see H. L. Mencken to Alain Locke, February 10, n.d., Alain Locke Papers, Howard University.

Paul Kellogg Papers, University of Minnesota. Letters of Paul Kellogg to George Peabody, Jan. 28, 1925, April 19, 1925; Locke to Paul Kellogg, February 19, 1926, February 23, 1926.

Alain L. Locke Collection, Moorland-Spingarn Research Center, Howard University is the major repository and source for Locke materials.

The Arthur Schomburg Collection, New York Public Library, New York, is an invaluable resource for information on the Harlem Renaissance.

Survey Associates Papers, Archives of Social Welfare History, University of Minnesota.

WORKS ABOUT LOCKE OF PARTICULAR RELEVANCE TO HIS PHILOSOPHY

Braithwaite, William S., "Alain Locke's Relationship to the Negro in American Literature," *Phylon* 18 (1957), 166–173.

Butcher, Margaret J., *The Negro in American Culture* (New York: Alfred A. Knopf, 1956).

Crane, Clare Bloodgood, "Alain Locke and the Negro Renaissance" (Ph.D. dissertation, University of California, San Diego, 1971).

Epps, Archie, Nathan I. Huggins, Harold Cruse, Albert Murray, and Ralph Ellison, "The Alain L. Locke Symposium," *Harvard Advocate* (December 1, 1973), 9–29.

Gayle, Addison, *The Black Aesthetic* (New York: Doubleday Anchor, 1972).

Gouinlock, James, Review of Johnny Washington's *Alain Locke and Philosophy*, in *Transactions of the Charles S. Peirce Society* 23 (1987), 320–326.

Harris, Leonard, "Identity: Alain Locke's Atavism," *Transactions of the Charles S. Peirce Society* 24 (Winter 1988), 65–83.

Harris, Leonard, "The Legitimation Crisis in American Philosophy: Crisis Resolution from the Standpoint of the Afro-American Tradition of Philosophy," *Social Science Information* 26 (March 1987), 57–73.

Hatcher, Wesley J., "The World of Interracial Relations," Lectures of Alain Locke, *The Berea Alumnus* 6:8 (1931), 252–257.

Helbling, Mark, "Alain Locke: Ambivalence and Hope," *Phylon* 40 (1979), 291–300.

Johnson, Charles, *Being and Race: Black Writing Since 1970* (Bloomington: Indiana University Press, 1988).

Kallen, Horace, "Alain Locke and Cultural Pluralism," *Journal of Philosophy* 54 (February 1957), 119–127.

Linnemann, Russell J. (ed.), *Alain Locke: Reflections on a Modern Renaissance Man* (Baton Rouge: Louisiana State University Press, 1982).

Mason, Ernest D., "An Introduction to Alain Locke's Theory of Value" (Ph.D. dissertation, Emory University, 1975).

Mason, Ernest D., "Alain Locke on Race and Race Relations," *Phylon* 4:4 (1979), 342–350.

Mason, Ernest D., "Black Art and the Configurations of Experience: The Philosophy of the Black Aesthetic," *College Language Association Journal* 27 (1983), 1–17.

Mason, Ernest D., "Alain Locke's Social Philosophy," *Dictionary of Literary Biography* (Winter 1978–1979), 25–34.

Stewart, Jeffrey C., *The Critical Temper of Alain Locke: A Selection of His Essays on Art and Culture* (New York: Garland Publishing, 1983).

Wacker, Fred, "The Fate of Cultural Pluralism Within American Social Thought," *Ethnic Groups* 3 (1981), 125–138.

Washington, Johnny, *Alain Locke and Philosophy: A Quest for Cultural Pluralism* (Westport, Conn.: Greenwood Press, 1986).

Washington, Johnny, "Alain L. Locke's 'Values and Imperatives': An Interpretation," in Leonard Harris (ed.), *Philosophy Born of Struggle, Anthology of Afro-American Philosophy from 1917* (Dubuque, Iowa: Kendall-Hunt, 1983), pp. 148–158.

Wright, W. D., "The Cultural Thought and Leadership of Alain Locke," *Freedomways* 14 (1974), 35–50.

WORKS ON LOCKE'S HISTORICAL CONTEXT
AND INTELLECTUAL ASSOCIATIONS

Aptheker, Herbert (ed.), *The Correspondence of W. E. B. Du Bois*, 2 vols. (Amherst: University of Massachusetts Press, 1973).

Barry, Faith, *Langston Hughes, Before and Beyond Harlem* (Westport, Conn.: Lawrence Hill, 1983).

Bell, Bernard, "Folk Art and the Harlem Renaissance," *Phylon* 39 (Spring 1975), 155–163.

Childs, John B., "Afro-American Intellectuals and the People's Culture," *Theory and Society* 13 (January 1984), 86.

Cooper, Wayne F., *Claude McKay: Rebel Sojourner in the Harlem Renaissance* (Baton Rouge: Louisiana State University Press, 1987).

Cruse, Harold, *Plural But Equal* (New York: William Morrow, 1987).

Fontaine, William T., "Josiah Royce and the American Race Problem," *Reflections on Segregation, Desegregation, Power and Morals* (Springfield, Ill.: Charles C. Thomas, 1967), pp. 66–73.

Frederickson, George M., *The Black Image in the White Mind: The Debate on Afro-American Character and Destiny, 1817–1914* (New York: Harper & Row, 1971).

Fullinwider, S. P., *The Mind and Mood of Black America*(Homewood, Ill.: Dorsey Press, 1969).

Hemenway, Robert E., *Zora Neale Hurston: A Literary Biography* (Urbana: University of Illinois Press, 1977).

Huffman, Frederick L., *Race Traits and Tendencies of the American Negro* (New York: Macmillan, 1896). See W. E. B. Du Bois' critique in "Race Traits and Tendencies of the American Negro, by F. Huffman," *Annals* 9 (January 1897), 127–133.

Huggins, Nathan I., *Harlem Renaissance* (London: Oxford University Press, 1971).

Huggins, Nathan I. (ed.), *Voices from the Harlem Renaissance* (New York: Oxford University Press, 1976).

Itzkoff, Seymour W., *Cultural Pluralism and American Education* (Scranton, Penn.: International Textbook, 1970).

Johnson, Abby Arthur, and R. M. Johnson, *Propaganda and Aesthetics: The Literary Politics of Afro-American Magazines in the Twentieth Century* (Amherst: University of Massachusetts Press, 1979), pp. 69–70.

Kent, George E., "Patterns of the Harlem Renaissance," *Black World* 21 (June 1972), 78.

Levine, Lawrence W., *Black Culture and Black Consciousness* (New York: Oxford University Press, 1980).

Lewis, David Levering, *When Harlem Was in Vogue* (New York: Alfred A. Knopf, 1981).

McKay, Claude, *A Long Way From Home: An Anthology* (New York: Harcourt, Brace & World, 1970), pp. 321–322.

Mason, Edna W., *Descendents of Captain Hugh Mason in America* (Franklin Park, N.J.: Tuttle Company, 1937).

Myers, Ardie Sue, "Relations of a Godmother Patronage During the Harlem Renaissance" (M.A. thesis, George Washington University, 1981), p. 55.

Royce, Josiah, *Philosophy of Loyalty* (New York: Hafner, 1908).

Royce, Josiah, *Race Questions, Provincialism, and Other American Problems* (New York: Macmillan, 1908).

Stoddard, Lothrop, *Re-Forging America: The Story of Our Nationhood* (New York: Scribner Publishing, 1927). Locke argues against Stoddard's views of biracial segregation in "Should the Negro be Encouraged to Cultural Equality?" *Forum* 78 (October 1927), 500–519.

Stoddard, Lothrop, *The Rising Tide of Color* (New York: Scribner Publishing, 1920).

CONTEMPORARY DISCUSSIONS CONCERNING THE ROLE OF
AFRICAN-AMERICAN PHILOSOPHERS AND THE NATURE OF
THE AMERICAN PHILOSOPHIC ENTERPRISE

Boxill, Bernard, *Blacks and Social Justice* (Totowa, N.J.: Rowman & Allanheld, 1984).

Harris, Leonard, "Select Bibliography of Afro-American Works in Philosophy," *Philosophy Born of Struggle: Anthology of Afro-American Philosophy from 1917* (Dubuque, Iowa: Kendall-Hunt, 1983), pp. 289–316.

Johnson, Charles, "Where Philosophy and Fiction Meet," *American Visions* 3 (1988), 36, 47–48.

McClendon, John H., "The Afro-American Philosopher and the Philosophy of the Black Experience: A Bibliographical Essay on a Neglected Topic in Both Philosophy and Black Studies," *Sage Race Relations Abstracts* 7 (1982), 1–49.

McDade, Jesse, Lesnor, C., Wartofsky, M. W., eds., "Philosophy and the Black Experience," special edition of *Philosophical Forum* 9: 2–3 (1977–1978).

McGary, Howard, Jr., "Teaching Black Philosophy," *Teaching Philosophy*, 7 (April 1984), 129–137.

Washington, Johnny, "What is Black Philosophy," in Washington, *Alain Locke and Philosophy: A Quest for Cultural Pluralism* (Westport, Conn.: Greenwood Press, 1986), pp. 1–22.

West, Cornel, *Prophesy Deliverance: An Afro-American Christianity* (Philadelphia: Westminister Press, 1982).

For discussion of various conceptions of American philosophy, see Bruce Kucklick, "The Changing Character of Philosophizing in America," *Philosophical Forum* 10 (Fall 1978), 4–13; Herbert W. Schneider, *A History of American Philosophy* (New York: Columbia University Press, 1963); Norman S. Fiering, "Early American Philosophy vs. Philosophy in Early America," *Transactions of the Charles Sanders Peirce Society* 13 (Summer 1977), 216–237; Elizabeth Flower and M. G. Murphey, *American Philosophy*, 2 vols. (New York: Capricorn Books, 1977); and Barbara MacKinnon (ed.), *American Philosophy: A Historical Anthology* (New York: State University of New York Press, 1985), pp. 667–679. For a view that *does* take into account national identities to formulate a conception of American philosophy, see John J. McDermott, *The Culture of Experience: Philosophical Essays in the American Grain* (New York: New York University Press, 1976).

Index